The

American
Culture
Wars

Current Contests and Future Prospects

Edited by
JAMES L. NOLAN, JR.

University Press of Virginia
Charlottesville and London

THE UNIVERSITY PRESS OF VIRGINIA
Copyright © 1996 by the Rector and Visitors of the University of
Virginia

First published 1996

A different edition of this work appeared as the *Virginia Review of
Sociology* 2 (1995) under the title *America at War with Itself: Cultural
Conflict in Contemporary Society.*

⊗ The paper used in this publication meets the minimum
requirements of the American National Standard for Information
Sciences—Permanence of Paper for Printed Library Materials, ANSI
Z39.48–1984.

Library of Congress Cataloging-in-Publication Data
The American culture wars: current contests and future prospects /
    edited by James L. Nolan, Jr.
        p.   cm.
    "A different edition of this work appeared as the Virginia review
of sociology 2 (1995) under the title America at war with itself"—
T.p. verso.
    ISBN 0–8139–1697–6 (pbk.: alk. paper)
    1. United States—Civilization—1970– 2. Culture conflict—
United States.   3. Social problems—United States.   4. United
States—Social conditions—1980–   5. Hunter, James Davison,
1955– Culture wars.   6. Multiculturalism—United States.
7. Pluralism   (Social sciences)—United States.   I. Nolan,
James L., Jr.
E169.12.A4185   1996
973.92—dc20   96-26136
                                                            CIP

Printed in the United States of America

CONTENTS

Contributors   vii

Preface
James L. Nolan, Jr.   ix

I. FIELDS OF CONFLICT

The Battle of the Books at Berkeley:
In Search of the Culture Wars in
Debates over Multiculturalism
David Yamane   3

Teachers and Preachers: The Battle over Public School
Reform in Gaston County, North Carolina
Kimon Howland Sargeant and Edwin L. West, Jr.   35

Public Television and the Culture Wars
William Hoynes   61

Cultural Conflict and Art:
Funding of the National Endowment for the Arts
Beth A. Eck   89

The American Abortion Debate:
Culture War or Normal Discourse?
Michele Dillon   115

Same Sex Politics:
The Legal Controversy over Homosexuality
J. David Woodard   133

II. THE CULTURE WARS AND BEYOND

Contrasting Styles of Political Discourse in America's Past
and Present Culture Wars
James L. Nolan, Jr. 155

Crossing Cultural Divides: Moral Conflict
and the Cairo Population Conference
Joseph E. Davis 189

Truth, Not Truce: "Common Ground" on Abortion,
a Movement within Both Movements
James R. Kelly 213

Reflections on the Culture Wars Hypothesis
James Davison Hunter 243

CONTRIBUTORS

Joseph E. Davis

Doctoral Candidate in Sociology
University of Virginia

Michele Dillon

Assistant Professor of Sociology
Yale University

Beth A. Eck

Assistant Professor of Sociology
James Madison University

William Hoynes

Assistant Professor of Sociology
Vassar College

James Davison Hunter

William F. Kenan Professor of
Sociology and Religious Studies
University of Virginia

James R. Kelly

Professor of Sociology
Fordham University

James L. Nolan, Jr.

Assistant Professor of Sociology
Williams College

Kimon Howland Sargeant

Sorokin Post-Doctoral Fellow
University of Virginia

Edwin L. West, Jr.

President, Masonboro Group Inc.
Wilmington, North Carolina

J. David Woodard

Associate Professor of Political Science
Clemson University

David Yamane

Doctoral Candidate in Sociology
University of Wisconsin

PREFACE

From the controversy over the acceptance of gays in the U.S. military, to debates over public funding of the arts, to arguments over the introduction of multicultural curricula in America's schools, to political disagreement over what really constitutes "family values," cultural conflict remains a prominent feature of contemporary public life. To refer to these various contests as individual parts of a larger societal-wide "culture war" has become part of the common parlance. Social scientific efforts to understand the roots of the contemporary *Kulturkampf* have focused not only on the changing structure of American religion (Wuthnow 1989)—a likely context for considering different systems of belief—but on transformations in the broader cultural landscape (Hunter 1991).

As the basic argument goes: Before World War II the most distinctive cultural differences in American religion were between Protestants, Catholics and Jews, with the birth of Christ and the Protestant Reformation being the historical moments from which these traditional divisions originated. Expanding pluralization and accompanying social change in American society have increasingly made these conventional dividing lines less relevant. With waning denominational and political party loyalties and the proliferation of special interest and para church organizations, a new cultural divide has emerged—one historically rooted, this time, in the Enlightenment. One side of the cleavage is represented by those who remain committed to "an external, definable, and transcendent authority," while the other side is represented by those who are committed to a "resymbolization of historic faiths according to the prevailing assumptions of contemporary life" (Hunter 1991). These ideological allegiances supersede denominational distinctions. As a result, Protestants holding to a traditional code of moral understanding have more in common with Jews and Catholics with a similar world view than they do with fellow Protestants with a more progressive orientation.

Earlier efforts to understand the underlying causes of modern cultural conflicts approached the matter from varying, though related, theoretical vantage points. Richard Merelman, for example, pointed to the tension created by society's movement away from the influence of "traditional cultural codes" toward a condition of "loose boundedness." In the latter, the individual is the basic cultural unit (Merelman 1984). Cultural conflict, according to Merelman, is rooted in the historically unique juxtaposition of these two cultural orientations.

Varying slightly from Merelman, Daniel Bell proposed that the raging cultural tensions, which first appeared in the 1960s, arose from the conflict between those adhering to traditional notions of societal life and those with more modern views (Bell 1976). Bell pointed to the 1920s as the beginning of this struggle and the 1960s as the time when the conflict became more visible. According to Bell: "From a cultural point of view, the politics of the 1920s to the 1960s was a struggle between tradition and modernity. In the 1960s the new cultural style denounced bourgeois values and the traditional codes of American life" (Bell 1976).

Related to these depictions of individualism's conflictual affront to binding societal obligations and of modernity's challenge to tradition, more recent works point to the fundamentally divergent world views out of which Americans operate—again, both within America's denominational landscape and in the culture more broadly. The cultural standoff has been semantically characterized in different ways: as between orthodox and progressivists (Hunter 1991), conservatives and liberals (Wuthnow 1989), fundamentalists and moderates (Ammerman 1990), and traditionalists and modernists (Bell 1976). The differences in nomenclature notwithstanding, each offers a similar heuristic framework, one that identifies the significance of a cultural division rooted in fundamentally divergent world views or cultural orientations.

According to the culture wars thesis, individuals on either side of the divide see their world view as absolute and the opposition's as illegitimate and "utterly alien to the American way" (Taylor 1990). The "rights"-based emphasis of contemporary discourse along with the polarizing nature of modern public debate (fostered through sound-bite long news accounts and the inflammatory language of computerized direct mailings) serves to exacerbate the cultural chasm. The result is a climate where activists engage the battle with a winner-takes-all mentality and where the more nuanced voices of the "muddled middle" are eclipsed by the sensationalized pronouncements of the extremes. Pointing to the absolutized certainty with which the different sides hold to their positions, Taylor observes that "the very nature of the Kulturkampf resides in [the] certainty that only one solution is defensible" (Taylor 1990). As a consequence the opposition is vilified and a rational search for common ground becomes increasingly untenable. Public debate, consequently, is dominated by the "reciprocal bellicosity" of the extremes, each battling within various societal institutions for the symbolic legitimacy of their view of the world.

Formulating a theoretical construct that makes sense of this polarized divide, James Hunter departs from conventional sociological understandings of conflict (typified as they often are by materialist explanations of the power struggle between those with and those without economic resources). Instead, Hunter draws on the work of the Marxist revisionist and social philosopher Antonio Gramsci to highlight a view of cultural discord that takes more seriously the independent import of ideological factors. Gramsci identifies distinctions between certain types of cultural elites: "traditional" intellectuals who maintain an affinity with the "truths of the past" and "organic" intellectuals, who advocate the "new and dynamic sources of progressive social reform" (Hunter 1991, p. 61). Hunter sees this dimension of Gramsci's work as the most salient for understanding the nature of conflict in the contemporary American context. And it is, no doubt, obvious how Gramsci's differentiation between the "traditional" and "organic" intellectuals parallels the aforementioned typologies of the warring cultural camps.

According to the culture wars thesis, then, conflict ultimately stems from groups and individuals with fundamentally different views of the world. Over a host of cultural issues groups like the National Association of Evangelicals, Concerned Women for America, and the National Right to Life Committee square off against groups like the National Organization of Women, the ACLU, and the National Education Association. The division between the "orthodox" and the "progressivist" impulses not only transcends economic class divisions and denominational differences, but also differences between gender, race, and region as well. If this is really the case, it bids us to explore these issues in greater detail. In other words, if there is indeed a profound and historically significant cultural divide as described by these various scholars, then a closer look at different cultural forums should reveal evidence of an observable cultural fault line, consistent with its theoretically purported significance.

The strength of Hunter's *Culture Wars* is that it provides an overarching theory for making sense of what a number of social theorists have identified, in one fashion or another, as a historically unprecedented cultural battle. Reception to the thesis, though largely favorable, has also received some criticisms (elements of which are discussed in this volume). Regardless of whether one agrees with the basic tenets of the argument, it is difficult to ignore the popular acceptance of the term for describing cultural conflict in contemporary American society. *Culture Wars,* as one reviewer notes, "is a book whose title has become a generic term for the contemporary dispute over cultural values in America" (Gilbert 1993). Not only has it been taken up by activists (Republican Presidential candidate Pat Buchanan being just one rather visible example), but also by academics advocating one or the other side of the debate—Peter Kreeft's *Ecumenical Jihad* would be an example from the orthodox side while Richard Bolton's edited collection on the arts (1992) would be one from the progressivist.

Even Supreme Court Justice Antonin Scalia invoked the term in his dissenting opinion in the 1996 *Romer v. Evans* decision where he accused the court of taking sides in the "culture wars." "The Court has mistaken a Kulturkampf for a fit of spite," Scalia argued in the case that overturned Colorado's controversial amendment regarding the legal status of homosexuals.

Largely missing from discussions of the concept both within academic circles and in the broader world of political and cultural punditry, however, are more dispassionate, empirically grounded investigations into the details of the various conflicts. In other words, where the culture wars thesis and discussions about it invite further work is in the empirical particularities of the various battle fronts. The incendiary nature of the conflict manifests itself in a number of different contexts, which have yet to be fully explored. Hunter devotes some one hundred pages to the various "fields of conflict" in *Culture Wars*. However, each of the different fields identified could be individual studies on their own.

For example, an entire book has been devoted to the battle between fundamentalists and moderates within the single denomination of the Southern Baptist Convention (Ammerman 1990). Others have analyzed hostile disputes in education (Graff 1992; Jacoby 1994; Gitlin 1995). Still others have focused exclusively on the controversial abortion issue (Luker 1984; Hunter 1993). Interestingly, Kristen Luker finds in her study of the abortion debate that the hostile differences between the "pro-life" and "pro-choice" activists "reflect the fact that the two sides have two very different orientations to the world and these orientations, in turn, revolve around two very different moral centers" (Luker 1984). Luker argues that the abortion controversy cannot be understood without an understanding of this deeper cultural conflict. According to Luker, "attitudes toward abortion rest on these deep, rarely examined notions about the world" which when looked at closely explain why "the abortion debate is so heated and why the chances for rational discussion, reasoned arguments, and mutual accommodation are so slim" (Luker 1984). While employing different terminology, her conclusions essentially confirm the culture wars thesis. Does a closer look at the abortion debate and other conflicts reveal the same? This is the research question that this collection of articles addresses.

Through empirical analyses of varying cultural skirmishes, this volume endeavors to further investigate the viability of the culture wars thesis on a case by case basis. As such, the first six chapters of the volume are devoted to examining in greater depth the substance of cultural conflicts within education, the media, the arts, the abortion debate, and the legal controversy over homosexuality. The next three chapters, in addition to considering individual cases, suggest certain possibilities about the future of the culture wars. The final chapter summarizes the various contributions to this volume in light of the larger intellectual discussion about the culture wars thesis.

Findings from two of the empirical studies—Michele Dillon's work on the abortion debate and David Yamane's analysis of the introduction of a multicultural curriculum at the University of California–Berkeley—suggest limitations in the applicability of the culture wars thesis to these particular conflicts. Beth A. Eck and James D. Woodard both combine the culture wars thesis with a status politics theoretical model to explain conflicts over public funding of the arts and the legal status of homosexuals, respectively. Studies on the controversy over the introduction of outcome-based education in Gaston County schools by Kimon Howland Sargeant and Edwin L. West, Jr., and the debate over public television by William Hoynes essentially work within and reaffirm the culture wars thesis, while adding interesting nuances particular to each case.

The last four chapters of the volume consider where the culture wars may be turning next. My comparative analysis of the 1992 elections highlights certain rhetorical tendencies in contemporary political debate that may portend the eventual victory of progressivism. Joseph E. Davis, in analyzing the Cairo Population Conference, considers the possibility of the culture wars as a global phenomenon. James Kelly, through an assessment of the abortion debate, investigates the prospect of common ground efforts in resolving cultural conflict, and James Davison Hunter offers summary reflections on the culture wars hypothesis while defending its cogency against recent criticisms.

Beyond providing more focused analyses on specific areas of cultural conflict, these chapters raise larger questions about the usefulness of qualifying the culture wars thesis with other theoretical models; about how best to conceptualize and measure the collective qualities of culture, in particular as it concerns the evident silence of the majority of Americans who find themselves unrepresented by either polarized extreme of the cultural divide; and about the relevance of the culture wars thesis to different levels of analysis (i.e., local, national, or global). Contributors to this volume vary in their viewpoints on these issues. Taken together, however, the chapters demonstrate the independent import of culture in understanding conflict in the contemporary context and promise to advance our understanding of the American culture wars.

I am grateful to the editorial board of the *Virginia Review of Soci-*

ology for supporting this work. In particular I wish to thank John Herrmann, Jeff Mullis, Karin Peterson, and Edith Raphael. The work was also made possible through Donald Black's role as editor of the JAI series in which this volume was originally published. Completing the project in a timely fashion was aided through fellowship assistance from UVa's Graduate School of Arts and Sciences and through support from the Post-Modernity Project. I owe a special thanks, too, to Carol Sargeant for editorial assistance. Finally, I'm grateful to Richard Holway at the University Press of Virginia for his helpful input and assistance in making possible this revised paperback version of *The American Culture Wars*.

James L. Nolan, Jr.

REFERENCES

Ammerman, N. T. 1990. *Baptist Battles: Social Change and Religious Conflict in the Southern Baptist Convention*. New Brunswick, NJ: Rutgers University Press.

Bell, D. 1976. *The Cultural Contradictions of Capitalism*. New York: Basic Books.

Bellah, R. N., R. Madsen, W. M. Sullivan, A. Swidler, and S. M. Tipton. 1991. *The Good Society*. New York: Alfred A Knopf.

Bolton, R. 1992. *Culture Wars: Documents from the Recent Controversies in the Arts*. New York: New Press.

Gilbert, J. 1993. "Cultural Skirmishes." *Reviews in American History* 21:346–51.

Gitlin, T. 1995. *The Twilight of Common Dreams: Why America Is Wracked by Culture Wars*. New York: H. Holt.

Glendon, M. A. 1991. *Rights Talk: The Impoverishment of Political Discourse*. New York: Free Press.

Graff, G. 1992. *Beyond the Culture Wars: How Teaching the Conflicts Can Revitalize American Education*. New York: W. W. Norton.

Hunter, J. D. 1991. *Culture Wars: The Struggle to Define America*. New York: Basic Books.

————. 1994. *Before the Shooting Begins*. New York: Free Press.

Jacoby, R. 1994. *Dogmatic Wisdom: How the Culture Wars Divert Education and Distract America*. New York: Doubleday.

Kreeft, P. 1996. *Ecumenical Jihad: Ecumenism and the Culture Wars*. San Francisco: Ignatius Press.

Luker, K. 1984. *Abortion: The Politics of Motherhood*. Berkeley: University of California Press.

Merelman, R. M. 1984. *Making Something of Ourselves.* Berkeley: University of California Press.

Taylor, C. 1990. "Freedom of Conscience or Freedom of Choice." *Articles of Faith, Articles of Peace,* edited by J. D. Hunter and O. Guinness. Washington, D.C.: The Brookings Institute.

Wuthnow, R. 1988. *The Restructuring of American Religion: Society and Religion Since World War II.* Princeton, NJ: Princeton University Press.

Wuthnow, R. 1989. *The Struggle for America's Soul: Evangelicals, Liberals, Secularists.* Grand Rapids, MI: William B. Eerdmans Publishing Company.

PART I

FIELDS OF CONFLICT

THE BATTLE OF THE BOOKS
AT BERKELEY:
IN SEARCH OF THE CULTURE WARS
IN DEBATES OVER MULTICULTURALISM

David Yamane

In *Culture Wars*, James Davison Hunter elaborates a general framework within which to examine contemporary cultural conflicts. According to Hunter, a culture war exists when two competing moral visions—"orthodox" and "progressive"—clash in the public sphere. In this respect, both the national debates over multiculturalism and local debates about curricular diversity in higher education can be understood as culture wars. I explore this assertion by applying Hunter's framework to the conflict over a proposed course requirement at the University of California Berkeley which focused on American cultural diversity. My analysis suggests that although the dimensions of the public debates at the U.C., Berkeley are somewhat similar to those suggested by Hunter, in the final analysis they deviate from his framework in important respects. While advocates of the requirement can be understood as organic intellectuals forwarding a progressivist vision of a pluralistic and diverse American identity, opponents of the requirement were *not* predominantly traditional intellectuals forwarding an orthodox vision of a culturally unified American identity. Few claimed that the Western tradition was the sole or primary source of American identity and unity, and therefore should form the core of liberal learning. On this essential point, opponents deviated from the impulse which provided the moral foundation for the orthodox alliance in the national culture war in education. I conclude by suggesting that the value of Hunter's framework for studying culture wars is as an ideal type which allows us to see in an instructive way what Weber called the "characteristic uniqueness" of the social world.

The recent work of James Davison Hunter represents an important codification of and intervention into the cultural struggles taking place in various institutions of American life, including politics, family, law and education. In *Culture Wars* (1991), Hunter elaborates a general framework within which to examine these conflicts. My purpose in this study is to explore the usefulness of Hunter's framework by considering its applicability in a potentially important case of cultural conflict: the movement to infuse multiculturalism into higher education, and more specifically, the debate over the institutionalization of a course requirement at the University of California, Berkeley which focuses on American cultural diversity, the "American Cultures Requirement."

According to Arthur Levine and Jeanette Cureton (1992) of the Harvard Graduate School of Education, the incorporation of multiculturalism in colleges and universities has been nothing less than a "quiet revolution." While I strongly disagree that it has been quiet,[1] there has indeed been a multicultural revolution in American higher education. A key element in this revolution has been the institutionalization of mandatory courses in multiculturalism (cultural pluralism, diversity, ethnic studies, etc.). In a recent survey conducted by Levine and Cureton (1992), fully 48 percent of four-year colleges and universities reported having a multicultural general education requirement.[2] Despite the prominence of this phenomenon, multicultural general education requirements have been inadequately studied by social scientists.[3] This application of Hunter's framework, therefore, is also an effort to redress the dearth of scholarship on this issue.

While it has become fashionable of late to characterize conflicts over the curriculum in higher education as "culture wars" (e.g., Gates 1992; Graff 1992; Jacoby 1994; Jay 1992; VLS 1989), these works tend to be position pieces *in* the conflict rather than sociological analyses *of* the conflict. These interventions into the cultural struggles in higher education are consequently much more limited than the nonpartisan and general view of cultural conflict afforded by Hunter's work.

In this application of Hunter's framework to the conflict over the American Cultures Requirement at the University of California, Berkeley, I will proceed as follows. I briefly summarize my understanding of Hunter's general framework for the study of cultural conflict as presented in *Culture Wars*. Next, I discuss his application of the framework to multiculturalism in higher education, generally agreeing that these conflicts seem to correspond well with his anatomy of contemporary cultural conflict. Having thus framed the issue, I turn to the case which constitutes the empirical core of this paper: the debates over multiculturalism in the curriculum at Berkeley. My analysis of the case suggests that although the dimensions of the public debates at Berkeley are somewhat similar to those suggested by Hunter for cultural conflict generally, they deviate from his framework in important respects. In closing, I briefly assess the general value of Hunter's work on culture wars for understanding debates over multiculturalism in American higher education.

HUNTER'S FRAMEWORK FOR STUDYING CULTURE WARS

Although it is impossible to fully appreciate *Culture Wars* without looking at the historical dimension of Hunter's work (Chapter 3) and without appreciating his attempt to address cultural conflict in a variety of institutional settings (Chapters 7-11), I would stress that it is a mistake to *only* see the work as concrete historical and comparative sociology. While Hunter's specific argument about the historical roots of the contemporary cultural fault lines and his tracing of the texture of those fault lines in several social institutions is certainly central to this overall project, what concerns me here is the framework for the study of culture wars generally which he has elaborated (Chapters 1,2,4). What Hunter calls "the anatomy of contemporary cultural conflict" is in fact a self-conscious attempt to use Max Weber's strategy of ideal types to shed light on an exceedingly intricate and multifarious social reality, without claiming to mirror that reality. It is an application of this general framework, not his specific historical argument, which concerns me here.

The Anatomy Of Contemporary Cultural Conflict

According to Hunter, at the heart of the contemporary culture wars are *"relatively* distinct and competing visions of public life." These moral visions appear as "cultural tendencies" amid a great deal of complexity in debates over national identity and the public life of the nation in a variety of institutional settings including the family, education, media and the arts, law, and electoral politics. Hunter is concerned with codifying these "distinct and opposing cultural impulses," recognizing that in sketching out their general contours, he is elaborating "ideal types" (pp. 107-108).[4] In Hunter's framework, "the cleavages at the heart of the contemporary culture war" are created by what he calls *"the impulse toward orthodoxy and the impulse toward progressivism"* (p. 43).

Fundamental to these two divergent impulses are "allegiances to different formulations and sources of moral authority" (p. 118). For the orthodox, *moral authority* is external and transcendent, definable and universally valid. Hunter is quick to note that the commitment to transcendent authority does not mean all committed to orthodoxy thus understood are "religious" in the traditional sense of believing in God(s). There are on the orthodox side many conservative and neoconservative secular intellectuals, such as Sidney Hook and Leo Strauss. For the secular proponents of orthodoxy, the transcendent foundation for moral judgment is not "God" but Natural Law, appeals to which are a functional equivalent to appeals to God in the contemporary culture wars (pp. 120-122).

In contrast to the universally valid and definitive conception of truth in the orthodox view, for the progressivist, *moral truth* is always understood and expressed in human terms and is therefore limited, conditional, relative, "perpetually unfolding." As opposed to the orthodox understanding of moral authority as transcendent, in the progressivist view, authority is primarily "this-worldly." While the orthodox look back to Athens and Jerusalem for guidance,[5] the progressivists look no further than the Anglo-European Enlightenment in both its "naturalist" (Hobbes) and its "subjectivist" (Kant) varieties (pp. 123-125).

Central to Hunter's framework is the observation that these moral visions are not simply confined to the private sphere, but are articulated in public life (p. 53). Because this cultural dynamic is located in public culture, the conflict becomes a contest over national identity, "over the meaning of America, who we have been in the past, who we are now, and perhaps most important, who we, as a nation, will aspire to become in the new millennium" (p. 50).

The primary carriers of these moral visions, put forth as they are in the public culture, are the elite. According to Hunter, "the development and articulation of the more elaborate systems of meaning, including the realm of public culture, fall almost always to the realm of elites." The relevant elites, for Hunter, are not simply university-based intellectuals. They also include, more importantly, "practically oriented 'knowledge workers.'" Among the significant knowledge workers named by Hunter are public policy experts, special interest lobbyists, public interest lawyers, independent writers and ideologues, journalists, community organizers, and social movement activists (pp. 59-60).

Hunter argues, following Antonio Gramsci, that at times of extensive social change, a particular cleavage develops among these cultural elites, a cleavage between *traditional* and *organic* intellectuals. Traditional intellectuals "present themselves as heirs to the truths of the past. Their legitimacy derives from their appeal to historical continuity." Organic intellectuals, on the other hand, "present themselves as the new and dynamic sources of progressive social reform" (pp. 60-61). Returning to the contemporary culture wars, we can see that the "orthodox alliance" in the culture wars is led by traditional intellectuals, while the "progressive alliance" is led by organic intellectuals (p. 63).

Armed with the anatomy of cultural conflict briefly sketched above, Hunter proceeds to examine the contemporary culture war as it manifests itself in a variety of institutional settings. As he notes, cultural conflict crystallizes in institutions, and without question one of the battlegrounds on which the culture wars have been fought most vigorously in recent years is education, and in particular, the curriculum (pp. 173-174). The particular setting which concerns us here is the formal educational system, especially institutions of higher education, and the particular substantive issue is *multiculturalism*. There is, without question in my view, a culture war being waged among intellectuals and activists around the issue of multiculturalism in higher education. Since Hunter himself applies his anatomy of contemporary cultural conflict to debates over multiculturalism in higher education, it is to that application that I now turn. Though his coverage of the issue is necessarily brief, the ideal type concepts Hunter has developed for the analysis of contemporary cultural conflict accurately describe the central cleavage in the national debate over multiculturalism in higher education.

Multiculturalism in Higher Education as a Culture War

Hunter correctly identifies schools as a primary site of cultural conflict (p. 174). The historical record overwhelmingly evidences this, and David Cohen and Barbara Neufeld (1981, p. 86) have memorably described it thus: "The schools are a great theater in which we play out [the] conflicts in the culture." In particular, the curriculum—what books and ideas are taught and how—provides an important stage for such conflicts because the curriculum contains the substantive definition of "an education." This is why so many of the culture wars of the 1980s have been, variously put, literary "canon wars" (Graff and Cain 1989), a "Battle of the Books" (Atlas 1992), or a "Quarrel of the Canons" (Bloom 1990, p. 23).

To debate the curriculum in *higher* education is, as Hunter (1991, p. 211) makes clear, to question what cultural representations will "shape the ideals and values as well as the categories of analysis and understanding that will guide the next generation of American leaders." Thus, the question of multiculturalism in higher education—more specifically, whether and how to include issues of race in the curriculum—is of great importance (but see Jacoby 1994). Gerald Graff and William Cain (1989, p. 310) recognize this importance and the consequent passion which surrounds the issue when they argue that "the great curriculum controversy [of the 1980s] ... would not have provoked such angry emotions—or such a stream of polemical books, editorials and official reports—if it were just an academic squabble over reading lists." But, they continue, the "curriculum is a microcosm of the culture: its inclusions and exclusions are an index of what the culture deems important. A conflict over 'the canon,' over what books to teach and how to teach them, is *a conflict over society's vision of itself*" (emphasis added). Judging from the curricular battles waged in the 1980s over "multiculturalism" in American higher education, our culture is very divided over where we stand and where we should go as a nation on racial issues.

Recalling that contemporary culture wars are clashes between orthodox and progressive moral visions, and that the carriers of these visions are traditional and organic intellectuals, respectively, Hunter shows that recent debates over multiculturalism in higher education should, in fact, be considered culture wars (pp. 215-20).[6] Briefly put, the movement for multiculturalism in higher education is a movement by progressivists for a curricular recognition of the pluralism and diversity which characterizes America racially. From its founding, according to this view, America has been a multicultural society. A curriculum dominated by the writings and history of "dead white European males" is, therefore, a biased reflection of the American experience (p. 215).

As Barbara Herrnstein Smith (1990, p. 71) argues in opposition to E.D. Hirsch's (1987) call for a *Cultural Literacy* based on the Western tradition, there is "no single, comprehensive macroculture in which all or even most of the citizens of this nation actually participate, no numerically preponderant majority culture in relation to which any or all of the others are 'minority' cultures, and no culture that, in Hirsch's terms, 'transcends' any or all other cultures." America is in fact multi-cultural, and only an incorporation of this diversity into the national identity can foster the type of appreciation necessary for inter-cultural harmony. The curriculum in higher education is taken to be an important vehicle for fostering such an identity and appreciation of diversity. One of the intellectual leaders of this movement, Harvard University Afro-American Studies professor Henry Louis Gates, Jr., has called the organic intellectual carriers of this vision "the cultural left" (1992, p. 17).

Opposed to this "Rainbow Coalition of contemporary critical theor[ists]" is what Gates (1992, p. 17) calls the "new cultural right." These traditional intellectuals are led by the "Killer-B's" (Pratt 1990, p. 9): Allan Bloom, best-selling author of *The Closing of the American Mind*, and William Bennett, the former Chair of the National Endowment for the Humanities and former Secretary of Education under Ronald Reagan. The moral vision advanced by these intellectuals is one of American cultural unity firmly rooted in the Natural Law (Bloom) and Judeo-Christian (Bennett) traditions of Western Civilization.

In his concluding remarks in the 1984 NEH report, "To Reclaim a Legacy," Bennett (1984, p. 30) lays out his vision of American identity and its relationship to the curriculum in higher education:

We are a part and a product of Western civilization. That our society was founded upon such principles as justice, liberty, government with the consent of the governed, and equality under the law is the result of ideas descended directly from great epochs of Western civilization... These ideas... are the glue that binds together our pluralistic nation. The fact that we as Americans— whether black or white, Asian or Hispanic, rich or poor—share these beliefs aligns us with other cultures of the Western tradition.

The curricular consequence of this understanding of the unification of American culture under the Western tradition is that "the core of the American college curriculum—its heart and soul—should be the civilization of the West, source of the most powerful and pervasive influences on America and all of its people" (Bennett 1984, p. 30).

In *The Closing of the American Mind*, Bloom (1987, p. 27) also engages the question of "what it means to be an American," and like Bennett locates his answer in the "unity and sameness" which results from the recognition and acceptance of "man's natural rights." In Bloom's view, "Class, race, religion, national origin or culture all disappear or become dim when bathed in the light of natural rights, which give men common interests and make them truly brothers." Openness to cultural diversity is a threat not simply to education but to society. As Bloom puts it, "when there are no shared goals or vision of the public good, is the social contract any longer possible?" The cultural unity necessary to forge a shared vision of the common good can be fostered by a liberal education based on "reading certain generally recognized classic tests," that is, by adopting "the good old Great Books approach" (Bloom 1987, p. 344). While Bloom wouldn't necessarily proscribe non-Western authors, his list of Great Books would certainly be dominated by the great thinkers associated with Western Civilization: Plato, Aristotle, Hobbes, Locke, the U.S. Founding Fathers, *inter alia*.

The particular curricular conflict on which Hunter focuses in *Culture Wars* is the debate over the Western Civilization requirement at Stanford University, which was revised in the late 1980s to include "the contributions of cultures disregarded and/or distorted by the present program" (p. 215). At its peak, the conflict over the new, diversified "Cultures, Ideas, and Values"—or "CIV"—requirement at Stanford pitted Rainbow Coalition leader Jesse Jackson against then Secretary of Education Bennett. At a rally led by Jackson, students memorably chanted "Hey, hey, ho, ho, Western Culture's got to go," to which Bennett responded that the CIV program exemplified "the closing of the Stanford mind."

This multicultural curriculum conflict is a "parable," according to Hunter, "repeated in different ways at most colleges and universities across the country." On this point, Hunter specifically names UC-Berkeley (pp. 215-216). It is my intention here to take this assertion by Hunter and treat it as a hypothesis which is open to empirical examination through a case study of the debates over the American Cultures Requirement at UC-Berkeley. The balance of this paper seeks to do just that.

THE BATTLE OF THE BOOKS AT BERKELEY

Hunter is not the only scholar to implicate ethnic studies requirements generally, or the American Cultures Requirement at UC-Berkeley specifically, in the contemporary culture wars. In *The Battle of the Books,* James Atlas (1992) seeks to understand "the curriculum debate in America" and acknowledges at the outset the vital importance of such debates, noting that "books alter the way we see ourselves. They form our collective character. We are what we read" (p. 19). The issue of who we are, therefore, comes to the fore in such cultural conflicts. In the course of his description and analysis, Atlas (1992, p. 35) makes the now familiar move of connecting the American Cultures Requirement at Berkeley to the more general movement for cultural diversity in higher education.

In his polemic, *The Hollow Men: Politics and Corruption in Higher Education*, Charles Sykes (1990) argues that "by 1990, many of the radicals of the 1960s had been transformed into the tenured gurus of American higher education" (p. 19), and these tenured radicals steadfastly adhere to and promote "the new official ideology of 'diversity'" (p. 18). As a result, this moral vision of diversity carried by organic intellectuals in the university "is often a curriculum as denuded of value as if it had, in fact, been created by a curriculum committee of Vandals with doctorates" (Sykes 1990, p. 18). Sykes later ensnares "mandatory ethnic studies requirements" in his criticisms (pp. 48-49), pointing a finger directly at the "recycled militants" at UC-Berkeley, among other schools (p. 310).

Finally, in a journalistic style similar to Sykes and in alignment with his more orthodox perspective on the issue, Dinesh D'Souza

(1991) also challenges the curricular politics of race on campus in his best-seller, *Illiberal Education: The Politics of Race and Sex on Campus*. Although his analysis is focused mostly on the debates over CIV at Stanford, D'Souza (1991, pp. 67-68) also specifically names the American Cultures Requirement at Berkeley as part of the same movement driving the diversification of curricula in institutions of higher education nationally.

What is the reality of the case? Did the specific local debate over the American Cultures Requirement at Berkeley articulate with Hunter's analytical framework as well as the larger national debate over multiculturalism? It is to these questions which this paper speaks. Before turning to the case study which constitutes the empirical core of this paper, I first give a brief history of the American Cultures issue at UC-Berkeley and discuss the data used in my analysis.

American Cultures: A Brief History

Although the proposal for an American Cultures Requirement (hereafter ACR) was not passed until 1989, the idea of a required course in ethnic studies was considered at UC-Berkeley—mostly in private among members of the Ethnic Studies faculties—as early as 1981.[7] Shortly thereafter, the issue became more public when in January 1983, California State Assemblymember Teresa Hughes (D-Los Angeles) introduced a bill which called on the Regents of the University of California (UC) to consider adopting an ethnic studies graduation requirement. Assembly Bill (AB) 383 eventually died in committee, but in July 1984 Assembly Concurrent Resolution 71—a toned down, non-binding version of AB 383 also sponsored by Hughes—was passed and succeeded in forcing UC schools "to review their policies and programs concerning the nature and extent of courses examining the cultural and historical experiences of those nonwhite ethnic groups which have been excluded from the core curriculum." The concurrent resolution also suggested that the UC schools *consider* adopting an ethnic studies requirement. No immediate action resulted at UC-Berkeley from Hughes's efforts. Progressivist faculty and students would have a long march still through the well-fortified bureaucratic trenches of the Academic Senate, Berkeley Division.

In the years following the July 1984 Concurrent Resolution 71, students actively lobbied the Berkeley Academic Senate on behalf of an ethnic studies requirement. Records from the Academic Senate reveal that the issue was considered by the Committee on Educational Policy (CEP) on 26 November and 10 December 1985, though it is unclear what about the requirement was discussed at those meetings. The issue was raised again in the spring of 1986 following two memoranda from the Associated Students of the University of California (ASUC) which urged the CEP to "recommend to the Chancellor the formation of a Task Force to explore the implementation of a campuswide Ethnic Studies breadth requirement." The CEP responded by forming a subcommittee to investigate the issue. This subcommittee reported that it discussed the ASUC proposal and dismissed the idea of a course requirement. It did, however, recommend that "the Senate Policy Committee establish an ad hoc study committee, including faculty, students, and administrators, to plan and implement a study of curricular and extra-curricular options for promoting better inter-racial understanding."

That same spring, the CEP as a whole decided a subcommittee of its own committee would be a more appropriate vehicle for this study, and resolved that "it agrees with the ASUC that the Campus should expand its efforts to create increased knowledge of, and better understanding among, the various ethnic and cultural groups that comprise our Campus community and the larger society." *However* and *above all*, a unanimously approved resolution declared, "The CEP does not believe that there should be an ethnic studies course requirement for graduation." In the fall of 1986, a CEP subcommittee was indeed formed, and rather than looking at how the university could "expand its efforts" with respect to education generally, the subcommittee considered the idea of an ethnic studies requirement. It eventually filed a report at the end of the semester rejecting the idea of such a requirement.

Such rejections did not deter the advocates, who continued to pressure the faculty to act on the issue. Before the February 1987 Academic Senate meeting, about 60 students and faculty held a "teach-in" on the requirement on Dwinelle Plaza. Later, Edwin Epstein, Chair of the Senate, agreed to allow three students from the newly formed "Ethnic Studies Coalition"—an umbrella organization which included the United People of Color, the African Students Association, *Movimiento Estudiantil Chicano de Atzlan* (MEChA), and the Asian Student Union—to share ten minutes in addressing the Representative Assembly on their proposal. Later that spring, the United People of Color and other student groups successfully worked to have an initiative put on the April ASUC election ballot asking students whether they favored an ethnic studies graduation requirement. In what was characterized by the student newspaper, *The Daily Californian* (20 April 1987), as an "unprecedented level" of voter turnout, about 7,000 students cast ballots, 53 percent favoring the principle of a requirement. Soon after, the Berkeley City Council got on the bandwagon and "unanimously endorsed and supported the proposal for an ethnic studies requirement" (Letter from City Clerk Edythe Campbell to the ASUC Senate and Officers, 24 April 1987).

These continuing efforts resulted in a crucial decision, one which ushered in the most active period of conflict around the issue of multiculturalism in the Berkeley curriculum. At the Academic Senate meeting of 28 April 1987, the faculty accepted a proposal to appoint an Ad Hoc Committee, which later became the Special Committee on Education and Ethnicity (hereafter, Special Committee). It was the Special Committee which ultimately drafted the American Cultures Requirement. The Special Committee's official charge from the Academic Senate was to "analyze the academic issues that are relevant to education about cultural diversity and ethnicity in the undergraduate curriculum," and to "identify approaches which would enhance current educational efforts in this area, including encouragement of academic innovations" (Simmons 1988, p. 1). However, the context in which the committee was created—in the midst and as a consequence of student demands for a course requirement—left little doubt among the members that they would attempt to draft a proposal for an ethnic studies requirement. Most members of the Special Committee I spoke with would agree with their colleague's recollection that "it was more or less assumed from the start that a requirement was desirable, not only to answer student demands, but because we recognized that there were appalling gaps in Berkeley's general curricula which left the whole area of ethnicity untouched."

The Special Committee eventually drafted a proposal for an "American Cultures" requirement, and in its final report to the Academic Senate recommended "the adoption of an American Cultures Requirement for all Baccalaureate degrees on the Berkeley campus." The type of courses seen as appropriate to fulfill the requirement would emphasize the cultural and political experiences and contributions of racial minority groups such as Native Americans, Chicano/Latino Americans, Afro-Americans, and Asian Americans in their relations with Euro-American and other ethnic groups which resulted in the shaping of the United States. The courses which the committee envisages are integrative and comparative. They should, for example, include in depth coverage of at least two of the above mentioned American minorities, so that the greater part of the semester should be committed to coverage of such groups (Simmons 1988, p. 1).

These guidelines proved to be very contentious issues, especially the specification of four racial minority groups and the dictate that at least two of them should be dealt with for the greater part of the class (see below). There were many objections to the requirement, however, and those faculty who opposed the requirement came to the May 1988 Academic Senate meeting determined to defeat the proposal.

The Senate meeting began ordinarily enough. After an introduction by Senate Chair Edwin Epstein, CEP Chair Jacob Lubliner moved the adoption of the Special Committee's ACR proposal. The body then debated the proposal in a spirited but cordial manner for nearly two hours, after which the Senate entertained two motions to make minor amendments to the proposal, both of which were defeated. Then, seemingly out of nowhere, Philosophy Professor Hans Sluga—one of the most identifiable opponents of the requirement—moved to submit the proposal to a mail ballot, a motion which was apparently intended to kill the proposal.

Though the huge majority of the faculty cherish their academic freedom more highly than any other value, when it comes to faculty governance, most would prefer not to be involved. Thus, although this Senate meeting had an extraordinarily high turn out—with more than three hundred faculty attending—this represented only a small fraction of those eligible to vote at Senate meetings (some 2100 faculty at the Berkeley campus). By securing a mail ballot many faculty members who would normally not be involved in a vote would, with little inconvenience to their preferred academic pursuits, be able to express their voice on the matter. However, this larger group of faculty members, who by the very virtue of their lack of engagement are more satisfied with the status quo, would thus be more likely to vote against it. Among supporters there was little doubt that the motion was a premeditated plan to kill the ACR.

Immediately following Sluga's motion, in a move both brilliant in its timing and disorienting in its consequences for most at the meeting, Physics Professor and Nobel Laureate Owen Chamberlin moved the previous question on all motions. This motion, if passed, would close debate on all motions and bring them up for an immediate vote. Amidst growing confusion on the floor, the motion to call the previous question was passed 213 to 73 (286 total votes). Thus, no debate could take place on the mail ballot question. This was significant, according to Special Committee member Lawrence Levine, because not having the opportunity to debate the mail ballot, "some professors who supported the proposal voted for the mail in ballot without realizing the implications" (*Daily Californian*, 11 May 1988).

The mail ballot motion, it was ruled by the Chair, needed to pass by a two-thirds majority. In calculating the number of votes necessary to pass the mail ballot, 286 was used as the total number of faculty voting. Based on this figure, it was determined (by an unidentified person who was sitting near Chair Epstein) that one-third of 286 is 92, and thus two-thirds is 184.[8] The Chair thus announced that 184 votes would be needed to pass the mail ballot. The actual vote on this motion was 185 ayes, 155 nays, and no abstentions. The motion for a mail ballot had passed.[9]

To return to May 1988 again, the mail ballot was widely seen to spell doom for the requirement, especially in the eyes of many supporters. According to one Academic Senate leader with whom I spoke, "everyone realized that sending [the proposal] to a mail ballot was simply a matter of killing it." Said Special Committee member Levine after the meeting, "It has lost" (*Daily Californian*, 11 May 1988).

In the wake of this Senate meeting, the Special Committee and other supporters of the requirement decided to pursue the withdrawal of their first proposal and to work on a new one to be considered in the Spring of 1989. To that end, they were aided by the new Senate Chair John Heilbron who delayed in sending out the mail ballot to the faculty, and by Engineering Professor Jacob Lubliner, an early supporter of the requirement as Chair of the CEP, who worked hard as Chair of the Committee on Rules and Jurisdiction to determine that the amendments to the Division's By-Laws could not be referred to mail ballots. The requirement thus gained a second life.

In reflecting on the opposition to the April 1988 proposal, it became apparent to many members of the Special Committee and supporters of the requirement that although its language was more suggestive than definitive—for example, the "for example" clause in the passage given above—the few guidelines it did provide were very contentious. Especially contentious was the specification of *four racial minority groups* for attention and the perceived *exclusion of white ethnics* from consideration in the courses which would be required. Indeed, in an analysis of a sample of arguments against the American Cultures proposal, I found that fully 36 percent (42 of 115) of the faculty opposed to the requirement cited the exclusion of whites as a reason for their opposition (see Appendix).

The Special Committee met again through the winter of 1988 and into the spring of 1989. In April 1989, the Special Committee, having then worked for some 16 months, again recommended to the Academic Senate that an American Cultures course be required as a prerequisite for every Baccalaureate degree awarded on the Berkeley campus. In what was obviously a concession to the largest group of opponents of their previous proposal, the new proposal suggested that courses which would fulfill the requirement should be "integrative and comparative.

> We intend that each racial or ethnic group be studied in the larger context of American history, society, and culture. Such courses should substantially consider at least *three of the five* main racial/cultural groups in American society: African American, American Indian, Asian American, Chicano/Latino, *and European American*. To be adequately comparative, no one of these groups may be the focus of the greater part of the course (Simmons 1989, p. 4, emphasis added).

This change in the language to include Euro-Americans undermined the most widely cited argument against the requirement. One vocal opponent of the first proposal said this about the key change the Special Committee made: "the Committee improved [the proposal] in one respect a great deal...It improved it so much that I hated to still be against it, because someone should be rewarded when they do such a good job....To my mind they improved it by including all ethnicities in it instead of specifically leaving out whites. In some sense, instead of a racist proposal it became a non-racist proposal. And so you had to judge it on other grounds."

Even this toned-down proposal passed only by the narrow margin of 33 votes (227-194) in what many said was the best attended meeting of the Berkeley Academic Senate since the trying times of the Vietnam War.[10]

Data

Much of the work I have done on this project can be considered
"natural history," in the sense forwarded by anthropologist Jules
Henry (1965). It has involved interviewing, reading official and
personal documents, scouring newspapers, and generally attempting
to get a feel for the campus climate at the time of the debates over
the ACR. The bulk of the data I argue from below are original
documentary sources and, to a lesser extent, newspapers. In the
process of agitating for and debating the various ethnic studies
requirement proposals (including the ACR), a variety of
documentary sources were produced—including meeting minutes,
committee reports, written testimony, letters, speeches, papers,
presentations, memos, proposals, pamphlets, and newspaper articles
and editorials—which provide excellent texts for analyzing the public
debate over multiculturalism.

Other important sources of information upon which I have
drawn are tapes (audio and video) of two important events: "The
Educated Californian" symposium of October 1987 and the May
1988 Berkeley Academic Senate meeting at which the ACR
proposal was first debated by the faculty as a whole. Another source
of data for this paper is 28 semi-structured interviews I conducted
in 1991 with students, faculty, and administrators at Berkeley who
were involved in the debates either by virtue of their institutional
position (e.g., committee membership, Faculty Senate office) or
because they chose to involve themselves (either as advocates or
opponents).[11] All uncited quotations in the text below are from
these interviews; as I promised my interviewees anonymity in
exchange for their cooperation, I identify them only by their general
institutional characteristics.

Finally, the "sample" of Berkeley faculty opinions to which I refer
is built upon the sources named above *plus* 147 completed survey
questionnaires which were sent out to the faculty in December 1988
by the Special Committee. These questionnaires asked the faculty to
comment on the Committee's first proposal. This collection of
documents is surely the largest single body of information about
faculty attitudes toward the proposed ACR. While they, like the
interviews I conducted, are not a "real-time" expression of public
discourse, they are a necessary and useful supplement to the public
record. I identify them in the text parenthetically as "Survey."

IN SEARCH OF THE CULTURE WARS

Let me assert at the outset the basic point I hope to make in my consideration of the conflict surrounding multiculturalism in the curriculum at UC-Berkeley. The dimensions of the conflict over various ethnic studies and American Cultures requirement proposals deviated in crucial ways from the dimensions suggested for culture wars generally in Hunter's ideal type. As I have already noted, the divide over multiculturalism is seen by Hunter as a divergence in conceptions of national identity: *"over the meaning of America*, who we have been in the past, who we are now, and perhaps most important, who we, as a nation, will aspire to become in the new millennium"* (Hunter 1991, p. 50). In the course of the long march toward a multicultural course requirement, advocates at Berkeley elaborated a clear vision of America as a racially diverse, pluralistic nation in character and culture (cf. Yamane 1992). While the advocates of the ACR at UC-Berkeley are well-understood as organic intellectuals advancing a progressivist moral vision, the opponents of the requirement *never articulated any coherent moral vision* of American character and culture. To be sure, there were some traditional intellectuals who rejected the multicultural ACR because they held a culturally orthodox view of American identity. This, however, was a minority position in the public discourse against the requirement.

Advocates: The Progressivist Moral Vision

Over the years 1984 to 1989, there were many serious efforts both by faculty and by students to develop a strategy and an argument for implementing an ethnic studies requirement. Thus, there exists an overwhelming number of statements which reveal the progressivist moral vision undergirding the movement for an ethnic studies requirement.

In October 1987, a major symposium was organized by supporters of an ethnic studies requirement on "The Educated Californian: Racial and Ethnic Pluralism in the Curriculum of the 21st Century." This symposium, which drew an audience of 1000 and generated considerable momentum for the movement, was the first major, sustained effort by proponents to draw the Berkeley debates into the national culture war over "liberal education,"—in E.D. Hirsch's (1987) terms, over "what every American needs to know."

Proponents, playing the role of cultural progressives, tried to cast opposed faculty in the role of cultural traditionalists. For example, Julie Chang, Vice President of the ASUC and a member of the United People of Color, argued in her opening address that the Eurocentric curriculum at Berkeley did not relate to the lives of people of color. "Old world values" were dressed up in the curriculum as universal and objective, when in fact objectivity "is merely white subjectivity." She implored her audience to "strive toward mutual respect and understanding in our multicultural community" by supporting the ethnic studies requirement, through which American cultural diversity would "be appreciated and celebrated." Later, Ronald Takaki charged Allan Bloom with cultural bigotry for the views he expressed in *The Closing of the American Mind*, and—in a play on E.D. Hirsch's work—stressed the "multicultural illiteracy" which plagued the Berkeley campus. A course requirement, Takaki argued, "has great *symbolic* value. It represents the university's commitment to the study of the diversity of American society." Moreover, according to Afro-American Studies Professor Margaret Wilkerson, an ethnic studies requirement "has serious implications for our national identity, the way we see ourselves, for it proposes a fundamental restructuring of our metaphorical framework: no longer that of a melting pot or a mainstream, but a people of many streams striving to find the common source." And we cannot assume that the common source is in the tradition of Western Civilization. In his keynote address, Mario Garcia of UC-Santa Barbara argued that "there is no single cultural center on which to build a core curriculum" in the United States. We are many cultures and many diverse experiences. "These cultures and experiences," he continued, "are the fundamental and most valuable part of what it means to be an American."

These same themes were reiterated by advocates of a multicultural course requirement throughout the process. Though he was not a member of any Academic Senate committees, Ronald Takaki played a major role in the movement for an ethnic studies requirement at Berkeley from the outset. He was involved in the earliest discussions among Ethnic Studies faculty, and he remained a catalyst and publicist for the movement until the passage of the ACR in 1989. It is no surprise, then, that he articulated the moral vision of advocates as clearly as anyone. In an essay published in the *Chronicle of Higher Education* (8 March 1989), Takaki argues that "an educated, culturally literate person must study America's multicultural reality." Drawing once again on Bloom's contention that "there are some things one must know about if one is to be educated" and Hirsch's insistence that there is some cultural information that "every American needs to know," Takaki asserts that the content of education appropriate to America's racial and cultural diversity is multicultural.

The Special Committee on Education and Ethnicity also elaborated the moral vision of the ACR in terms of the question of liberal education in America. In their first proposal to the Academic Senate, the Special Committee raised the issue in this way:

> In recent years the traditional content of a liberal education has come under increasing criticism and scrutiny among the nation's leading universities and in public debates. The key question is: as the world becomes a global village and the population of the U.S. becomes increasingly multiracial and multicultural, what knowledge, skills and values are essential to enable educated individuals in our democratic society to live intelligently, productively, sensitively, and responsibly? (Simmons 1988, p. 9).

The Committee's answer to this key question is that students need "to develop a more informed understanding of the racial and cultural diversity of U.S. society" (Simmons 1988, p. 12), and that the ACR would contribute to such development.

In the Academic Senate debate over this first proposal, advocates of the requirement argued similarly for an understanding of American diversity. William Simmons, the Chair of the Special Committee, argued early in the debate against the orthodox view that the foundation for the curriculum was in any way transcendent:

> Until recently, we have had a situation where students of majority cultural background have attended to a curriculum that reflects majority interests. As long as this situation remained unchanged, it seemed like the God-given, natural order of things. But our students are changing. The increasing number of minority students on this campus and across the country, they see our curriculum differently. They have a feeling that something is missing. They feel that there are some assumptions here that may have been going unnoticed. And it seems to us as a committee that there is something to their perception, because our curriculum was not constructed with them in mind. ... This is where the emphasis on American cultures comes in. These students that we're talking about represent a range of subcultural traditions: Asian American, Afro-American, and so on.

Jewelle Taylor-Gibbs, a professor of Social Work, also clearly articulated the multicultural moral vision of America in her speech at the May 1988 Academic Senate meeting:

> The University should educate students to adapt to the changing American society as we approach the 21st century. The demographic imperative in the United States predicts that early in the 21st century, one-third of Americans will be non-White or Spanish speaking. Thus it is essential that the University's curriculum and general ethos should educate *all* of its students to live in a society which is becoming increasingly non-White and in a world which is increasingly interdependent economically and politically. The major way to implement this is to include information about the contributions of minority ethnic groups in this country and in all spheres, as well as the contributions of their original countries to the heterogeneity of the American culture. Unless students can gain some understanding of the vitality and the richness of other non-European cultural groups they will never develop positive attitudes and an interest in mutual interactions with these groups. ... How many [Berkeley students] are aware of the contributions made by blacks, Hispanics, and American Indians? Most of these contributions have in fact been minimized by historians, misinterpreted by social scientists, and misrepresented by the mass media. So students are not given at any educational level in this country a broad perspective on the history and cultures of minority groups in America.

The vision of American identity underlying this perspective is well-summarized by Simmons when he states: "we are reaching toward a perspective that takes *diversity* as its premise, and that is concerned with the relations between particular traditions and the whole. The *Pluribus* as well as the *Unum*."

Though the second proposal of Special Committee was considerably longer than the first, responding in detail to criticisms of the first proposal, the core vision undergirding the American Cultures Requirement remained unchanged:

> American society is distinctive if not unique in the diversity of racial and ethnic groups that shaped its early formation and that continues to shape its identity in the present. This identity ... reflect three processes, two of which are encoded in our national motto, *E Pluribus Unum*. First, we are constituted by people with historical traditions from Africa, Asia, Europe, North America, and elsewhere. Second, these traditions have been reshaped by New World experience which has impressed a new level of identity upon the whole. Thus, American culture derives from its many constituent groups, but in their interaction on American soil it has been redefined, both within each racial and ethnic tradition and at a level that transcends all such traditions. The third process may be described as exclusion. The experiences of exclusion and

isolation have affected most groups in the United States although some have experienced this over a longer time period and in qualitatively different ways than others (Simmons 1989, p. 2; also Simmons 1988, p. 2).

In sum, American identity is fundamentally diverse and pluralistic. While the committee writes as if they were simply *describing* what American identity *is*, we can clearly recognize that theirs is a *normative* vision of what American identity *should be*.

Advocates of the ACR at UC-Berkeley, in my view, clearly articulated a progressivist cultural vision which takes as its central value *diversity*. This side of the debate, therefore, articulates well with Hunter's framework. Unlike the advocates, opponents did not adhere to an overarching, compelling moral vision of America which was fundamentally different than the vision supporting the requirement. Opponents of the requirement do not fit Hunter's framework as well as the advocates.

Opponents: Ideological Fragmentation

As I have noted above, the reports of the Special Committee on Education and Ethnicity recommending an American Cultures Requirement represented the first concrete proposals considered by the Berkeley faculty as a whole (in the Academic Senate). These reports provided a focus and forum for the public debates over multiculturalism in the UC-Berkeley curriculum, and thereby ushered in the most active period of conflict around the issue on the Berkeley campus. Although opponents had a common focus in this period, this did not lead to a commonly articulated justification for their antagonism toward the requirement. Quite the opposite happened, in fact. Arguments against the requirement proliferated, and some of those argument were directly contradictory.

To take but one example, some faculty opposed to the ACR argued for a total reconceptualization of Berkeley's core requirements with a view toward a more coherent overall structure; others argued that at the college level there should be no requirements at all (i.e., they wanted *less* overall structure). Despite being diametrically opposed in their educational principles, on the issue of the ACR, they came down on the same side. This lack of a unifying belief on the part of the opponents contributed to their inability to mount sufficient organized resistance to the proposal. Unlike the proponents who emerged from the "organized autonomy" which characterizes university life to form a solid interest group working for a common goal, most opponents never overcame their autonomy and ended up losing by less than 10 percent of the final vote as a result.

In order to organize the vast assortment of dissimilar arguments against the requirement, I examined a sample of 115 statements by professors raising objections to either of the two ACR proposals and coded *fifteen different reasons* given for opposing the ACR. (I believe that further differentiation would reveal even more categories.) A table summarizing the distribution of these objections is given as an Appendix to this paper. Due to space constraints, I cannot discuss all of these arguments in detail. My goal in including this information is simply to empirically establish the lack of a coherent moral vision underlying the proliferation of arguments against the ACR.

To be fair, ideological fragmentation on either or both sides of the cultural divide is not ruled out by Hunter, who recognizes that his conceptualization highlights impulses toward orthodoxy and progressivism amid considerable complexity in the public struggles to define America. If Hunter's argument is to have any force, however, we should be able to locate beneath the proliferation of various arguments evidence of a concrete single impulse. In this case, among the opponents of the ACR we should see an impulse toward orthodoxy identifiable by the following features: (1) acknowledgment of God or Natural Law as the source of moral authority; (2) appeals to historical continuity and the truths of the past; and (3) a vision of an American culture and identity unified under the traditions of Western Civilization (see above). In my view, while not indiscernible, such an impulse is both faint and not common to the arguments against the ACR.

God and Natural Law (or other functional equivalents) were not cited as sources of moral authority by those opposing the requirement, and in fact, some opponents would agree with their adversaries that moral truth is limited, conditional, and perpetually unfolding. Furthermore, ideas such as "the Great Books," "the Canon," "Western Civilization," and "the closing of the American mind" were rarely if ever voiced by those opposed to the requirement. Thus, while ACR proponents' arguments articulated well with the national debates, opponents failed to engage such central questions as "what every American needs to know." Finally, although there were some appeals to the past—for example, "the spirit of intellectual inquiry a university stands for"—they were not combined with foundationalist claims to universally valid truth. Nor was the past linked to a moral vision of American identity or culture. In these important respects, the fragmentation among opponents of the ACR at Berkeley is a marked divergence from what is expected based on Hunter's framework.

As mentioned earlier the most often cited reason for opposing the measure was the exclusion of whites from the curriculum. That it was *politically motivated* was the second largest category of reasons for opposing the ACR, with 28 percent of the sample (32 of 115) raising this objection. This second objection merits further attention. According to the faculty opposed on these grounds, the proposed requirement was motivated by politics and ideology rather than academic, intellectual, or educational concerns. A few examples from the faculty *Survey* should serve to illustrate this response:

> An anonymous survey respondent requested some "assurance that not all of the courses meeting the requirement will conform to left-wing ideology. It's clear that most of them will."

> A professor in the social sciences felt that the ACR would legitimate courses, some existing already, whose message is "to paraphrase Che Guevara, People of Color, Yes. White Man, No."

> A departmental colleague of the social scientist just cited concurred that the "whole notion of a requirement concerning 'ethnicity'... smacks of indoctrination rather than serious higher education."

> Another professor in the social sciences thought "the new requirement will be not much different from courses on Marxism-Leninism offered at the universities of Communist societies."

> An assistant professor in a professional school made his point clear: "I do not think a committee external to a department should regulate course content to achieve political objectives extrinsic to the spirit of intellectual inquiry a university stands for."

This is an important type of argument because, as Hunter (1991, p. 218) himself argues, with respect to the larger national culture wars, the orthodox believe that the progressivist "idea of diversity is defined by political criteria." We saw above that writers representative of the orthodox side of the divide, such as Charles Sykes and Dinesh D'Souza, criticize movements for racial and cultural diversity precisely for politicizing the curriculum.

The question, then, is this: If 28 percent of the faculty opposed
to the requirement charged that it was politically motivated, does this
not constitute an *impulse to orthodoxy*? I must concede that there
is some merit to the claim that these 28 percent of the faculty harbor
the orthodox impulse. Because they want to defend traditional
notions of "serious higher education," these professors can be seen
as defenders of cultural orthodoxy in the university. Although they
are more critical than constructive in their arguments, Hunter notes
that "discourse of adversaries" in the culture wars is often *negative*.
The tone and temper of the conflicts at Berkeley certainly manifests
this "*negative face* of moral conflict: the deliberate, systematic effort
to discredit the opposition" (p. 136). In a university what could be
more discrediting than suggesting that your opponents are
ideologically rather than intellectually motivated?

But for Hunter, the negative face of adversarial discourse is only
half the story. What about the positive face? In my view, the fact
remains that beyond simply charging advocates with playing politics,
these opponents of the ACR never took steps to articulate a coherent
and comprehensive alternative vision to that advanced by advocates
of the requirement. Listening to these critics, we have no idea of the
quality or source of their moral truths, and no firm grasp of their
understanding of American identity, much less any idea of whether
they believe that identity to be unified by the tenets of Western
Civilization. There was no public voice among these faculty even
closely approximating the vision of American identity forwarded by
an Allan Bloom or William Bennett.

In the final analysis, while we can see the seeds of a full blown
vision in many of these arguments, they remained only seeds. That
is perhaps the major reason why, to the end, arguments against
the requirement simply continued to proliferate without gaining
any coherence.

CONCLUSION

A culture war exists when two competing moral visions clash in the
public sphere. According to James Davison Hunter, both the
national debates over multiculturalism and local debates about
curricular diversity in higher education can be understood as culture
wars. Recalling that Hunter characterized the debates over the core

curriculum at Stanford as a "parable" repeated at other campuses, we would expect the debate over the American Cultures Requirement at Berkeley to be a perfect case in which to see the culturally "orthodox" square off against the culturally "progressive" in a public debate over American identity.

In this paper, I have tried to argue that, upon further investigation, the debate over the ACR at U.C.-Berkeley does not correspond precisely to the terms of the culture wars as Hunter has laid them out. While advocates of the requirement can be understood as organic intellectuals forwarding a progressivist vision of a pluralistic and diverse American identity, opponents of the requirement were *not* predominantly traditional intellectuals forwarding an orthodox vision of a culturally unified American identity. Opponents of the requirement never made exclusivist appeals to the great intellectual tradition of Western Civilization as embodying the proper content of an education. When Western Civilization was brought into the debate, it was stressed that students should learn this tradition *in addition to* the pluralistic cultural traditions of the United States. In this crucial respect, they deviated from the impulse which provided the moral foundation for the orthodox alliance in the national culture war in education (as exemplified by the ideas of Bloom and Bennett). Few claims were made that the Western tradition was the sole or primary source of American identity and unity, and therefore should form the core of liberal learning.

Given this divergence from the Culture Wars framework, what are we to make of Hunter's work on this issue? In my view, while Hunter's argument about the *historical* development of the *particular* cultural cleavage in America today is open to empirical investigation and criticism, his *general* framework for analyzing cultural conflict should be evaluated in terms of Hunter's intention in elaborating it. Hunter, as I have already mentioned, sees his framework as an *ideal type* (p. 108). We know from the master elaborator of ideal types, Max Weber (1949), that ideal types cannot be judged true or false; they can only be more or less *useful*.

In Weber's (1949, p. 72) view, "the way in which life confronts us in immediate concrete situations" is characterized by "an infinite multiplicity of successively and coexistently emerging and disappearing events." The way social scientists handle the "absolute infinitude of this multiplicity" is by elaborating general concepts and formulations widely known as ideal types. According to Thomas

Burger (1987), "Ideal types are statements of general form asserting the existence of certain constellations of elements which are empirically only approximated (and then to varying degrees) by concrete instances of the class of phenomena to which the type refers" (see Weber 1949, p. 90). The "testing" of ideal types—that is, the determination of how closely the constructs reproduce or mirror reality—should not be taken as the *ends* of investigations; rather, applying ideal typical constructs to concrete individual phenomena are a *means* of shedding light on certain aspects of infinitely complex phenomena.[12]

Evaluating Hunter's framework according to these standards reveals not that it inadequately characterizes cultural conflict in the concrete institutional setting considered here, but that it usefully allows us to see that the culture wars which are fought nationally in speeches, books, and magazines manifest themselves differently in different "local" contexts. On the national stage, the divisions in the culture war are quite distinct. On the local level, in contrast, considerably more diversity of opinion is apparent, as Hunter recognizes. It is only because Hunter's conceptualization highlights key aspects of the sharply crystallized national debate over multiculturalism that we can use it to grapple with the more equivocal, messy debates over curricular diversity played out on local stages. Hunter's *Culture Wars* allows us to see in an instructive way the "characteristic uniqueness" of the social world. Whatever insights this paper provides into the nature of the debates over multiculturalism at Berkeley are due largely to the usefulness of Hunter's framework in emphasizing certain important aspects of the debates and thereby helping to organize an infinitely complex empirical phenomenon.

APPENDIX:

Distribution of Reasons for Opposition to American Cultures[13]

Category	Count	Percent of Total	Example[s]/ Explanations
Whites Excluded	42	36	According to an anonymous survey respondent, "Any proposal which focuses on particular minorities and excludes others (Armenians, Jews, Italians, Irish) is divisive. Several of the above have faced severe discrimination—as severe or more severe than several of the currently included categories."

(continued)

APPENDIX (Continued)

Political	32	28	One assistant professor in one of the professional schools made this point: "I do not think a committee external to a department should regulate course content to achieve political objectives extrinsic to the spirit of intellectual inquiry a university stands for" (*Survey*). Also see text.
Not a Solution	30	26	The requirement was portrayed by advocates as a vehicle for reducing racial antagonism by promoting inter-racial understanding. This associate professor in the natural sciences disagreed: "'Appreciation' requirements never work. ... Such courses don't engender appreciation. They engender resentment. That is the quickest way to make sure race relations degenerate on campus" (*Survey*).
Mickey Mouse Courses	17	15	Many professors (mostly in the natural sciences) believed that courses dealing with the history and experience of ethnicity would be intellectually inferior. This professor recounted to me the main sentiment of many of his scientific colleagues: "It is far more important to have another physicist than to set up these Mickey Mouse, bullshit [programs]. One more of them doing nothing but spinning their wheels and bullshitting. And this university is a place for serious business. More money should go for the serious business."
Narrowly Focused	15	13	By focusing exclusively on the U.S., the requirement is parochial, even dangerously nationalistic. One professor in the humanities argued, "We surely cannot get rid of racism or instruct very successfully by wrapping ourselves in the American flag and giving 4 units. ... Nationalism is as grave and murderous a problem as racism and directly related to it" (*Survey*).
Other Priority Subjects	14	12	History Professor Roger Hahn in the text of his speech at the May 1988 Academic Senate meeting gave the archetypical example of this argument: "I happen to think that all students should know about World History, including the U.S., but particularly about Third World problems, and about cultures *other* than American ones. I happen to think a citizen of this world needs to know of the opportunities and dangers posed by our scientific and technological age. I happen to think every student needs courses in religious or ethical values. But we don't have requirements to that effect. Why should we pick on American Cultures with a mandated emphasis on minorities? Why not World History? Why not Science and Technology? Why not Philosophy and Religion?"
No Required Courses	13	11	There were two subgroups in this contingent. One argued that there should be no required courses for educational reasons (educational libertarians), and the other simply saw requirements as unfeasible in a university the size of UC-Berkeley. (1) A professor in the social sciences and leading opponent told me, "I just know I would see if I could get

(continued)

APPENDIX (Continued)

Category	Count	Percent of Total	Example(s)/Explanations
			across the point of breadth without impinging on the students' freedom quite as much as I think it [the core curriculum] presently impinges on them." (2) A 15+ year veteran in the humanities told me, "we have more than 30,000 students, we have 4000 [freshmen] a year roughly, and how can you really implement [a core curriculum]? I think that's why we have given up."
Burden on Students	11	10	Not against requirements *per se*, as above, but see students—especially in science and engineering—as already having enough requirements; they don't need and can't handle any more.
Redo Whole Core	7	6	One faculty member argued that the ACR "might be an appropriate part of an overall core curricula" and suggested to his colleagues, "It's time we had a proper 'core.' Let's do the whole job" (*Survey*).
Pedagogical Problems	7	6	Requiring a course in a field which didn't exist—"American Cultures"—is problematic. One leading opponent, a professor in the humanities, told me, "I kept saying to myself, it's like Newton saying. 'Wouldn't it be nice to have something called the Calculus. Well, let's make a requirement and see what comes out of it, and maybe we'll invent it.' It's just putting the cart before the horse because we don't have this field of comparative studies."
Resources are Zero-sum	6	5	According to a professor in the natural sciences, some of his departmental colleagues told him, "if this is going to cost a faculty position, we must all vote against it." This argument follows Hazard Adams's (1988, p. 45) "Third Stereotypical Principle of Faculty Behavior": "an educational principle is fine as long as it does not interfere with a departmental program."
Committee is Self-Serving	3	3	An associate professor in the natural sciences argued that the Committee could gain "credibility" by expanding its membership to include "some who did not appear to have a vested interest in such a required course."
Doesn't Go Far Enough	3	3	A professor in the natural sciences argued that a racist faculty could not teach classes about race. The courses, he argued, "should *only* be taught by people with appointments in 'ethnic studies' (i.e., experts)" (*Survey*). This would be a more radical requirement than the Committee forwarded.
Other	2	2	Miscellaneous and sundry reasons
None	15	13	Respondent gave no specific argument or was non-responsive to the question, "Why do you oppose the American Cultures requirement?"

ACKNOWLEDGMENTS

This line of inquiry was inspired by debates with my good friend Boaz Roth. The research was undertaken thanks to early help from Jerome Karabel, early and continuing support from Michael Olneck, and a critical audience provided by Orly Levy and Jim Nolan. Financial support was provided initially by the Ford Foundation through a grant to the ASA's Minority Opportunity Summer Training (MOST) Program. Further support was provided by an NIMH-funded Graduate Minority Fellowship from the ASA (#MH15722-13), and with partial support by a grant from the National Institute of Health (#HD25592-0251). The views in this paper should not reflect negatively upon the ASA, Ford Foundation, NIMH, NIH, or the individuals named above.

NOTES

1. Taking as my starting point Frederick Douglass's comment that "there is no progress without struggle," I have elsewhere explored the central role played by student social movements in agitating for multicultural general education requirements (Yamane 1993). Astin et al. (1975) do the same in their study of "the power of protest" in facilitating the multicultural curricular changes of the late-1960s and early-1970s (e.g., the institutionalization of ethnic studies departments and courses).

2. Among four-year institutions, these course requirements are evenly distributed among "research and doctoral universities" (48 percent), "comprehensive colleges" (50 percent), and "liberal arts colleges" (45 percent). The survey was based on a random sample of 270 chief academic officers at two-and four-year colleges and universities in the United States, for which there was a 72.6 percent response rate, for a final n=196.

3. For example, the published work of Sucheng Chan (1989) and Estelle Disch (1993) are more personal reflections on ethnic studies requirements than systematic analyses of them.

4. This and all further page references are to Hunter (1991) unless otherwise noted.

5. I am indebted to Boaz Roth for his guidance on this point.

6. A full mapping of this vast terrain in terms of the framework provided by Hunter would be fascinating and useful. Unfortunately, such a major task cannot be undertaken here.

7. Many people I spoke with suggested that the idea existed even at the time of the Third World College strike at UC-Berkeley in 1969. There is some evidence that at other colleges in the late sixties (e.g., Beloit College in Wisconsin), one of the black student strikers' demands was to require that whites take classes about black history and culture (Astin et al. 1975).

8. This process of calculation is audible on a tape recording of the meeting which was given to me by a member of the Senate.

9.   It is interesting to note that in the bedlam which characterized this part of the meeting, a critical mathematical error was made which undoubtedly had a major impact on the future of the requirement. Whoever calculated 184 as the number of votes necessary to pass the motion made a mistake. One-third of 286 is 95.3, not 92; and two-thirds is therefore 191, not 184. By my calculation, the final vote of 185 in favor of the motion should not have been a sufficient number of ayes to pass the mail ballot. It was, in fact, six votes shy. Moreover, the nay vote on the mail ballot was 155. 185 plus 155 equals 340 total votes cast. This is far more than 286, the number from which 184 as two-thirds was mistakenly calculated in the first place. Since 185 is less than two-thirds of 286, it is definitely far less than two-thirds of 340. In sum, it appears by these calculations made after the fact that the mail ballot should never have passed in the first place, and the first ACR proposal should have been voted on by the faculty that day. While we will never know what would have happened if the faculty had voted on the ACR that day, many involved suspect that the delay of the faculty vote on the requirement was the best thing that could have happened. It allowed the Special Committee to get further input from those faculty who were on the fence, and draft a more palatable second proposal.

10.   See the Minutes of the Special Meeting, University of California Academic Senate, Berkeley Division, 25 April 1989. Over 400 faculty members attended the meeting, as did some 700 students, 350 in the auditorium where the vote was held, and another 350 who listened to the debate broadcast in the Student Union (*Daily Californian*, 26 April 1989).

11.   While what was said during the interviews I conducted certainly should not be mistaken for *public* discourse, everyone I interviewed was an important actor in the conflict over American Cultures. To locate these individuals, I snowballed a sample, first by drawing names of people involved from relevant official documents, then by pulling them from the campus paper, and finally by asking people who were involved if they knew of other important actors. In the course of my research, I found the attitudes they expressed in our private conversations articulated very well with what was generally understood to be their public positions. Because not all publicly articulated positions are captured in print, these interviews are a necessary and useful supplementary source of data in this analysis.

12.   Charles Camic's intelligent reading of Weber has been instructive here.

13.   Most of the 115 professors whose statements I coded gave more than one reason for opposing the requirement.

REFERENCES

Adams, H. 1988. *The Academic Tribes*. Urbana: University of Illinois Press.

Astin, A., H. Astin, A. Bayer, and A. Bisconti. 1975. *The Power of Protest: A National Study of Student and Faculty Disruptions with Implications for the Future*. San Francisco: Jossey-Bass.

Atlas, J. 1992. *The Battle of the Books: The Curriculum Debate in America*. New York: W.W. Norton.

Bennett, W. 1984. *To Reclaim a Legacy: A Report on the Humanities in Higher Education*. Washington, DC: National Endowment for the Humanities.

Bloom, A. 1987. *The Closing of the American Mind*. New York: Simon and Schuster.

————. 1990. "Western Civ." Pp. 13-31 in *Giants and Dwarfs: Essays 1960-1990*. New York: Simon and Schuster.

Burger, T. 1987. *Max Weber's Theory of Concept Formation: History, Laws, and Ideal Types*. Durham, NC: Duke University Press. Expanded edition.

Chan, S. 1989. "On the Ethnic Studies Requirement, Part I: Pedagogical Implications." *Amerasia Journal* 15:267-80.

Cohen, D., and B. Neufeld. 1981. "The Failure of High Schools and the Progress of Education." *Daedalus* 100:69-89.

Disch, E. 1993. "The Politics of Curricular Change: Establishing a Diversity Requirement at the University of Massachusetts at Boston." Pp. 195-213 in *Beyond a Dream Deferred: Multicultural Education and the Politics of Excellence*, edited by B. Thompson and S. Tyagi. Minneapolis, MN: University of Minnesota Press.

D'Souza, D. 1991. *Illiberal Education: The Politics of Race and Sex on Campus*. New York: Free Press.

Gates, H. L. 1992. *Loose Canons: Notes on the Culture Wars*. New York: Oxford University Press.

Graff, G. 1992. *Beyond the Culture Wars: How Teaching the Conflicts Can Revitalize American Education*. New York: W.W. Norton.

Graff, G., and W. Cain. 1989. "Peace Plan for the Canon Wars." *The Nation* (6 March):310-313.

Hirsch, E.D. 1987. *Cultural Literacy: What Every American Needs to Know*. Boston: Houghton Mifflin.

Hunter, J. 1991. *Culture Wars: The Struggle to Define America*. New York: Basic Books.

Jacoby, R. 1994. *Dogmatic Wisdom: How the Culture Wars Divert Education and Distract America*. New York: Doubleday.

Jay, G. 1992. "The First Round of the Culture Wars." *Chronicle of Higher Education* (26 February):B1-2.

Levine, A., and J. Cureton. 1992. "The Quiet Revolution: Eleven Facts About Multiculturalism and the Curriculum." *Change* 24 (January/February):25-29.

Pratt, M. L. 1990. "Humanities for the Future: Reflections on the Western Culture Debate at Stanford." *South Atlantic Quarterly* 89:7-26.

Simmons, W., Chair. 1988. "Report of the Special Committee on Education and Ethnicity." Prepared by the Special Committee on Education and Ethnicity, University of California Academic Senate, Berkeley Division.

————. 1989. "Proposal for an American Cultures Breadth Requirement." Report by the Special Committee on Education and Ethnicity, University of California Academic Senate, Berkeley Division.

Smith, B. 1990. "Cult-Lit: Hirsch, Literacy, and the 'National Culture'." *South Atlantic Quarterly* 89.

Sykes, C. 1990. *The Hollow Men: Politics and Corruption in Higher Education*. Washington, DC: Regnery Gateway.

VLS. 1989. "Culture Wars: Knowledge, Power, and the Loaded Canon." *Village Voice Literary Supplement* (January/February):12-35.

Weber, M. 1949. *The Methodology of the Social Sciences*. New York: Free Press.

Yamane, D. 1992. "Melting Pots and Salad Bowls at Berkeley: Discourses of Multiculturalism and the American Cultures Course Requirement." Paper presented at the annual meeting of the American Sociological Association, Pittsburgh, PA.

_____. 1993. "Challenging the Curricular Color Line: A Processual Model of Student Movements for Ethnic Studies Requirements in Higher Education." Paper presented at annual meeting of the American Sociological Association, Miami, FL

TEACHERS AND PREACHERS:
THE BATTLE OVER PUBLIC SCHOOL REFORM IN
GASTON COUNTY, NORTH CAROLINA

Kimon Howland Sargeant and Edwin L. West, Jr.

This paper will examine a proposed public school reform initiative—entitled the Odyssey project—and the sources of the religious right's opposition to Odyssey. Following Wuthnow (1983), we argue that in order to enter the political arena, religious groups must negotiate the symbolic barrier between religion and politics. This involves a two-stage process. First, religious groups must translate their religious concerns into moral ones (e.g., we are concerned about parents' rights, not teaching Christian values in school) and, second, they must then legitimize moral crusading in the public sphere. Religious groups justify their political activity by linking it with procedural rationality (e.g., the duty of parents to educate their children) or the public interest (e.g., we're concerned for the welfare of all the children). In Gaston county, symbolic issues such as the religious heritage of America and the content of education, whether local people or cosmopolitan elites make the decisions, rather than the specific content of the proposed program, were at the center of the struggle over Odyssey.

EDUCATION AND THE CULTURE WARS

The culture wars in American public life are being waged over a diverse and controversial range of issues, from the definition of life itself to the limits, if any, on free expression. The extensive media exposure given to dilemmas such as whether or not to allow gays to serve openly in the military, whether the National Endowment of the Arts should have funded Robert Mapplethorpe's photography, and the seemingly constant conflicts over abortion indicate that the culture wars have become a permanent fixture of our national life. Cultural issues such as the debate over abortion threaten to divide political conventions and party politics as much as the more "bread and butter" issues of tax policy, job creation, and economic growth. Special interest groups on both sides of the culture war—the National Organization for Women and People for the American Way on the left and Concerned Women for America and the Christian Coalition on the right—square off on a host of volatile subjects. The culture wars, it would seem, are here to stay.

To be sure, the culture wars in American society revolve around profound questions of national import, and therefore involve nationally based special interest groups representing both sides of the political and cultural spectrum. Yet the culture wars are also regional in nature, and may flare up over localized matters such as the content of school textbooks (see Bates 1993 for an in-depth analysis of one such local school battle). Local issues frequently provide the origins of national disputes, as was the case in Cincinnati when some local citizens attempted to bar the Mapplethorpe exhibit. Many local issues, however, never attain national prominence. We suggest that, more often than not, cultural conflicts occur at the local rather than the national level. The reason for this is simple. National issues involve disputes that are happening away from home. They are problems in someone else's backyard, so to speak. Local conflicts, however, are not someone else's problem. Because their potential impact is immediate, these local conflicts mobilize people to take sides. Many special interest groups recognize the appeal of local issues. For example, Ralph Reed, the director of the Christian Coalition, argues that "the real battles of concern to Christians are in the neighborhoods, school boards, city councils, and state legislatures."[1] The culture wars, then, are not simply a national or federal phenomenon. They involve clashes over important questions at the local as well as the national level.

Of all the issues that are likely to generate controversy, no issue hits closer to home than the education and care of children. A cursory glance at many of the most heated issues in the culture wars reveals just how pivotal education is. Multiculturalism, sex education, condom distribution, guns in schools, textbook selection, creationism, values clarification—controversies over these issues demonstrate how educational institutions have become a primary focus of the culture wars. Schools transmit cultural and national values to the next generation. The battle over the schools then is nothing less than a struggle for the future of America, a contest between competing visions of how to fulfill this nation's democratic promise.

In this article, we examine one instance of the culture wars coming to a local public school district. The site of this controversy was Gaston County, North Carolina, which earned a degree of sociological fame with Liston Pope's classic study *Millhands and Preachers* (1942). Pope analyzed the attitudes of church leaders toward the transformation of the local economy from a predominantly agrarian system to an industrialized textile manufacturing center. Pope was interested in learning how the churches responded to these economic changes and whether the churches supported or resisted the transformations in economic life.

In contrast to Pope's inquiry, the controversial issues in our study are cultural and moral, rather than economic. While Pope found that the local preachers were highly supportive of the economic changes occurring in Gaston County earlier this century, in 1993 some of Gaston County's conservative preachers strenuously resisted what they perceived to be the "radical" changes the local school board was proposing. Industrialization was welcomed by Gaston County preachers in the 1930s for its economic benefits, but recent efforts to prepare students for another major economic transformation— the shift to an information-based society in the twenty-first century— raised the suspicions of preachers and others concerned with the pace of cultural and moral change in Gaston County and the nation. Our aim in this paper is to explain and interpret the opposition to the proposed changes in Gaston County's school system in terms of the contemporary culture wars.

A PROFILE OF GASTON COUNTY

Gaston County is located a few miles west of Charlotte, North Carolina and two hours east of the Blue Ridge mountains. The Gaston County school district, with an approximate student enrollment of 31,000, is the fifth largest school system in North Carolina and is among the largest 150 districts in the United States. The total operating budget of the school system is $120 million and the school system is the second largest employer in Gaston County with more than 3300 part and full-time employees. The school system in Gaston County is clearly one of the most important local institutions. In fact, its supporters claim that, given the size of its mission, the school system requires more local resources to operate effectively. As evidence for this, school supporters cite the fact that though Gaston County ranks twelfth in the state in terms of median family income, county financial support for the school system ranks only ninety-first (out of 120).

In response to these concerns, community leaders spearheaded the election in 1988 of a reform-minded Board of Education. The new Board searched for ways to improve both the physical condition of the schools and the academic performance of the students. Before 1988, the performance of Gaston County students had been so poor that the school district was targeted for takeover by the State Board of Education. Moreover, the district was ranked in the bottom seventeen school districts in the state (out of 120) due to its students' poor academic performance, high dropout rates, and other unfavorable outcome measures. According to the reform-minded Board elected in 1988, a significant change in the district's philosophy of education would be required in order to achieve substantial improvements in academic performance.

In response to this crisis, the school board adopted an innovative pedagogical approach called outcome-based education (OBE). What is outcome-based education? In general, OBE refers to a change in the assessment of student performance based on a demonstration of skills rather than on traditional testing. Some OBE curricula go so far as to eliminate grades and grade levels in order to promote "attitudinal" outcomes. The Gaston County reform proposal included both of these elements and was christened the *Odyssey Project*. This project proposal incorporated "an outcome-based education model that focused on the knowledge, skills, and attitudes that students should possess when they graduate," as well as a longer school day and year; coordinated education, health, and social services; and early childhood education at three of the district's 54 schools (*Odyssey Project* 1922, p. 1). Grades were to be eliminated and replaced with four levels of formal schooling. In order to advance from one level to another, students would have to demonstrate their accomplishment of a set of performance outcomes specifically related to the five main goals (or "exit outcomes") of the program. These five goals of the *Odyssey Project* were "to produce lifelong learners capable of being effective communicators, collaborators, critical thinkers, creative producers, and concerned and confident citizens" (Odyssey Project 1992, p. 3).

Noble goals and intentions do not assure the success of any endeavor and the *Odyssey Project* was no exception. Before the first experimental program was implemented, the program encountered organized and often vitriolic opposition. The opponents of *Odyssey* objected to the use of outcome-based education as the principal means of instruction. Opponents also raised concerns about whether students would suffer in their applications to colleges because of OBE's untraditional approach, whether teachers could be retrained to use this unique curriculum, and whether OBE would interfere with the district's existing athletics' schedule. By far the most important objections raised were concerned with the overall philosophy and intention of the program. The leading opponent of the *Odyssey Project* likened it to Nazism, quoting Adolf Hitler and warning that "the program seeks to conquer children's minds" and was a form of behavior modification.[2] A letter to the editor of the local newspaper referred to the program as the work of the "Antichrist." Another opponent labeled outcome-based education "a fiasco" (Somerfield 1993, p. 1). Notably, opposition to outcome-based education has not been limited to Gaston County. Organized dissent to OBE, not all of it stemming from the religious right, has developed in at least a dozen states, including California, Washington, Colorado, Texas, Minnesota, New York, and Pennsylvania.[3]

What was so controversial about this reform program? Gaston County had earned a $20 million grant in a highly competitive national bidding process for the specific purpose of implementing this innovative project; yet, instead of celebrating, the district was soon torn by strife. For many parents, the program's proposed elimination of grade levels and letter grades was ample cause for alarm. But hysteria over the program was generated not so much by its pedagogical method as by its philosophical basis. Put simply, the program's opponents saw outcome-based education as promoting "secular humanism." Thus, while the catalyst for the battle over the Gaston County public schools was this proposed shift to outcome-based education, we argue that the underlying cause of unrest in Gaston County was the parents' grassroots reaction to what they perceived to be a "secular" threat to their traditionalist world view. They were fighting to protect their children from the interference of professional "outsiders," outsiders whom they deemed to be antagonistic to their religious convictions. In other words, the rallying cry for the opposition to outcome-based education was not so much "no grades" as it was "no God."

THE GENESIS OF CONFLICT

The election of the reform-minded Gaston County Board of Education in 1988 marked the beginning of educational change in the Gaston County schools. In 1990, a new school superintendent was hired and given a mandate from the board to improve the schools. Under his leadership, Gaston County submitted a proposal to the New American Schools Development Corporation (NASDC) in 1992 to fund the county's proposed school of the twenty-first century.[4] In July, Gaston County's *Odyssey Project* proposal was one of 11 proposals selected by NASDC in a national competition. By November of 1992, Gaston County had received $2 million in order to implement the first phase (a planning year) of the *Odyssey Project*. According to the stipulations of the grant, NASDC would evaluate in May of 1993 Gaston County's progress in implementing the *Odyssey Project* and determine whether Gaston County would receive any of the remaining $20 million grant.

This auspicious beginning to the *Odyssey Project* was quickly overshadowed by the attack of a religiously motivated pressure group.

It all started with a videotape. While visiting her relatives in Pennsylvania, a resident of Gaston County was presented with a videotape—"Who Controls the Minds of Children?"—produced by *Citizens for Excellence in Education*, a California-based lobbying group that actively opposes outcome-based education. Eventually, this video found its way into the hands of Reverend Gregory Dry, pastor of Ranlo Baptist Church. According to Reverend Dry, one of the primary faults of the *Odyssey* program was that it imposed a set of non-Christian values on the public schools. Dry, whose child attends a private church school, claimed that he was fighting the new program "because the values taught in *Odyssey* schools won't be those taught in Christian homes...I don't want values taught my children that contradict the values I teach my children...They don't want us to teach the Bible in schools... *Odyssey* is trying to teach children to move away from their moral underpinnings like the church."[5] At a meeting held at Dry's church in February 1993, approximately 500 people watched the video in which programs such as *Odyssey* were accused of using computers to spy on families, and of condoning homosexuality.[6] From this initial viewing of the video, an active and vocal opposition to *Odyssey* developed. The battle over *Odyssey* had begun.

The opposition to *Odyssey* packed school board meetings where they monopolized the use of the microphone, harassed school board members, wrote letters to local newspapers, distributed fliers urging parents to act swiftly in order to save their children from the dire effects of this "radical" school program, circulated warnings on *Prodigy*—the home electronic mail network, and gathered signatures on petitions. School board staff members were spat upon and were subjected to name calling and verbal abuse. Intimidating phone calls were made until the early hours of the morning to an 83 year old member of the Board of Education whose spouse had recently died. And, on a few occasions, they, it was alleged, threatened the lives of board members by phone at home.

In addition, leaders of Concerned Citizens for Public Education, an organization formed to fight *Odyssey*, appealed to the County Commissioners (who control local school funding) and members of the General Assembly to put pressure on the Board of Education to rescind its support of *Odyssey*. These tactics met with some success as two members of the General Assembly and some members of the County Commission took a public stand against the *Odyssey Project*.

While the controversy over the *Odyssey Project* was largely a local affair, national advocacy organizations also played an important role in framing the debate and fanning the flames of discontent. One especially active opposition group was *Citizens for Excellence in Education* (CEE), which produced the video critical of outcome-based education, and is the activist arm of the National Association of Christian Educators. CEE's goals, as stated in its literature, are:

> [T]o return faith to public schools.... to change the atheist dominated ideology of secular humanism in our school texts, curriculum, and teachers' unions.... to return Christians to control of public schools.[7]

Outcome-based education is, according to CEE, one of the programs that most threatens to impose the ideology of secular humanism in public schools. Dr. Robert Simonds, the founder of CEE, claims that in OBE "children will be taught racial guilt, multiculturalism, and environmentalism that teaches the worship of rocks, birds, plants, and self instead of God."[8] The objects of the CEE's wrath are the alleged secular humanism and new age thinking promoted by programs such as outcome-based education. Worse yet, outcome-based education, as described in CEE literature, "is without a doubt, the end of academic education in America" (Simonds 1992, p. 3). As a result of programs like OBE (as well as self-esteem curriculums), "the battleground of testing for the church is in the public schools" (Anti-Defamation League 1992, p. 2). CEE is not alone in its opposition to outcome-based education. The Reverend Pat Robertson has also joined the nationwide struggle; he has shown the Pennsylvania video on his television program and actively supports attacks on outcome-based education in other states.

Although initially unprepared for such a virulent opposition to *Odyssey*, the Gaston County school board defended its program and attempted to foster support for *Odyssey* through an information campaign. For example, the board distributed an *Odyssey Fact Book* to help parents learn more about *Odyssey*. It also held public meetings, wrote letters to local newspapers, and fought to convince parents of the benefits of the proposed school reforms. Pro-OBE national interest groups involved themselves in the debate. *People for the American Way* provided a complete analysis of CEE tactics nationally. With this assistance of *People for the American Way*, the school board had reason to believe the

Odyssey Project could be successfully defended. On March 23, 1993, when the Gaston County School Board gave its final approval for three schools to implement the *Odyssey Project*, it seemed that the proposal would become a reality.

The Symbols of Cultural Conflict

Was there something fundamentally unsound with outcome-based education to draw such controversy? Was the soundness of outcome-based education even at issue in Gaston County? Why did conservative Christians feel especially threatened by the *Odyssey Project* and, what was the role of special interest groups in escalating the conflict?

In order to make sense of the conflict over outcome-based education, it is important to understand the symbolism inherent in the culture war. Each side in the culture war invokes particular symbols within a particular historical context. Each side "struggles to monopolize the symbols of legitimacy by labeling the opposition an extremist faction," marginal to the mainstream of American life (Hunter 1991, p. 147). Thus, CEE accuses outcome-based education of promoting secular humanism and manipulating unsuspecting children. Meanwhile, People for the American Way claims that the religious right poses a dire threat to freedom and tolerance in the United States.

Organizations actively involved in the culture war not only use negative symbolism to discredit their opponents but also seek to associate themselves with positive or legitimating symbols. For conservative Christians (and others on the orthodox side of the cultural divide), these symbols of legitimacy may include the traditional family, the flag, morality, and religious devotion. Not surprisingly, organizations promoting the orthodox agenda in the culture war will seek to embody these symbols in their names. Examples abound. Consider "Concerned Women for America," the "Moral Majority," the "Christian Coalition," and even "Citizens for Excellence in Education." All of these organizations invoke the favored symbols of the orthodox side and suggest, by implication, that those who disagree with them are either unconcerned about America, immoral, unchristian, or in favor of mediocrity in education. On the progressive side, organizations such as "People for the American Way," the "American Civil Liberties Union," and the "National Organization for Women" imply through their organizational names that they uphold the values of America, of freedom, or of women. The contestants in the culture war are fighting over the symbolic meaning attributed to the family, America, or the nature of freedom. Cultural conflict in America today is about "the uses of symbols, the uses of language, and the right to impose discrediting labels upon those who would dissent. It is ultimately a struggle over the right to define the way things are and the way they ought to be" (Hunter 1991, p. 155).

The perception of reality is largely defined by symbols. It is therefore those who most effectively manipulate these symbols who will succeed in framing the American perception of reality. For example, is our health care system "in crisis" or the "best system in the world" that needs some minor adjustments? To take another example, what is a family? In the United States, the term "family" represents a revered symbol of hearth and home. But will "family" connote the traditional bourgeois model of a working father and a (at least part-time) stay-at-home mother with children or is it any possible combination of persons united by bonds of love? How this question is answered—or what symbol of the family gains public legitimacy—will have profound implications for public policy and our common life together.

The clash between the progressives and the orthodox over the definition of symbols is ultimately a clash over the nature of America itself. The progressives' and the orthodox's differing visions of America are based upon their profoundly different understandings of moral authority. For progressives, moral authority "tends to reside in personal experience or scientific rationality, or either of those in conversation with a particular religious or cultural tradition." For the orthodox, moral authority "is the commitment on the part of adherents to an external, definable, and transcendent authority" (Hunter 1991, pp. 44-45). Because of these fundamentally different understandings of moral authority, progressive and orthodox groups tend to talk past each other in the culture war, rarely understanding the other's positions, and perhaps even more rarely, convinced that there is merit to the opposing side's views. In sum, it is not money but morals—to borrow Lamont's (1992) terms—that fuels the culture war in America.

The vehemence of the culture wars is inextricably linked to the fact that what people hold most sacred—their conception of the Good—is often at stake in disputes over matters of moral authority. On the orthodox side, a fear of the spread of secular humanism among the religious right reflects a growing concern about the ability of conservative Christians to maintain their beliefs and pass them on to the next generation. As Steve Bruce argues, "the New Christian Right is a movement of cultural, rather than status, defense. It is concerned with the politics of lifestyles rather than status" (Bruce 1988, p. 16). One of the primary goals of the New Christian Right is to help its followers maintain their orthodox world view. This task, however, is becoming increasingly difficult because of the continuing advance of "carriers" of modernity such as bureaucracy, technology, and cultural pluralism (Berger, Berger, and Kellner 1973). The formation of the religious right thus can be understood "as a reaction to changes in the social, moral, cultural, and political environment which [threaten] to undermine the ability of a particular group to maintain its shared culture" (Bruce 1988, p. 16).

Let us now examine the context of how fundamentalists have come to be active in the political realm and how they justify their political involvement. To begin, the emergence of conservative Christian political activism in the late 1970s and especially in the 1980s through organizations such as Reverend Jerry Falwell's *Moral Majority* was an unexpected—and in many quarters, an unwelcome—development. Fundamentalists and evangelicals had not had an active political presence in the United States for decades and it was believed that their theology precluded public involvement. Conservative Christians were thought to be so involved with matters of personal piety, morality, and evangelism as to have neither the inclination toward, nor the justification for, political activism. Empirical research conducted through the 1960s and early 1970s (see Wuthnow [1983] for a summary of these findings) confirmed that evangelicals were less likely to be politically active than were their less evangelical counterparts. One reason for the relative political quietism of evangelicals and fundamentalists during this time was that many of the popular movements of this period, such as the civil rights movement and the anti-Vietnam war protest, were not broadly supported within conservative churches.

Contrary to the perception that the religious convictions of fundamentalists precluded or at least strongly discouraged political involvement, the political developments of recent years have made quite clear that there is room within the fundamentalist world view for political activism. Robert Wuthnow suggests that the reason many analysts inaccurately predicted that fundamentalists would remain politically aloof is due to their misunderstanding of the nature of religious symbol systems in general. The problem with many analyses of religion, according to Wuthnow, is that "religious systems are regarded as static clusters of beliefs organized around simple tenets, such as the quest for individual salvation." A more accurate view is that "[r]eligious systems are dynamic configurations of symbolism and ritual whose character has scarcely begun to be comprehended" (Wuthnow 1983, p. 17). Thus, in order to understand religion, we must understand its symbolism, as well as the constraints on religious symbols in the public sphere. First, let us turn to the constraints upon religious symbolism in the public sphere.

One of the most important constraints on religion in modernized societies has been the separation of the public realm from the domain of morality and religion. For example, the state legitimizes its activity through procedural rationality, not through the traditional forms of authority used by religion. Thus, for Christians to be politically active in the modern world, they must find ways to negotiate the symbolic barrier between religion and politics. Wuthnow argues that there are in fact two types of symbolic barriers to be negotiated: the first is between religion and morality and the second is between morality and politics (Wuthnow 1983, p. 180). As an example of how the first boundary is negotiated, groups such as the Moral Majority and the Christian Coalition are able to attract a broad following because they do not develop a specifically religious (or theological) basis for their organization. They have no statement of faith or position on infant baptism. Instead, their agenda is based on moral positions (albeit with clearly religious justifications) on issues ranging from abortion and homosexuality to school choice. Thus, Baptists, Presbyterians, Pentecostals, Catholics, Jews, and secularists who agree with these positions may join such political pressure groups. Framing religiously based opposition in moral terms is a necessary, and common, activity for Christians involved in politics at every level of society.

Based on this premise, we would expect the Christian activists in GastonCounty publicly to articulate their opposition to the *Odyssey Project* in non-religious or moral terms. And, in fact, in their dealings with the press, leaders of the *Odyssey* opposition were careful to frame their concerns in terms of the moral or public policy implications of the program. One of the parents upset with the proposed *Odyssey* program, for example, exemplified this strategy by arguing: "This is not a religious issue. This is a parental rights issue."[9] The implication is that all parents, religious or otherwise, should be concerned with the effects of *Odyssey* on their children.

In addition, Christian activists must also find a way to legitimize moral crusading in politics—the second of Wuthnow's symbolic boundaries. Two of the most common ways to bridge the symbolic boundary between morality and politics is to legitimate political claims by associating them with procedural rationality or by linking them symbolically with the public interest. Let us take one of Reverend Dry's statements as an example of how a religious issue may be framed in a manner acceptable to the public sphere. In response to criticisms of the religious motivation behind the *Odyssey* opposition, Reverend Gregory Dry asserted, "We're not going to come primarily from the religious aspect. We're more concerned about other issues related to this program," such as the legal duty of parents to educate their children and the responsibility of schools to be responsive to parents' wishes.[10] In the first part of his statement, Dry claims that his concerns are moral, rather than religious. In the second part, Dry legitimizes his political activism by appealing to procedural rationality ("the legal duty of parents"). Elsewhere, Dry argues that *Odyssey* will harm the children of Gaston County by providing an inferior education; this is an appeal to the public interest. Thus, by framing its religiously based objections in moral terms, and by linking these moral concerns to broader issues such as the public interest and the legal duty of parents, the opposition to *Odyssey* developed its strategy for challenging the program in the public sphere.

Behind the rhetoric, the *Odyssey* opponents' primary objections to OBE were quite subtle, having to do with their concern for the future course of this country, the meaning of America, the future of their children, and the ability of local citizens to define and maintain their way of life without undue interference from outsiders. Of course, much of the vitriolic rhetoric of *Odyssey's* opponents seems to have little to do with such lofty notions as the meaning of America or preserving the autonomy of local communities. But it is precisely the intensity of their attacks that reveals just how critical these issues were to the *Odyssey* opposition. In the next section, we will examine their opposition to *Odyssey* by taking a closer look at three specific symbolic issues.

THE MEANING OF AMERICA: CHRISTIAN OR SECULAR?

The clash over the *Odyssey Project* in Gaston County can be interpreted as one part of a larger cultural battle which James Hunter has termed "the struggle to define America."[11] As indicated earlier, this struggle is especially fierce in the context of public school reform because schools serve as the primary institutions responsible for reproducing community and national identity for succeeding generations of Americans. Through courses in history, civics, geography, literature, and so on, schools ultimately teach what it means to be an American.[12] In addition to Hunter, Donald Heinz (1983) also suggests that the battle over the public schools represents "a struggle to define America." Heinz argues that the religious right is engaged in a contest over the meaning of America's story and therefore is attempting to establish a counter mythology to the established liberal and secular mythology predominant in schools today. "For the new Christian Right, the public school stands as a primary symbol of their control, or lack of control, over decisions that directly affect their lives" (Heinz 1983, p. 139). From this perspective, the school is a symbol of the community. The federal government's intervention in the practices of local schools over the last few decades (banning prayer and Bible reading, for example) alarms some citizens and incurs the hostility of those who support local control. Furthermore, federal intervention raises the suspicions of many individuals toward any type of school reform proposal. In the case of Gaston County, many opponents of *Odyssey* wanted nothing less than a speedy return to the traditional curricula that had been displaced. As Reverend Dry wrote, "What we want is for our schools to get back to teaching true academics, love for our country, and a fear of Almighty God.... [W]e want prayer and Bible reading in the classroom. You want to 'reinvent' our schools? This is the only way to do it that we'll accept" (Day 1993b).

It is our contention that the conflict in Gaston County over the Odyssey project can best be understood as an expression of hostility toward governmental reforms and an appreciation for the importance of schools in transmitting shared cultural values. For example, although certain elements of the *Odyssey* proposal were specifically attacked—such as the replacement of grades with mastering outcomes—the specifics of the program were objected to less frequently than were the program's alleged philosophical underpinnings. In other words, the primary source of opposition to *Odyssey* was not its lack of letter grades but the perception that the program inculcated anti-Christian moral values. Does *Odyssey* condone homosexuality? Does it teach "secular humanism?" Does it undermine the moral values of the church and of Christian homes? These were the concerns that mobilized the opposition. At their root all these questions express a basic concern for the meaning of America: Is America a secular or a Christian nation?

Typically, the religious right voices its concern that a secular humanistic philosophy is now predominant in America's public schools. Such a concern can be seen as a reaction to a more general sense that the country has been moving in an increasingly secular direction. Thus, for the religious right, the symbol (or specter) of secular humanism represents much that has gone wrong with the United States in recent decades. In a national survey conducted in 1987, over two-thirds (69 percent) of the evangelical respondents familiar with the term agreed that "public schools [were] teaching the values of secular humanism" compared to only one-quarter (27 percent) of those identified as secularists. An even greater number of evangelicals (82 percent compared to only 21 percent of the secularists) described secular humanism's "impact on this country" (presumably in large measure through the public schools) as "bad" (Hunter 1991, p. 203). Conservative Christians have a tendency to blame secular humanism for many of the evils of the modern world, from abortion on demand to declining church attendance. Thus, it is not surprising that the fear of secular humanism prompted some Gaston County residents to vehemently oppose *Odyssey*. One mother, for example, called the *Odyssey* program "secular humanism," and claimed that "they're taking my baby, my child, and giv[ing] them the choices they want. We send the kids in and they want to teach them morals."[13] From this viewpoint, the state is seen as intrinsically opposed to parental authority and the schools are viewed as the tools whereby the state can ideologically indoctrinate children. *Odyssey* was seen as a blatant example of such indoctrination. By labeling *Odyssey* as a propagator of secular humanism, fundamentalists categorically rejected the program.

In the view of the religious right, secular humanism represents a betrayal of America's purpose. Furthermore, the religious right views the possible courses for America in stark contrast: America is either secular or Christian. Therefore, when the opponents of *Odyssey* find that the program is not Christian, they conclude that it must be secular. Reverend Dry claimed that the overall philosophy of outcome-based education "was designated (*sic*) to teach opposition to Christianity.... It requires students to accept specific morals and values to progress and destroys traditional values."[14] What was his evidence? Dry based his objections on the information from the CEE video, as well as his own unique interpretation of specific *Odyssey* terminology. For example, *Odyssey* states as one of its goals the propagation of "humanistic" learning. In Dry's analysis, "humanistic" learning is "secular humanism."

One reason for Dry's blanket condemnation of OBE is his conflation of civic and religious values. Civic duties such as voting and obeying the law, and morals such as honesty, industry, and courtesy conceivably can be taught in a nonsectarian manner, without entering the morally charged terrain of issues such as sexuality. In Dry's view, however, all values are inextricably religious in nature. Similarly, Robert Simonds, the head of CEE, argues that "Government and true Christianity are inseparable!... Morality is based on the Christian Bible" (Anti-Defamation League 1994, p. 101). In denying the possibility of a nonsectarian approach to inculcating civic values, the religious right labels all that is not supportive of conservative Christianity as "secular humanism."

The Care of Children: Parents' Rights v. Education Reform

While preserving or restoring a "Christian" nation is a goal that not all fundamentalists share, preserving and perpetuating the Christian family is an almost universally accepted aim within this community. The family is, after all, the most important means through which a community's beliefs and values are inculcated in the following generation. It is therefore not surprising that some of the most vociferous attacks on *Odyssey* were made by those who feared *Odyssey's* impact upon their own parental authority. The religious right exploited this anxiety by voicing their concerns about the effect of the proposed reforms on families and children. Reverend Dry, as mentioned earlier, stated that one of his reasons for opposing Odyssey was that "the values taught in Odyssey schools won't be those taught in Christian homes.... I don't want values taught my children [in public schools] that contradict the values I teach my children."[15] Even though Dry's child attends a Christian school, many if not most of the children in the local churches attend the public schools. It is possible that the schools might try to teach Christian children "anti-Christian" values. To take another example, flyers distributed to parents labeled the *Odyssey* project "a radical program" and urged that parents have the right to review such a program before it is used in the classroom.[16]

Much of the hyperbolic rhetoric in this case was disseminated by national advocacy organizations, specifically Citizens for Excellence in Education (CEE). For example, one letter from the national office of CEE warned that public schools would continue "to sink deeper into the pit of illiteracy, immorality, and psychological indoctrination of every child's mind" if programs such as OBE were adopted.[17] Dr. Robert Simonds, the founder of CEE, warned that "OBE is, without a doubt, the end of academic education in America" (Simonds 1992, p. 3). Elsewhere, Simonds suggested that OBE "is nothing short of a communist system, only worse." This alarmist tone is reflected in the statements by the local chapter of CEE. In Gaston County, CEE passed out information critical of OBE, claiming that it was "a method of manipulating students through behavior modification."[18] According to these statements, not only was OBE academically inferior but its emphasis on psychological development and affective outcomes accomplished a sort of brainwashing.

It is important to note that while much of the rhetoric of the religious right in Gaston County was inflammatory, some of the information distributed by the *Odyssey Project* contributed to the development of a vocal opposition. The *Odyssey Project* proposed replacing grades with four formal levels of schooling. It also included a prenatal to age three component. Instead of using grades, Greek letters were assigned to each age range of learners at a particular center. "Alpha" designated children up to three years of age, "beta" referred to children between ages three and six. Learners ages seven to ten were designated "gamma"; "delta" referred to learners ages eleven to fourteen. The high school was to be renamed the *Odyssey* Center, to signify that learning is a lifelong journey. As with many proposals to revamp existing organizations, the *Odyssey Project* proposal developed its own extensive terminology. Unfortunately, the laudable goals of the project were often overshadowed by the overly technical and occasionally alarming terms used by the planners. For example, *Odyssey* planners wanted to ensure that preschool children would receive training at home that would help to prepare them for school. Because of the critical need for "pre-school learning opportunities for all children," the Gaston County Design Team (GCDT)—comprised of local educators with more than 170 years experience in the school system—urged that "these important learning years must not be allowed to lie dormant in environments which lack proper stimulation" (The Odyssey Project 1992 pp. 7-8). How was this to be done? The GCDT proposed that "health care workers and counselors will visit Alpha homes to ensure that health care needs are being met, [and] that adequate cognitive stimulation is being provided."

This combination of passive voice, the imperative ("must not be allowed"), and unusual terminology (Alphas and Betas) contributed to an almost Orwellian sense of impending government intervention and regulation. The prospect of "Beta center learning facilitators" visiting the homes of Alpha children may have fanned the flames of opposition among a group already suspicious of the government's involvement in education. Though the Gaston County educators made numerous efforts to clarify their terminology and discuss the specifics of the program—they held public meetings, wrote letters to the editor, published an information guide to summarize the program, and so forth—their efforts were rebuffed. One explanation for this was that, even though the project had been designed by local educators, the staff hired for the *Odyssey Project* by the design team lacked credibility with their opponents—they were "outsiders" to the community, i.e., not longtime residents of Gaston County.

Who Decides?: Cosmopolitan v. Local Control

The controversy over the *Odyssey* program in Gaston County was in many ways a referendum on change. Is change good? Is it necessary? And who decides what kind of change to bring—local parents or outside experts? One's view of the desirability of change greatly influenced one's view of the *Odyssey Project's* terminology. For example, while "change," "radical" restructuring, and "world class" education represented to the educators the best aims of a school system, these very terms signified to *Odyssey's* opposition much that had gone wrong with the world.

The opposition to the *Odyssey Project* was catalyzed by conservative Christians' profound distrust of change. Fundamentalists are, after all, part of a religious group dedicated to preserving an unchanging truth.

And preserving a religious truth is intimately connected with preserving a way of life because ideas of any sort are sustained and transmitted by communities with similar lifestyles. This is what Steve Bruce (1988) has called the "politics of lifestyle choice." Fundamentalists are fighting to preserve their way of life, which they perceive (with some justification) to be threatened by changes in the culture. Nancy Ammerman, in her study *Baptist Battles*, suggests that the fundamentalists are defined by their rejection of modernity. "Fundamentalism only exists where there is conscious opposition to the forces of change, and conscious opposition can only exist where there are forces of change" (Ammerman 1990, p. 155). Fundamentalist groups are likely to mobilize when change is proposed. The opposition to the Odyssey project in Gaston County provides an excellent example of the nature of fundamentalism's resistance to the modern world.

The religious right has been one of the most vociferous opponents of proposed changes in the schools, criticizing programs such as "whole language, global education, self-esteem, values education, critical thinking, holistic education, multicultural education, site-based management, mentoring, non-graded classes, and cooperative learning." Furthermore, according to *School Board News*, school districts that adopt innovative reform proposals are likely to be accused of embracing programs rooted in "New Age religion," which teach children to defy their parents (Sorohan 1991, pp. 1-5). Many of these criticisms were levelled against *Odyssey* in Gaston County.

One element of the *Odyssey Project* that came under particularly heavy criticism was the Board's goal of developing a "world class" education. The board's intent was to develop a first-rate educational program, one that could be a national and even an international model of twenty-first century education. Unfortunately, "world class" turned out to be a term loaded with negative connotations for the opponents of *Odyssey*. In the parlance of the religious right, "world class" is associated with a "one world" government—a monolithic, anti-Christian entity promoted by secular humanists and alluded to in Christian apocalyptic literature. Thus, when Gaston County educators proclaimed the worthiness of their intentions to bring a "world class" education to Gaston County, they actually confirmed many of their opponents' worst fears. "World class" education was viewed as nothing less than a plan by secular cosmopolitan outsiders to replace the traditional, and locally acceptable, methods of teaching children.

This predisposition toward interpreting educational terminology in terms of conspiratorial efforts by "secular humanists" is by no means unique to Gaston County. Fritz Detwiler, a professor of religion who follows the religious right closely, suggests that there are recognizable patterns in the way educational terms acquire negative connotations. Detwiler finds that in the parlance of the religious right, "'global education' becomes 'globalism' (a push toward one-world government), character education becomes 'moral relativism,' critical thinking becomes 'challenges to parental authority,' and 'affective education' becomes 'New Age religion'" (cited in Soadren 1991, p. 5). The mere presence of suspicious terms in an educational proposal may be enough to mobilize opposition. Unfortunately, the creators of the *Odyssey* proposal in Gaston County were unaware of this danger. They extolled the virtues of creating a "world class" education system (a term which, as we have seen, galvanized *Odyssey's* opponents).

In order to create a "world class" educational system, the *Odyssey* plan promised—or threatened, depending upon one's point of view—to radically restructure public school education. For example, the Gaston County design team, according to *The Gaston Gazette*, wanted to create "a radical new way to teach children."[19] For the Gaston County educators who designed the new program, the radical part of their approach was that it offered a new means to achieve the fundamental and essential aims of education. Their radical proposal was a way to *return* to the aims of education, not break with the goals of the past. Unfortunately, what was "radical" in the sense "of pertaining to the root or foundation" to the educators was instead understood by the active opposition as radical in the sense of "extreme." OBE was perceived not as a program that might "radically" improve the education of children in Gaston County but rather as a "radical" plan to teach secular or anti-Christian values to children.

The *Odyssey Project* was presented as a major change in education, a change that the planners thought would be welcomed. However, terms that the planners used to promote the program actually incited the ire of the program's opposition. To take another example, the *Odyssey* proposal states that all learning centers will use "paideia" concepts as the primary instructional delivery system. What is paideia? It is Mortimer Adler's concept of seminar training. However, Reverend Gregory Dry, writing in *The Gaston Gazette*, links paideia with "secular humanism," in part due to the description of paideia as a form of "general humanistic learning" and to a reference to the Aspen Institute for Humanistic Studies in a teacher's booklet on how to use the paideia approach (Dry, 1993a). The "humanism" of paideia combined with the "radical" plan to create "world class" schools led Dry to conclude that the *Odyssey* project is "nothing less than a new world view. They know that we aren't likely to change, so their only hope is to seek changes through our school children. They've been doing it for years with their sex-ed programs, values clarification programs, holistic health programs and the like." The opposition to *Odyssey* was thus based not solely on the proposal to implement outcome-based education but on a resentment of all of the educational changes that have threatened the fundamentalist world view.

In retrospect, the *Odyssey* planning team recognized some of the mistakes it made that contributed to misunderstandings of the new program. Educational jargon—such as outcome-based education, paideia, core and core-plus curriculum, and global education—made the *Odyssey Project* less attractive to those uninitiated in such terminology. Even the *Odyssey* fact book, which was specifically prepared for parents, contained jargon. For example, the benefits of *Odyssey* were summarized as follows:

> By using an outcome-based model, specifying exit outcomes, determining a set of performance outcomes for each level of schooling, subscribing to the theory of multiple intelligences, and identifying common and special features for core curriculum areas, the *Odyssey Project* will produce world class learners who can function effectively in a diverse global society (The Odyssey Fact Book 1993, p. 7).

Use of such jargon, particularly in a county with a 52 percent illiteracy rate, promoted an atmosphere of suspicion and provided a focal point for the opposition's attacks. In addition, as we mentioned earlier, suspicion of the new program was exacerbated by the fact that all staff members of the Odyssey project were new to the county and the project director himself had only been a resident for eighteen months. Not only did the staff lack knowledge of Gaston County's culture and community, but local opponents could then portray the staff as "outsiders" coming to impose their "secular" or "radical" ideas upon the county. Put differently, the local opposition was able to cultivate a resentment of "cosmopolitan" educators who were coming in to tell the people how a school system really should be run while ignoring the fact that local educators had designed the program.

Searching for Common Ground in Public Education

The furor over the *Odyssey Project* in Gaston County is a clear and unfortunate example of the grassroots nature of the culture wars. Conservative Christians reacted against the perceived takeover of their local schools by "secular humanism" and against the "cosmopolitan" educational experts. Outcome-based education alone was not the problem in Gaston County. School reform had a decidedly negative connotation in Gaston County, as it was associated with removing prayer and the Bible from public schools and introducing controversial programs such as sex education. Eventually, the proposed "radical" restructuring of three of the county's 54 schools catalyzed enough of a groundswell of opposition to reform that the *Odyssey Project* was terminated, the remaining funds from the NASDC grant were forfeited, and the school superintendent was forced to resign. The school board members face a difficult reelection campaign this fall. Culture wars often have very concrete results.

Although the conservative Christians of Gaston County did have important concerns with the *Odyssey Project*, many of their concerns could have been addressed if there had been a forum for reasoned debate and discussion. The "paideia" method of "general humanistic learning" is not a front for "secular humanism" but a teaching method that uses seminars to allow students to actively participate in class discussion. The details of how Beta center learning facilitators were going to help parents of Alpha children enhance their preschool learning were not firmly fixed and conceivably could have included assistance that some conservative Christian parents may have welcomed. In these and other areas of the controversy over *Odyssey*, it might have been possible to find common ground between the concerned parents and the *Odyssey Project* team about the benefits and liabilities of the program, such as allowing children whose parents objected to the program to transfer to another school. Yet reasoned debate was unable to take root in the soil of acrimonious shouting spawned by conservative Christians who vehemently opposed the program and who refused to meet and discuss the program unless it was an open forum with the media present.

One reason for this lack of dialogue and the resulting inability to find common ground was that national advocacy organizations such as CEE and People for the American Way became involved in the dispute. Each of these national organizations is opposed on principle to "compromise." Each paints the other as the enemy of the Good— whether the Good is understood to be God in the public schools or liberty and tolerance. Because each of these organizations has a national base, each has an interest in heightening the conflict so that they can alert their supporters to the dangers posed by their antagonists in the culture war. Escalation of rhetoric makes for good publicity but bad relations among those engaged in the dispute. The tragedy in Gaston County was that a substantive debate about the merits of the reform proposal was never broached.

What the furor over the *Odyssey Project* shows is that the only way to resolve the culture war is through the difficult task of arguing substantively—rather than by invective or inflammatory images and statements—about our deepest differences (see Hunter's *Before the Shooting Begins* for an extended discussion of how the culture war might be mediated). In other words, the issues in Gaston County could not be sidestepped. They needed to be addressed directly, with each side willing to consider possible compromises. Clearly, this did not happen. Second, the furor in Gaston County also demonstrates how concerns over public education are likely to continue to play an important role in the culture wars. Any innovation that affects children—children who will lead our nation into the twenty-first century—will always generate controversy. Last, the *Odyssey Project's* untimely demise should not convince us that school reform is impossible. The real lesson from *Odyssey* is that any reform effort must anticipate misunderstandings of its aims and substantive disagreements over educational philosophy and be prepared to mediate those conflicts that may arise. In sum, the only hope for resolving the culture war is if civic institutions such as the schools find ways to address the substantive differences that divide us by identifying compromises based on what we share in common.

NOTES

1. *The New York Times*, October 27, 1992, p. A1.
2. *The Gaston Gazette*, April 14, 1993, p. 8A.
3. *Sunday Patriot News*, Harrisburg, PA, Sunday March 7, 1993.
4. The goal of NASDC, a nonprofit corporation conceived at the October 1989 education summit at the University of Virginia and funded by contributions from major corporations such as Johnson and Johnson, is to support the development of world-class schools that will serve as models for educational reform.
5. *The Gaston Gazette*, February 21, 1993, p. 5A.
6. *The Gaston Observer*, February 14, 1993, p. 4.
7. "Citizens for Excellence in Public Education," produced by *People for the American Way*, 2000 M Street, N.W., Washington, D.C.
8. *The Gaston Gazette*, February 28, 1993, p. 7A.
9. *The Gaston Observer*, February 15, 1993, p. 3A.
10. *The Gaston Gazette*, Wednesday, February 17, 1993.
11. This is the subtitle to Hunter's *Culture Wars*.
12. See Hunter, *Culture Wars*, pp. 197-198 for more discussion of this issue.
13. *The Gaston Gazette*, February 15, 1993, p. 1A.
14. *The Gaston Gazette*, March 1, 1993, p. 2A.
15. *The Gaston Gazette*, February 21, 1993, p. 5A.
16. Flier distributed by Concerned Citizens for Excellence in Public Education, Gaston County, NC.
17. Letter provided by People for the American Way, 2000 M Street, N.W., Washington, DC.
18. *The Gaston Gazette*, February 22, 1993, p. 3B.
19. *The Gaston Gazette*, July 10, 1992, p. 1A.

REFERENCES

Adler, M. 1982. *The Paideia Proposal: An Educational Manifesto*. New York: Macmillan.
Ammerman, N. 1990. *Baptist Battles*. New Brunswick: Rutgers University Press.
Anti-Defamation League. 1994. *The Religious Right: The Assault on Tolerance and Pluralism in America*. New York: Anti-Defamation League.
Bates, S. 1993. *Battleground: One Mother's Crusade, the Religious Right, and the Struggle for Control of Our Classrooms*. New York: Poseidon Press.
Berger, P., B. Berger, and H. Kellner. 1973. *The Homeless Mind*. New York: Vintage Books.
Bruce, S. 1988. *The Rise and Fall of the New Christian Right*. New York: Oxford University Press.
Dry, G. 1993a. "School Board Should Rescind Program." *The Gaston Gazette* (March 7).
_____. 1993b. "Taking Issue with Odyssey." *The Gaston Gazette* (March 20).

Heinz, D. 1983. "The Struggle to Define America." In *The New Christian Right*, edited by R. C. Liebman and R. Wuthnow. New York: Aldine Publishing Company.

Hunter, J. 1991. *Culture Wars*. New York: Basic Books.

————. 1994. *Before the Shooting Begins*. New York: Free Press.

Lamont, M. 1992. *Money, Morals, and Manners*. Chicago: University of Chicago Press.

Norris, B. 1993. "Bible Belt Chokes Odysseus." *The Times Educational Supplement* 4004 (March 26): 18.

The Odyssey Fact Book. 1993. Gastonia, NC: Gaston County Design Team.

Odyssey Project. 1992. A Proposal submitted to the New American Schools Development Corporation by the Gaston County Design Team. Gastonia, NC.

Pope, L. 1942. *Millhands and Preachers*. New Haven: Yale University Press.

"Religious Right Says Reform Ends." 1993. *Sunday Patriot News*, Harrisburg, PA: March 7.

Simonds, R. 1992. *President's Report*. Costa Mesa, CA: National Association of Christian Educators (July).

Sommerfeld, M. 1993. "Christian Activists Seek to Torpedo NASDC Project." *Education Week* 12 (March 10): 1,18-19.

Sorohan, E. 1991. "Schools Leaders Face 'New Age' Charges." *School Board News* 11 (October 1).

Wuthnow, R. 1983. "The Political Rebirth of American Evangelicals." Pp. 167-185 in *The New Christian Right*, edited by R. C. Liebman and R. Wuthnow. New York: Aldine Publishing Company.

————. 1987. *Meaning and Moral Order*. Berkeley and Los Angeles: University of California Press.

————. 1988. *The Restructuring of American Religion*. Princeton: Princeton University Press.

PUBLIC TELEVISION AND
THE CULTURE WARS

William Hoynes

This article examines the 1992 debate over federal funding for public television, suggesting that it must be understood as part of the broader "culture wars" in the United States. The paper explores the underlying assumptions behind the widely publicized conservative critique of public television and argues that this specific case of cultural politics represented an emergent alliance between economic conservatives and cultural conservatives against a vulnerable, public sector target. While public television emerged with renewed federal funding after the 1992 skirmish, the paper argues that this resolution is temporary and subject to continuing cultural struggle. The paper closes by discussing the issues that are likely to resurface in future debates about public television funding.

Since the early years of television, the images broadcast on the small screen have been subject to a wide range of political challenges. From the struggle over "Amos 'n' Andy" (Ely 1991) to the debate over the impact of Vietnam war coverage (Hallin 1986) to the 1980s' challenge by conservative activists to images of sex and violence in prime time (Montgomery 1989), network television has faced a steady stream of organized political activity and been shaped by it. One of the principal reasons for the routine targeting of television by political actors is the widely shared belief that television images have powerful "effects" on their audiences.

While the scholarly literature is decidedly mixed on the nature and extent of television's impact (Lewis 1991), popular lore—which is widely accepted by both politicians and advertisers—identifies television as an influential force in contemporary American society. If, as various critics argue, television shapes Presidential elections (Hertsgaard 1988), is a central battleground in the waging of wars (Kellner 1992), and helps to define those with whom we have little face-to-face contact (Jhally and Lewis 1992), then it should come as no surprise that television is never far removed from the broadly defined world of politics. Nor, in an increasingly image-saturated society, should it be surprising that struggles over television have only become more intense in the 1990s.

Such broad generalizations about the fundamentally political nature of television, while a helpful corrective to the "minimal effects" model of media influence, do little to clarify either the underlying source of the conflict or the dynamics of how such struggles unfold. In particular, such assertions tell us little about what is at stake in these conflicts, as they shift from a narrower political focus to a broader cultural context. As then-Vice President Dan Quayle's 1992 remark criticizing television character Murphy Brown's choice to become a single mother suggests, there is something more than traditional politics involved in these ongoing skirmishes over television images. Hunter's (1991) conceptualization of the "culture wars"—in which culturally conservative and culturally progressive groups, organized around radically different visions of moral authority, compete over the definition of contemporary American society—provides a helpful framework for decoding these conflicts. In particular, Hunter alerts us to the fact that an understanding of the traditional liberal-conservative discourse is inadequate for interpreting the nature of the ongoing conflicts over television images.

In order to understand more fully television's part in the broader culture wars, it will be useful to examine a particular case in which television was the primary target of cultural activism. This will provide us with both a more specific window on the world of cultural politics and an opportunity to assess the analytic utility of Hunter's culture wars framework. One of the principal sites of activism in the 1990s has been public television. This paper explores the "battle" over public television, arguing that it should be viewed as an example of a contest in which the culture wars intersect with political-economic developments—in this case, a post-Cold War assault on the public sector.

HISTORICAL ROOTS OF THE CONFLICT

In November, 1967, President Johnson signed the Public Broadcasting Act, which created the Corporation for Public Broadcasting, setting the stage for the development of the system of public broadcasting in the United States. The Public Broadcasting Act, which was first discussed in Congress only nine months before its passage, was one of the final pieces of Johnson's Great Society program—and indeed, the only piece of communications legislation that was part of the Great Society. The rapidity with which it moved through the legislative process—now almost unheard of—reflected the firm consensus that the United States needed a healthy, federally-funded, non-commercial television system. One of the central mandates of this new system was to add diversity to the airwaves, providing "a voice for groups in the community that may otherwise be unheard," with programming that would "help us see America whole, in all its diversity" (Carnegie Commission 1967, p. 92). With its rhetorical commitment to broadening television to include marginalized groups and less-than-traditional perspectives, the very enterprise of public television can be seen as the work of cultural progressives, initiated at a time when cultural conservatives were not well mobilized. Within public television circles, however, there has been some confusion as to how such a commitment to diversity should be enacted. In addition, there has also been an underlying set of incentives—largely economic—that encourage culturally conservative, although still highbrow, programming. In this sense, from its inception, public television was an institution that was ripe for both internal and external cultural warfare.

Since its earliest days, public television has never been far from political controversy. In fact, shifting political pressures go a long way toward explaining the evolution of our public television system in its first twenty-five years. The history of public broadcasting has been well told elsewhere;[1] however, in order to understand the 1990s' challenge to public television, we need to begin with a brief historical overview. Since external political pressure has played such an important role in public television's history, helping to shape the evolving structure of our public television system, we should be particularly concerned with the changing political climate, and how public broadcasters have responded to it.

Since its earliest days, there has been a slow but steady movement toward the privatization of public television. This is partially a result of the fact that, within public television circles, fear of political control by the federal government has always outweighed the fear of commercialization. This should not be surprising given the broader political culture in the United States, in which intervention by "big government" in any arena of community life raises immediate suspicion.[2] Fears of government intervention, however, were not based simply on abstract popular notions about the dangers of government involvement. The formative experiences of many public broadcasters gave them good reason to be wary of government intervention, particularly from the White House.[3]

Rather than model American public television after the system of public service broadcasting in Europe, the designers of the American system sought to avoid state control and suggested both an administrative and financial structure to prevent it. The Public Broadcasting Act, however, only set up this separate administrative structure (CPB),[4] leaving the financing to the federal government's regular appropriations process. As a result, the funding of public broadcasting has always been a politically charged issue—even when money is authorized on a three-year basis, two years in advance. This has been the case since the late 1970s' with partisan debates about bias being a regular feature of the funding process.

Early proponents of public broadcasting suggested that the only way to prevent such a politicization of the funding process was to provide stable, long-term funding for public television. The initial proposal by the Carnegie Commission (1967), whose report led to the passage of the Public Broadcasting Act, recommended that an excise tax on the sale of television sets, to be placed in a trust fund specifically for the use of public television, would make it impossible to politicize the funding process.[5] While President Johnson indicated in 1967 that a long-range funding plan would be worked out in the coming year, the Vietnam War, the growing anti-war movement, and Johnson's ultimate withdrawal from the Presidential race left public broadcasting without such a plan. The 1968 election of Richard Nixon brought new problems for the fledgling public television system. From Nixon's perspective, particularly as the Vietnam War continued to drag on, public television was little more than a home for liberal journalists who produced biased news and public affairs programs with the assistance of federal funds.

By 1970, unhappy with the broadcasting of such documentaries as *Banks and the Poor*,[6] which critically examined banking practices that exacerbated poverty in urban areas and "closed with a list of 133 senators and congressmen with banking holdings or serving as directors of banks—while the Battle Hymn of the Republic played in the background" (Stone 1985, p. 29), the Nixon Administration made plans to reign in public television. Since public television was most vulnerable in the area of funding, the administration focused its attention on the appropriation of money for CPB. On June 30, 1972 President Nixon vetoed CPB's authorization bill, arguing that public television had become too centralized and was becoming a "fourth network." In criticizing CPB and its supposed over-centralization, the administration had hoped to capitalize on a growing confusion about the evolving relationship between CPB, the recently formed Public Broadcasting Service (PBS), and the local stations. In retrospect, it seems clear that Nixon's call for a return to "the bedrock of localism," as the administration put it, was simply cover for the administration's more political criticisms of the system, in particular its disapproval of several members of the CPB board, who were perceived as being too liberal and unwilling to work with the administration. Additionally, it held an aversion for CPB's relationship to National Educational Television (NET), one of the principal programmers for the young public television system, which had produced *Banks and the Poor*.

However, as Witherspoon and Kovitz (1987) suggest, the Nixon Administration was concerned about the political consequences of directly attacking public affairs programs. Its goal to change the makeup of the CPB board and to steer public television away from the production of nationally distributed public affairs programs could be accomplished by focusing an attack on the centralized power of CPB instead of the particular programs that the Nixon administration found politically problematic. This strategy was intended to shield the White House from charges that it was interfering politically with an independent public television system or that it intended any form of "censorship." To a great extent, the strategy worked; over the next two months the Chairman, President, and Director of Television for CPB all resigned. At the end of August, after these resignations had been accepted, Nixon signed a bill authorizing public broadcasting funding for 1973.

The political struggle between Nixon and CPB had three important, and lasting, consequences for the future structure of public television. First, it showed that public broadcasting was vulnerable to political pressure, particularly from the White House. As mentioned earlier, this vulnerability came from a predictable source: the fact that the federal government had to regularly approve public broadcasting's funding. Second, it meant that public television had to establish mechanisms to protect itself, as much as possible, from the political pressures it was likely to face in the future. This led to the development of a decentralized method for distributing production funds, the Station Program Cooperative (SPC), which would be a central component of the public television programming process from 1974 to 1990.[7] The creation of the SPC was but one sign of a broader trend to diffuse the potential targets of political pressure by shifting programming decisions away from CPB. Third, the public television system realized that it needed to look for additional sources of revenue, particularly from the private sector, in order to reduce its dependence on the highly politicized federal appropriations process. More specifically, the Nixon veto led public television producers to turn their attention to corporate underwriting, initially from major oil companies, as a new source of program financing.

These three consequences—vulnerability to Presidential political pressure, a reorganization of the relationship between local stations and the national public television system, and a growing reliance on corporate underwriting dollars—are recurring issues in the history of public television. The 1972 Nixon veto set the tone, and provided a framework, for the subsequent political struggles—including the 1990s' challenge—about the need for, and structure of, a public television system.

In contrast to the Nixon years,[8] Carter's presidency was largely uneventful for public television, which continued to grow, both in terms of the number of stations involved and the financial resources available to the system. Since Congressional Democrats had traditionally been supporters of public television, the absence of tension between public television and the Democratic administration served as a temporary respite from political pressure. When Ronald Reagan assumed the Presidency in 1981, however, public television faced renewed political and economic pressures from the White House. On one level, the hostility to public television was philosophical: the Reagan White House supported wide-ranging deregulation, and it frowned upon a host of federally funded programs. As a result, federally funded public television was, to say the least, not a favored institution in the Reagan administration. On another level, the hostility was more partisan, as the charge of a liberal bias in public television, last heard from the Nixon administration, was once again in the news. Such philosophical differences and partisan political charges did have material consequences. The Reagan administration urged funding reductions for public broadcasting through the 1981 Public Broadcasting Amendments Act.

The reduction of federal support and the simultaneous deregulation of commercial television were not the only signs of a renewed emphasis on a market orientation for the American broadcasting industry. In 1984, the Federal Communications Commission (FCC) broadened its guidelines for the identification of corporate underwriter support on public television programming, allowing commercial-like announcements at the beginning and end of programs. Rather than simply allow "advertising" on public television, the new regulations, labelled "enhanced underwriting," permitted "logos or slogans that identify—but do not promote or compare—locations, value-neutral descriptions of a product line or service, trade names, and product or service listings" (Witherspoon and Kovitz 1987, p. 56). Not only was the commercial television industry becoming less regulated, and therefore less accountable to any measure of the public interest beyond audience size, public television itself was—as a result of federal funding cuts and new underwriting codes—becoming increasingly commercialized.

RENEWED CHALLENGE IN THE 1990S

In the spring of 1992, public television was the subject of national
discussion once again. It made newspaper headlines, aroused a great
deal of attention on Capitol Hill, and even was the subject of
campaign advertisements by Republican Presidential candidate,
Patrick Buchanan. The attention was not, however, due to the release
of another highly acclaimed documentary series, such as *Vietnam:
A Television History or The Civil War*, both of which had catapulted
PBS into the national spotlight in the previous decade. On the
contrary, the attention in the first half of 1992 was neither triggered
by a particular PBS program, nor was it encouraged by public
television executives. It represented, to be sure, the most powerful
threat to the survival of a public television system since the 1972
Nixon veto and was the result of two simultaneous developments:
privatization and the heating up of the culture wars.

Privatization, as such, does not occur spontaneously, any more
than the initial creation of the public sector occurred spontaneously.
Nor is it simply the product of a particular *zeitgeist*, such as the
market fetishism emerging in the post-Cold War era in the United
States. Privatization must be understood as part of the larger ongoing
contest over how societies are to be organized—both the social
relations of production and consumption. During a historical period
in which the collapse of the Soviet Union is interpreted as the ultimate
victory for capitalism—and the economic and moral superiority of
the free market is celebrated uncritically—the call for privatization
must be seen as the work of the social strata, led by corporate
America, that have historically had little need for a public sector,
and will, not surprisingly, benefit most directly from privatization.
While the erosion of the public sector can appear to take on a life
of its own in a recessionary economic climate, particularly when such
an economic climate is combined with a growing perception that
some people are "dependent" upon the public sector and others are
not,[9] we must avoid the tendency to forget the actual human agency,
in the form of organized political activity, that is the driving force
behind the movement toward privatization.

At the same time that corporate forces were pushing privatization
forward, cultural struggles were intensifying in various arenas. College
campuses were abuzz with debates over so-called "political correctness,"
with each side charging the other with a series of moral violations. Local

school boards struggled over the challenge of multiculturalism and the content of sex education. Unlikely coalitions formed to oppose pornography and violence in films and television. Most relevant for the discussion of public television, the very existence of the National Endowment for the Arts (NEA) was challenged by cultural conservatives who perceived several NEA-supported projects as obscene. In the case of the NEA, the debate moved beyond a focus on art and obscenity to a broader discussion of the relationship between the public sector and cultural production, with conservative critics suggesting that the answer to the questions raised by the culture war—about the definition of art, the meaning of "public," and the question of censorship—was the abolition of taxpayer support for the arts.

This is the context in which public television made headlines in early 1992. Public television, much to the dismay of its principals, momentarily took center stage in two simultaneous debates: one over the future of the public sector and another over the core values of American society. The proximate source of this widespread attention was the organized attack on public television by a coalition of conservative organizations at a time when Congress was to consider the reauthorization of funding for public broadcasting. The substance of the critique had a familiar ring, although its increased vigor gave the impression of something different. The outcome, at least in the short run, was also reminiscent of previous debates, as a Democratic-controlled Congress passed the reauthorization bill but attached tighter strings. What was new was the historical context: a post-Cold War political climate that celebrated the market in a quasi-religious manner combined with a well-organized movement of cultural conservatives made the abolition of public television, for the first time, seem to be a viable option.

The 1992 debate about public television, much like the debates that occurred under Nixon and Reagan, illuminates the historical tensions—economic, political, and cultural—inherent in the public television system in the United States. The conservative critique of PBS came from two, apparently contradictory, directions, representing an emergent alliance between traditional economic conservatives and more recently organized cultural conservatives. Economic conservatives were represented most visibly by Laurence Jarvik, the Bradley Resident Scholar at the Heritage Foundation. The public face of the cultural conservatives was David Horowitz, of the Committee for Media Integrity.

Jarvik's January, 1992 report "Making Public Television Public," distributed by the Heritage Foundation and quoted widely in the mass media, argued, contrary to the title of the report, for the wholesale *privatization* of public television. The rationale for such an argument was twofold: (1) television, in principle, should be a private enterprise, and (2) the particular institutions that make up our public television system have outlived their usefulness. As such, Jarvik's plan for making public television public was to sell the Corporation for Public Broadcasting to the private sector. Ultimately, Jarvik (1992a, p. 12) argued that "privatization provides the means to clean up the public television mess by creating incentives for excellence, efficiency and accountability. It is time to privatize public television."[10]

Horowitz and the cultural conservatives focused their critique on the content of public television programming, arguing that public television had a liberal bias. In particular, Horowitz (1991, p. 27) claimed that "the protest culture, which everywhere else had withered at the end of the '60s when its fantasies of revolution collapsed, discovered a new base of operations in public television." These charges were widely repeated as the debate ensued. On a similar note, Robert Knight of the Family Research Council argued that public television "is consistently antifamily, it favors alternative lifestyles and is usually a mirror of the liberal democratic agenda." Likewise, Gary Bauer, also of the Family Research Council, wrote Senator Robert Dole to criticize "documentaries designed to destroy basic American institutions such as churches and families" (*Boston Globe* March 4, 1992, pp. 1, 14). At the same time, then-Presidential candidate Patrick Buchanan was running a television advertisement in southern states criticizing President Bush for permitting federal funds for "pornographic and blasphemous art" (*Time* March 30, 1992, p. 58). The ad showed a film clip from a documentary recently broadcast on some PBS stations. As a result, cultural conservatives argued that public television should be subject to more political control by the U.S. Congress, both to prevent indecency and to ensure objectivity and balance.

As the debate about federal funding of public broadcasting moved forward, cultural conservatives found powerful allies in the United States Senate. Much of the criticism of public television was directed at individual programs, generally documentaries, that apparently demonstrated the biased nature of the programming. Senator John

McCain, following Horowitz's lead, singled out the documentary *Maria's Story* as one that showed "the Communist guerrillas in El Salvador in the most heroic of depictions." Senator Jesse Helms criticized the documentary *Tongues Untied*, which he said "blatantly promoted homosexuality as an acceptable lifestyle" (*Time* March 5, 1992, A14). Senate Minority Leader Robert Dole charged that "the broadcasting apologists are hiding behind Big Bird, Mr. Rogers and *Masterpiece Theatre*, laying down their quality smokescreen while they shovel out funding for gay and lesbian shows" (Benz 1993). After the Senate had approved funding for public television, the tenor of the debate did not change; Senator Trent Lott made it clear that cultural conservatives were still not satisfied with PBS. Referring to the impending broadcast of *The Lost Language of Cranes*, a drama about a father's struggle with his homosexuality, Lott argued that "on June 24 they're going to have another show that's going to horrify many Americans" (*Times* June 4, 1992, pp. A, B10).

Two years later, the presentation of images of gays and lesbians on PBS made headlines once again. Longtime cultural activist Rev. Donald Wildmon and his American Family Association led a campaign denouncing the PBS broadcast of *Tales of the City*, a mini-series based on stories about life in San Francisco in the 1970s, because it contained prominent gay characters. Georgia's lieutenant governor urged his state's public television stations not to run the series. A bomb threat was made to the PBS affiliate in Chattanooga, Tennessee, leading the station to pre-empt *Tales of the City* an hour before its scheduled air-time. In the wake of this controversy, PBS declined to co-finance a sequel—despite the fact that the original series generated the highest ratings for a dramatic series in PBS history (Biddle 1994; Koplined 1994).

These charges against PBS, based on anecdotal evidence and drawing upon larger cultural debates about communism and sexuality, made for good newspaper copy and lively talk show debates. The call by cultural conservatives for Congress to reassert political control over public broadcasting—by ensuring "objectivity" and "balance" on public television—found a good deal of support in the U.S. Senate. While Jarvik's call for privatization helped set the tone for broader discussions about the future of public broadcasting, ultimately, these assertions of bias and indecency framed the immediate Congressional debate about public television.

The positions of the cultural and economic conservatives—one calling for the government to take a more active role in regulating the political content of public television, and the other suggesting the complete privatization of public television—may appear antithetical. In essence, one calls for increased state intervention, the other for a total end to government involvement. However, as Jarvik's heavy reliance on Horowitz's argument makes clear, they represent an alliance between two social forces with a common adversary: public television. What they share is a desire to impose new restraints—in one case political, in the other economic—on a public television system that had been at least partially removed from such constraints. Moreover, the strategy of increased state intervention can be seen as the centerpiece of an intermediate strategy, one that accepts the short-term existence of public television; the call for privatization is part of a longer-term strategy to eliminate public broadcasting altogether.

The combined argument for further state control of public television and total privatization, then, highlights the principal questions for the future of public television: What is the relationship between a *public* television system and both the market and the state? What, indeed, does it mean to be a *public* institution at a time of rapid privatization? And who is the public that this public television system is intended to serve? It will be useful to review, in some detail, the conservative argument, for it provides an important context for understanding the dilemmas facing the current public television system.

THE FOUNDATION OF CONSERVATIVE CRITICISM

The conservative critique—as articulated by Jarvik, Horowitz, several U.S. Senators, and later popularized by conservative newspaper columnist George Will[11]—rests on three central assumptions about the nature of mass communications systems in general and the makeup of public television in particular. First, the economic conservatives assume that the forces of the economic market will encourage the creation of a mass media with a representative marketplace of ideas. Put more bluntly, the quality of ideas should be measured by the demand they generate among an audience of media consumers. In the case of television, those programs that can attract an audience (and, presumably, the advertisers interested in selling goods to that audience) will find a home on the television schedule. Those programs that cannot attract a sizeable enough audience, the logic continues, have no business cluttering up the television schedule. Government support for a public television system, therefore, violates this central premise, for there would be no market mechanism to determine the necessity of a particular program.

Related to this first assumption is the argument, articulated most clearly by George Will and shared by cultural conservatives who perceive media professionals to be a liberal, out-of-touch elite,[12] that without any kind of market accountability, public television has become a taxpayer-supported luxury for a tiny elite. In an era characterized by a growing federal budget deficit, the argument that public television is oriented to elites gives the conservative critique a neo-populist tone, one that resonates well with the growing anti-tax sentiment across the United States.

A second assumption, asserted most clearly by economic conservatives, is that the television market in the United States has been burst open by the development of new technologies, particularly cable television, so that non-commercial television is no longer necessary. Without the artificial constraints posed by the limited broadcast spectrum—which allowed for only three or four channels in most areas prior to the development of cable—the market will provide for all of the needs of television viewers. Non-commercial television, perhaps necessary when competition was limited, is therefore obsolete.

Finally, a third assumption, most clearly articulated by cultural conservatives, is that public television broadcasts programming that is overwhelmingly liberal, in both political and cultural terms. From this perspective, programming is politically liberal because it is produced by liberal Democrats and is often critical of policies advanced by such conservative Presidents as Reagan and Bush. Programming is culturally liberal, out of touch with the mainstream, because it questions—even undermines—basic American institutions and values by giving routine access to a variety of non-traditional groups, including gays and lesbians, and feminists.

These three assumptions—the organization of the media on market principles, the "freeing" of the television market by the advent of new technologies, and the outlet public television provides for political and cultural critics of American society—are the driving force behind the conservative critique of public television—are the driving force behind the conservative of public television. They represent—in this case—two separate, but allied world views: on the one hand, the economic conservatives adhere to an ideology that reveres the market and distrusts institutions organized on non-market principles; on the other hand, cultural conservatives are committed to a different ideological perspective, one that is based on the defense of tradition in the face of cultural change—change which the national media promote.

In the case of the contest over public television, there was no visible tension between these two ideological stances. In fact, the two held so tightly together that there is reason to believe that, in the post-Cold War era, one may be the precondition for the other. In other words, a particular kind of reverence for the market may undergird the cultural conservative position, for it is "big government" that is perceived to be the source of so many of the incursions on traditional community life. As such, a defense of cultural orthodoxy can easily mix with a defense of free-market economics. Those economic conservatives who are committed to the free market find well-organized and potentially powerful allies, at least in the critique of public institutions, among cultural conservatives—even if they are likely to have different long-term agendas.

Decoding the Conservative Critique

The three assumptions underlying the critique of public television are not presented as propositions—to be analyzed and debated—but as inarguable assumptions about how the world works. In essence, they are served up as common sense, something which "we all know." Framing an argument as simple common sense can be a powerful political strategy. It also may represent the degree to which such arguments have been internalized by proponents. For sociologists, however, such common sense assumptions should serve as flags to issues which cannot simply be taken for granted. In this case, these common sense assumptions highlight the issues upon which the future of public television rests. It may not be overstating the case to suggest that the contest to have one's assumptions accepted, as truth not ideology, will be central in the broader cultural and economic struggles to come. As such, in order to understand the future prospects of public television in the United States, it will be useful to examine these "common sense" assumptions in some detail.

The first assumption, that the market is the most democratic basis upon which to structure a media system, is, in many ways, a peculiarly American position. Other advanced industrial countries have never accepted the premise that television should simply be organized as a commercial industry. Rather than serving as a guarantor of a vibrant idea market, the economic market has been seen by many analysts as the principal threat. Entman (1989), for example, has argued that there is a "contradiction between the logic of the economic market and the logic of the market place of ideas." In particular, scholars have argued that the for-profit orientation of commercial media organizations permeates all aspects of decision-making (cf. Epstein 1973; Kellner 1990; Herman and Chomsky 1988). Profit pressures provide strong incentives for news organizations to produce a least-common-denominator brand of news which will attract a large audience. And the for-profit orientation imposes severe cost-limiting pressures, leading news organizations to, for example, rely on political elites for most information and use resources to cover primarily preplanned, predictable happenings.

Critics of commercial media also argue that advertising, as the principal source of financial support for media organizations, sets limits on the range of expression. From this perspective, media content is linked not simply to competition between media outlets for viewers but also to the competition to please large advertisers. Although it does not wholly determine the nature of mass media products, critics argue that advertising serves as an important force—both as an external constraint and one that has been internalized by major cultural producers—toward the homogenization of imagery (cf. Gitlin 1985; Jhally 1989; Baker 1994). Others have focused on the increasing concentration of media ownership (Schiller 1989; Bagdikian 1990)—which continues to proceed apace in the 1990s with the occurrence of new, ever-larger corporate mergers—as the source of media uniformity. Schiller, for example, argues that mass media have become the central component of an "organic process by which the corporate 'voice' is generalized across the entire range of cultural expression" (1989, p. 44).

In one of the more evenhanded recent studies of contemporary American news media, Entman concludes by suggesting that "the first step to lasting improvements in journalism is isolating some outlets from the economic market altogether." This is precisely the opposite of the conservative argument that we should aim to restore market forces.[13] Notably, the economic conservative assumption—often presented without question in media accounts of the attack on public television—is, at minimum, far from an accepted truth. It is, in fact, a topic on which there has been great scholarly debate.

The second assumption, that cable television has opened up the television market, making public television obsolete, is more complex. Its most straightforward claim is that there is a greater volume of programming available to American television viewers. If the number of channels has increased by a factor of five, ten, or twenty in the past decade, then, or so the argument implies, this growth in volume brings with it an equivalent expansion in diversity of programming. Furthermore, such expanded diversity now satisfies virtually all known taste segments of the viewing population, leaving no justification for the existence of public television, which was created specifically to add diversity to the commercial television system.

The observation about increased volume is undoubtedly true, but the assertion of a corresponding increase in diversity is dubious. Though the simple equation of volume with diversity initially may not seem problematic, the expanded number of channels will still face the same economic constraints as the smaller number. Neuman (1991) has suggested that while new communications technologies provide enormous potential for increased diversity, "commercial market forces and deeply ingrained media habits pull back hard in the other direction." The result is a "pattern of common-denominator and politically centrist political communication. The new media will not change this in the main." Gitlin advances a similar argument, noting that the widely heralded potential of the new technologies is unlikely to be realized.

> The brave new cornucopia is likely to create only minor, marginal chances for diversity of substance—and fewer and fewer as time goes on.... Conglomeration proceeds apace. Homogeneity at the cultural center is complemented by consumer fragmentation on the margins. Technology opens doors, and oligopoly marches in just behind, slamming them. There can be no technological fix for what is, after all, a social problem (1985, p. 332).

Moreover, the argument that public television is obsolete ignores the high cost and limited availability of cable programming. As of 1992, only 60 percent of households even had basic cable service and only 28 percent had the more expensive "premium" cable channels. Such an argument also discounts the degree to which cable services have been dominated by entertainment, not public affairs, content. In this regard, Blumler has argued "[f]or the viewer *willing to pay for it*, there is an extension of choice in several senses, though the monetary terms of his or her access to it may change over time" (1991, p. 204; emphasis added). Still, he notes that "certain threats to the terms of choice cannot be discounted" (1991, p. 205), identifying the monopoly power of cable operators as a central concern. As a result, Blumler argues that there will still be programs "beyond the pale" in the "new television marketplace," particularly "productions that are relatively expensive to make but are unlikely to recoup their costs in viewer or revenue terms" (1991, p. 208).[14]

These kinds of analyses suggest that, in fact, the rise of new media technologies does not make non-commercial media obsolete. On the contrary, new technologies that are developed for commercial usage may make non-commercial media even more important, as an oasis for the use of these technologies in an environment that is partially insulated from the market. Again, the conservative assumption about the role of the new media is, in this case, an issue on which there is an ongoing debate.

Finally, the assumption about the biased nature of programming, which is subscribed to by culturally orthodox viewers, is also the subject of much debate. Notwithstanding a body of scholarship that raises serious questions about this assumption (Bennett 1988; Gans 1979; Croteau and Hoynes 1994) and questions the utility of the bias framework (Hacket 1984), the liberal nature of the mass media has taken on a mythical status. Easily invoked, widely accepted, and with a substantial history, this assumption is rarely, if ever, held up to critical scrutiny. When the content of public television is analyzed systematically, as it has been in two recent studies, the findings suggest that the cultural conservative position is, at best, the result of a selective viewing of programming.

A 1992 study by the Center for Media and Public Affairs, "Balance and Diversity in PBS Documentaries," suggested that despite difficulties in labelling a diverse set of topics and ideas as liberal or conservative, "...there can be little doubt that the ideas expressed on public affairs issues were far more consonant with the beliefs and preferences of contemporary American liberals than with those of conservatives" (Lichter et al. 1992, p. 159).

However, this study suffered from several serious methodological shortcomings. The study acknowledged that "many more hours of programming are offered to viewers by public broadcasting each year than any study could hope to analyze" (p. 17) and it went on to examine only a tiny slice of PBS programs. It did so by systematically excluding the overwhelming majority of programs broadcast by PBS stations. First, the study limited itself to "public affairs documentaries aired during the evening" over a one-year period between 1987 and 1988. This effectively eliminated the bulk of public affairs programs broadcast on public television, including news, talk shows, and business programs. The rationale for the exclusion of interview programs, talk shows, and panel discussions was that the *content* of such programs is not controlled by the producer. However, this ignores the basic fact that decisions concerning who to allow to speak on such programs are clearly in the hands of program producers.

Second, the study divided the documentaries examined into 35,094 small "segments" and then went on to ignore *98.3 percent* of these segments. It claimed that only 1.7 percent of the segments "clearly stated a thematic argument" (p. 50). Such a method excludes the underlying political themes when they are not "clearly stated"; it is probable that it is less necessary for those who support current social and economic arrangements to "clearly state" such positions than for those who are critical of the status quo. As a result, programming with "critical" content will be dramatically overrepresented in this kind of analysis. Moreover, the discussion of "balance" in PBS documentaries is, in fact, based on this tiny percentage of documentary programming—a genre of programming which, in turn, makes up only a small percentage of the overall schedule. On the face of it, the Lichter study supports the cultural conservative position—and was widely reported to do so in the news coverage of the 1992 Congressional debate. However, it is weak support at best. The study narrows the questions so dramatically, by focusing on such a small segment of programming and using a very limited analytic method, that it produces findings that may have had substantial practical value for cultural activists, but were of little value in illuminating the complex politics of public television programming.

A 1993 study (Croteau, Hoynes, and Carragee 1993) provided a broader examination of the content of public television programming, including documentaries along with news programming, talk/interview shows, and business programs. Using data from a composite national schedule over a six week period in 1992, the authors found that public affairs documentaries, the focus of the Lichter study, accounted for eight percent of programming on **PBS** stations. On such programs, the study found that "there is little evidence that the documentaries themselves exhibit the kind of political message that recent critics have claimed. Traditional sources still make up the bulk of the voices" (p. 28).

The study also reported that business programs are "the most highly politicized type of program, representing the interests of one social sector overwhelmingly" (p. 29). Additionally, the authors found that of the 1644 on-camera sources on the 114 programs in the sample period, none were representative of gay or lesbian organizations. The authors suggest that this finding could inform the ongoing cultural struggle over public television.

> Conservative critics pointed to the documentary *Tongues Untied*, Marlon Riggs' exploration of the lives of gay black men, as evidence of the highly visible gay presence on public television.... Regardless of one's view of this particular documentary, however, our data indicate a conclusion that is precisely the opposite of that advanced by conservative critics.... The focus on *Tongues Untied*, in fact, effectively obscured the larger source patterns on public television, in which representatives of gay and lesbian organizations have virtually no visibility (p. 25).

More generally, the authors argue that the source patterns on public television indicate that claims of bias by cultural conservatives—and by the Lichter study—do little to illuminate the complexity of the politics of public television. In particular, the study suggests that there is no systematic liberal bias. Nor is the bias framework theoretically or methodologically helpful for evaluating public television. Instead, the authors argue that "the challenges ahead for public television are to enhance the diversity of its programming and to refocus on the 'public' that public television is intended to serve" (p. 41).

The substantially different language used in these two studies—and the world views represented in this language—point to a wide cultural divide that is at the root of the battle between cultural conservatives and cultural progressives. The first study is likely to be appealing to cultural conservatives; it advances a language of bias, and provides support for those who would argue that particular programs, because of their subject matter or perspective, are not appropriate for public viewing. The second study is likely to be appealing to cultural progressives, as it draws upon the language of diversity, providing support for those both inside and outside of public television who believe that PBS should represent the multiplicity of perspectives and experiences in the United States.

LESSONS OF THE CONFLICT

What have we learned by looking at the underlying assumptions behind the conservative challenge to public television? First, we have seen that the apparently "common sense" truths upon which the conservative argument rests are ideological constructions rather than simple "facts." Second, and perhaps more important for scholarly purposes, we have seen that the taken-for-granted assumptions of the conservatives are actually central issues in the debate about the future of public institutions in general, and public television in particular. Any discussion about public television or communications policy more generally will have to take up these very points: the market orientation of mass media, the impact of new communications technologies, and the political and cultural content of media products. Ultimately, the analysis of public television becomes more than a technical or economic question; it becomes a normative question, for we end up talking about the kind of media system our country should have. The normative nature of the discussion can be obfuscated by the use of common sense assumptions, presenting them as simple fact. As a weapon in the culture war, as well as in the political-economic struggles that are unfolding, this is likely to be a widely used tactic.

Conservative efforts to decrease or even eliminate federal funding for public broadcasting in 1992 ultimately failed; however, their success in putting the focus on the alleged lack of balance and their call for privatization did have important consequences. The Public Telecommunications Act of 1992, which authorized funding for public broadcasting for 1994-1996, directed the Corporation for Public Broadcasting to review public broadcasting programming annually to ensure "objectivity and balance in all programs or series of programs of a controversial nature." The driving force behind this call for an annual review, and for the taking of "remedial" steps to correct any perceived imbalance, was the claim advanced by cultural conservatives of liberal bias on public television.

In essence, the cultural conservatives won a partial victory in this round, gaining a national forum for their position, new allies within the U.S. Congress, and new constraints on programmers that routinize the conservative critique as part of the decision-making process within public television. At the same time, such routinization in a large bureaucratic system like public television is likely to mean that the short-term benefits for cultural conservatives will be small. Further, the vague wording of the legislation, which permits the CPB board a good deal of interpretive leeway, certainly means that the cultural struggle over PBS is not over.

Economic conservatives won little from this skirmish, except for a seat at the table in the culture wars. The call for privatization, and the possibility that public broadcasting would receive a smaller federal appropriation or even none at all, helped pave the way for public broadcasters and cultural conservatives to agree on a compromise, but one that only temporarily halted the battle over public television. In the next round, in 1995 when privatization was raised again, the economic conservatives drew support from their 1992 allies, cultural conservatives, whom they rallied behind. To the extent that cultural progressives actively engaged in the 1992 contest, which was in the very limited manner of defending public broadcasting, they sustained substantial losses—as the cultural conservative argument received widespread attention and the cultural progressive argument often went unheard—but the continuing existence of non-commercial television means that the loss was far from complete.

In the end, there was no clear winner in this particular battle over public television. Instead, this battle may be most significant for what it suggests about future contests. At the most general level, it reminds us that the culture wars unfold in particular historical circumstances, and political-economic forces such as the current advance of privatization can play a central intervening role. In future skirmishes, the economic conservatives may not be satisfied with a background, supportive role in the cultural struggle; they may pre-empt the culture war over the content of public television by effectively abolishing it. Moreover, cultural conservatives are not likely to find the same allies when the target of their protests is network television, for economic conservatives have a different stake in commercial television. Public television, therefore, is likely to be a more permeable target for cultural warfare, because it already occupies a precarious position within an unstable public sector.

The long-term consequences for public television of this round of criticism depend upon the resolution of several dilemmas that have plagued public television since its earliest years. These dilemmas fall into two basic categories: (1) those based on what it means to be a public television system, particularly in an age when the public sector is under siege; and (2) those concerned with questions of "bias" and "diversity." Both sets of issues had a brief moment on center stage during 1992, as conservatives suggested their own resolution to these dilemmas and defenders of public television countered. The 1992 debate about the future of public television helped to clarify the nature of these dilemmas, but did little to resolve them. In 1995, public television was under siege, again, and the alliance between cultural conservatives and economic conservatives was stronger than it had been three years earlier. The difference, in the 1995 round, was that Republicans controlled both houses of the U.S. Congress. Public broadcasters no longer had majority support on Capitol Hill. More important, the new Republican majority promoted a culturally conservative agenda, and public television was a prominent target for new legislators. While cultural politics catapulted public television back into the spotlight in 1995, economic conservatives proposed a solution: cut the federal budget by ending federal support for a wide range of "non essential" programs, including public broadcasting. An end to federal government financing of public broadcasting, or "zeroing out" PBS as proponents dubbed it, could satisfy both economic and cultural goals. Cutting the size of government by ending support for programs that are identified as morally dubious helped to link the economic and cultural agendas within the Republican party. The result, in 1995, was a substantial decrease in— not a total cessation of—funding for public broadcasting. The battle over public television had changed course since 1992, as the position of PBS had become more precarious. Still, the battle is not over, there will be at least one more round in the cultural struggle over public broadcasting.

As we have seen, much of the recent discussion has focused on issues of bias and objectivity. These are familiar issues and they lead to even more familiar questions with which public television will continue to grapple. How is bias to be measured? Are there topics and perspectives that a federally funded public television system should exclude? What is the proper unit of analysis for claims of bias: the program, the series, or the overall schedule? Should all programming attempt to abide by the norms of objectivity or is it appropriate to present "point-of-view" programming? Who is to arbitrate claims of bias? Should public television be required to meet a specific set of requirements in regard to balanced programming? In many respects, the entire debate about bias is problematic. By focusing on the product, and ignoring the process, the bias paradigm tells us little about the causes of supposed shortcomings. Neither can it provide a theoretically informed analysis of how to move public television forward, or, in fact, where it should go. Still, if the bias paradigm is in decline, as Hacket (1984) has so persuasively argued, no alternative framework has emerged in the ongoing debate about the politics of public television. Without any alternative, and with the critique of the bias paradigm limited to the academic world, it is likely that the next challenge to public television will include a new round of arguments about the supposed bias of programming.

There are, of course, broader dilemmas raised by the conservative challenge. The most general question raised by this challenge is whether it is socially necessary to have non-commercial media institutions as the twentieth century comes to a close. Although the temporary answer in 1992 was a resounding "yes"—at least in the U.S. Congress—the specific structure of a public television system remains open to debate. How, for example, is public television to be funded? How should the funds, whatever their source, be distributed? What role should a public television system define for the public that it is intended to serve? Is it possible to create spaces where members of the public become more than an audience for programming, and actually participate—at the local and national level—in policymaking? And what are the goals of public television? To broadcast "quality" programming, or "diverse" programming, or "balanced" programming or "alternative" programming? What do these terms mean to those who are producing or consuming the programming?

Analyzing the assumptions underlying the attack on public television can help to illuminate the issues that will likely resurface in future bebates about public television funding. It also suggests that there are connections between the struggle over public television, the forward movement of privatization, and the broader culture wars of the 1990s, of which mass mediated images are a central component. Ultimately, the future of public television—its autonomy, perhaps its very existence—will be determined by the debate over a series of highly value-laden questions about our public culture. Until these kinds of questions are resolved, with at least temporary stability, public television will continue to be a prime battleground in the ongoing wars about the relationship between public and private in the contemporary United States.

NOTES

1. See Witherspoon and Kovitz (1987) for the "official" history of public broadcasting, a concise report paid for by CPB and distributed by the public broadcasting trade publication *Current*. Rowland (1986) provides a revisionist account of the history of public broadcasting. The 1979 Report of the Carnegie Commission on the Future of Public Broadcasting (known as Carnegie II) also provides a useful early history of public broadcasting. Stone's (1985) analysis of Nixon's relationship to public television includes a detailed history of the years between 1969 and 1974.

2. A large body of recent scholarship has examined the centrality of "individualism" in American political culture, and a corresponding fear of large state structures. See Gans (1988), Bellah et al. (1985, 1991), and Reinarman (1987) for discussion of these themes.

3. See Stone (1985) for an analysis of the Nixon Administration's efforts to pressure public television. Lashley (1992) argues that "executive turnover has profoundly influenced the strategic behavior of public television. Because performance preferences change with each administration, the organizational structure and strategic behavior of this public organization have been adjusted accordingly" (p. 64).

4. We should recognize, however, that even the administrative structure is not totally insulated from the federal government. The President appoints the members of the CPB board.

5. Witherspoon and Kovitz note that the idea of an excise tax was a political non-starter. "Legislators dislike excise taxes because they are hard to control; economists dislike them because there may not be a connection between the amount of money raised and the amount needed" (1987, p. 14). An alternative interpretation is that legislators opposed the excise tax precisely because it would have created a federally funded public television system that was, at the same time, financially autonomous of the federal government.

6. See Witherspoon and Kovitz (1987) and Stone (1985) for discussions of the reaction to this particular documentary.

7. Under the SPC, local stations, which received most of CPB's money through Community Service Grants, would decide which programs to support, through a

complex process of voting. See Reeves and Hoffer (1976) and Campbell and Campbell (1978) for a more thorough description of the SPC. Reeves and Hoffer (1976) also provide a content analysis of the SPC's first year. They found that "[t]he stations purchased two kinds of proposals: Those that were cheap and those already on the air. The first criterion was understandable; there was little money to spend. The second is difficult to reconcile with the lofty statements made by PBS officials and the Carnegie Commission regarding the necessity of risk-taking by public broadcasters. The SPC ventured and gained little" (p. 562). In 1990, the SPC was abolished and the program funding process was centralized.

8.   In 1974, public television was thrust into the middle of national politics again, as it broadcast live the entire Watergate Hearings. See Fletcher (1977) for a discussion of the audience for PBS's broadcast of the hearings and Stone (1985) for a discussion of what he calls the "poetic symmetry" of public television broadcasting the hearings that brought down its nemesis.

9.   See Coontz (1992) for a thoughtful analysis of the myths associated with the discourse on "dependence."

10.   See Jarvik (1992a, 1992b) and Horowitz (1991) for a fuller version of their own arguments. A variety of critics have responded directly to the substance of these arguments. See, for example, Daniel (1992), Grossman (1992), Schone (1992), and Ouellette (1991) for analysis and criticism of the conservative mobilization against PBS.

11.   Will's widely syndicated column helped to popularize the conservative argument. See his columns "Public TV Charades" (*Boston Globe*, April 23, 1992) and "$1.1 Billion for Public TV?" (*Washington Post*, May 12, 1992).

12.   See Lichter et al. (1990) and Medved (1992) for an elaboration of this argument.

13.   See Gamson et al. (1992) and Hoynes (1994) for a more detailed discussion of the political economy of mass media. Additionally, Kellner (1990) develops a "critical, institutional theory" of television, and Gitlin (1985) provides a thorough discussion of how market pressures influence the production of prime time, network television.

14.   Among those kinds of programs that Blumler suggests are "less favored" are "major documentary projects," ... "critical and controversial programs," ... "critical examinations of the role of television and other mass media in society."

REFERENCES

Bagdikian, B. 1990. *The Media Monopoly*, third edition. Boston: Beacon Press.

Baker, C. 1994. *Advertising and a Democratic Press*. Princeton, NJ: Princeton University Press.

Bellah, R., R. Madsen, W. M. Sullivan, A. Swidler, and S. M. Tipton. 1985. *Habits of the Heart*. Berkeley: University of California Press.

Bellah, R., R. Madsen, W. Sullivan, A. Swidler, and Steven M. Tipton. 1991. *The Good Society*. New York: Knopf.

Bennett, W. L. 1988. *News: The Politics of Illusion*. Second edition. White Plains, NY: Longman.

Benz, O. 1993. "In the Life: PBS Keeps its Distance from Gay Programming." *Extra!* 6:4.

Biddle, F. "Flap Erupts as PBS Refuses to Fund More Tales of the City." *Boston Globe*, April 13, 1994. p. 76.

Blumler, J. 1991. "The New Television Marketplace: Imperatives, Implications, Issues." Pp. 194-215 in *Mass Media and Society*, edited by J. Curran and M. Gurevitch. London: Edward Arnold.

Campbell, D. and J. Campbell. 1978. "Public Television as a Public Good." *Journal of Communication* 28: 52-62.

Carnegie Commission on Educational Television. 1967. *Public Television: A Program For Action.* New York: Bantam.

Carnegie Commission on the Future of Public Broadcasting. 1979. *A Public Trust.* New York: Bantam.

Coontz, S. 1992. *The Way We Never Were: American Families and the Nostalgia Trap.* New York: Basic Books.

Croteau, D., W. Hoynes, and K. M. Carragee. 1993. "Public Television 'Prime Time': Public Affairs Programming, Political Diversity, and the Conservative Critique of Public Television." Unpublished paper. Excerpted in *Extra!*, August/September, 1993.

Croteau, D. and W. Hoynes. 1994. *By Invitation Only: How the Media Limit Political Debate.* Monroe, ME: Common Courage Press.

Daniel, J. 1992. "Uncivil Wars: The Conservative Assault on Public Broadcasting." *The Independent*, August/September, 1992.

Ely, M. 1991. *The Adventures of Amos 'N' Andy.* New York: The Free Press.

Entman, R. 1989. *Democracy Without Citizens.* New York: Oxford University Press.

Epstein, E. 1973. *News From Nowhere.* New York: Vintage.

Fletcher, J. 1977. "Commercial Versus Public Television Audiences: Public Activities and the Watergate Hearings." *Communication Quarterly* 25 (4): 13-16.

Gamson, W., D. Croteau, W. Hoynes, and T. Sasson. 1992. "Media Images and the Social Construction of Reality." *Annual Review of Sociology* 18: 373-393.

Gans, H. 1988. *Middle American Individualism.* New York: Free Press.

Gans, H. 1979. *Deciding What's News.* New York: Vintage.

Gitlin, T. 1985. *Inside Prime Time.* New York: Pantheon.

Grossman, L. 1992. "PBS Funding Mix Helps Keep it Uniquely Free." *Boston Sunday Globe*, May 17, p. 84.

Hacket, R. 1984. "Decline of a Paradigm? Bias and Objectivity in News Media Studies." *Critical Studies in Mass Communication* 1 (3): 229-259.

Hallin, D. 1986. *The Uncensored War.* Berkeley: University of California Press.

Herman, E. and N. Chomsky. 1988. *Manufacturing Consent.* New York: Pantheon.

Hertsgaard, M. 1988. *On Bended Knee.* New York: Schocken.

Horowitz, D. 1991. "The Politics of Public Television." *Commentary* 92 (December): 25-32.

Hoynes, W. 1994. *Public Television For Sale.* Boulder, CO: Westview.

Hunter, J. 1991. *Culture Wars: The Struggle to Define America.* New York: Basic Books.

Jarvik, L. 1992a. "Making Public Television Public." Washington, DC: The Heritage Foundation.

Jarvik, L. 1992b. "What Price PBS?" *Boston Sunday Globe*, May 10, p. 73.

Jhally, S., and J. Lewis. 1992. *Enlightened Racism*. Boulder, CO: Westview.

Jhally, S. 1989. "The Political Economy of Culture." Pp. 65-81 in *Cultural Politics in Contemporary America*, edited by I. Angus and S. Jhally. New York/ London: Routledge.

Kellner, D. 1992. *The Persian Gulf TV War*. Boulder, CO: Westview.

Kellner, D. 1990. *Television and the Crisis of Democracy*. Boulder, CO: Westview Press.

Kopkind, A. 1994. "Chilling Tale." *The Nation*, May 2.

Lashley, M. 1992. *Public Television: Panacea, Pork Barrel, or Public Trust?* New York: Greenwood Press.

Lewis, J. 1991. *The Ideological Octopus*. New York: Routledge.

Lichter, S., D. Amundson, and L. Lichter. 1992. *Balance and Diversity in PBS Documentaries*. Washington, DC: Center for Media and Public Affairs.

Lichter, S., S. Rothman, and L. Lichter. 1990. *The Media Elite*. New York: Hastings House.

Medved, M. 1992. *Hollywood versus America*. New York: Harper Collins.

Montgomery, K. 1989. *Target Prime Time*. New York: Oxford.

Neuman, W. 1991. *The Future of the Mass Audience*. New York: Cambridge University Press.

Ouellette, L. 1991. "Right Wing vs. Public TV." *Media Culture Review. 1: 1*.

"Public Broadcasting Bill Is Sidelined." *New York Times*, March 5, 1992, p. A14.

"Public Broadcasting Wins Senate Battle for Federal Money." *New York Times*, June 4, 1992, pp. A1, B10.

"Public TV Under Assault." *Time*, March 30, 1992, p. 58.

Reeves, M. G. and T. W. Hoffer. 1976. "The Safe, Cheap and Known: A Content Analysis of the First (1974) PBS Program Cooperative." *Journal of Broadcasting* 20 (4): 549-565.

Reinarman, C. 1987. *American States of Mind*. New Haven, CT: Yale University Press.

Rowland, W. 1986. "Continuing Crisis in Public Broadcasting: A History of Disenfranchisement." *Journal of Broadcasting and Electronic Media* 30 (3): 251-274.

Schiller, H. 1989. *Culture, Inc.* New York: Oxford.

Schone, Mark. 1992. "The Jarvik Mart." *Village Voice*, February 25, pp. 46-47.

Stone, D. 1985. *Nixon and the Politics of Public Television*. New York/London: Garland Publishing, Inc.

"Targeting PBS." *Boston Globe*, March 4, 1992, pp. 1, 14.

Witherspoon, J. and R. Kovitz. 1987. *The History of Public Broadcasting*. Washington, DC: Current.

CULTURAL CONFLICT AND ART: FUNDING THE NATIONAL ENDOWMENT FOR THE ARTS

Beth A. Eck

Cultural conflict over federal funding for the National Endowment for the Arts is examined through a status politics/culture wars theoretical framework. Analysis of the rhetoric employed in 1989 and 1990 by both sides of the debate reveals that the religious right's battle to defund the NEA has little to do with art and everything to do with their perception that the influence of Christianity is waning and that traditional morals are under attack. These actors are engaging in a "symbolic crusade" in which art is simply one manifestation of all that is evil in society. The media's role in this struggle is analyzed as well. Spokesmen for the religious right are quoted less frequently than conservative members of Congress, suggesting the suspect level of legitimacy the former hold in defining and constructing reality.

Although in terms of budget matters this is of minor consequence, in terms of symbolic matters for the people themselves, it's very important. Isn't it morally correct to ensure that people's tax money is not taken from them in order to be spent for something they find morally objectionable? (Kantor 1989).
—Representative Dana Rohrabacher (R-CA), September 1989.

The NEA is lying there now almost like a wounded animal and there are a lot of jackals, maybe hyenas, that are waiting to tear it apart ... I am particularly concerned with those legislators who know better, who know what the implications are, who know that an attack on arts is always a precursor to other kinds of restrictions.
—Joseph Papp, Producer of the New York Shakespeare Festival, May 1990 (Masters 1990).

Can the NEA be expected to know something that sociologists, pollsters, researchers, scholars and other observers of American culture have never been able to identify—a single, permanent, immutable, orthodox standard of decency, true for all persons at all times in all places.
—from Brief filed by 60 literary, arts and broadcasting groups regarding the decency clause in NEA's funding (Trescott 1993).

I would like to raise a challenge to President Bill Clinton to meet with John Doe and sit down and watch the film [footage from the International Gay and Lesbian Film Festival which the NEA did not fund this particular year]... which graphically shows footage of a man licking the inside of a toilet bowl, and then tell Mr. and Mrs. John Doe that the sacrifices they must pay in higher taxes must go to the NEA because this type of film is considered art.
—Martin Mawyer, President, Christian Action Network
September 10, 1993 (Washington Post 1993).

In 1989 Congressional debate arose over federal funding for the National Endowment for the Arts. The NEA's budget was granted after much wrangling between the political and cultural left and right, but as illustrated by the comments above, the war still rages. This article focuses on a consideration of what constitutes the reasons for this fight and for the vitriolic fervor with which it is played out in the public realm. In order to gain insight into this matter, I examined the rhetoric each side used in the battle, both to garner support for itself and to vilify the efforts of the opposition. More specifically,

I considered the symbols which served as the rhetorical basis for the debate. What follows is a review of the cultural conflict as it evolved in 1989 and an explanation of how those events fit into the larger culture war.

THE CULTURE WAR

Hunter argues (1991) that the present day culture war provides a setting for unlikely alliances. Before World War II, moral conflicts took place between Catholics, Protestants and Jews. Today the debates are between those who hold to orthodox moral commitments and those who hold to progressive ones. Hunter suggests that at the "heart of the new cultural realignment are the pragmatic alliances being formed across faith traditions" (1991, p. 47). Beneath the surface of the smaller battles that revolve around such issues as prayer in school, abortion, etc., lies a deeper battle over the moral vision that will define contemporary American society. Disputes take place between "groups who hold fundamentally different views of the world. On all sides the contenders are generally sincere, thoughtful, and well meaning, but they operate with fundamentally opposing visions of the meaning of America: what it has been, what it is, and what it should be" (1991, p. 63).

Hunter argues that "cultural conflict is ultimately about the struggle for domination" (1991, p. 52). Similarly, Gusfield notes, in his study of Prohibition, that issues of moral reform can be analyzed

> as one way through which a cultural group acts to preserve, defend, or enhance the dominance and prestige of its own style of living within the total society... As his claim to social respect and honor are diminished... the citizen seeks for public acts through which he may reaffirm the dominance and prestige of his style of life (1986, pp. 3-5).

Actors engage in what Gusfield terms "status politics."

SYMBOLS AND SOCIAL MOVEMENTS

One way in which social actors publicly struggle for domination is through their involvement in social movements. A fight through political action, in particular, coerces the public definition of what is moral and respectable (Gusfield 1986). However, serious debate takes on the tone of simple rhetoric, each side choosing and exercising particular symbols to articulate their points and positions. Thus, the cultural battle becomes one of symbols: on the one hand symbols function as a short-hand definition of a movement while on the other they make true conversation, compromise or resolution unlikely. Utilization of symbols allows each side to emphasize its rights and identity; consequently these serve to elevate the tension of the original conflict. This cuts off debate and leads to further polarization.

Even though symbols can serve a dysfunction in attaining a movement's goals, I suggest that they are important nonetheless. Symbols communicate ideas, beliefs and claims that are important to movements. They identify and focus attention on its key issues and goals. Individuals who identify themselves with these symbols become followers of the movement. By analyzing the symbols of social movements and countermovements, it is possible to examine the world view each espouses. This is what I do here in an examination of the controversy over federal funding for the arts.

HISTORY OF THE CASE

This case study focuses on the controversy over federal funding for the National Endowment for the Arts (NEA) over an eighteen-month time period beginning in the Spring of 1989 and ending with reauthorization of the Agency in October 1990. Here I will review the general evolution of this debate (for a more detailed account, see Dubin 1992). The debate began when the Reverend Donald Wildmon, founder of the American Family Association, received a newspaper clipping alerting him to a photograph by Andres Serrano entitled "Piss Christ." The photo depicted a crucifix submerged in a jar of urine. Serrano had been given a grant by the NEA through its funding of the Southeastern Center for Contemporary Art (SECCA) in Winston-Salem, North Carolina. Through his monthly newsletter, the *American Family Association Journal*, Wildmon was able to garner the support of thousands who promptly wrote letters to members of Congress. The sentiment was the same. In Wildmon's words: "I find it extremely offensive that my tax dollars are used to promote anti-Christian bigotry." In response, Serrano said his work expressed rejection "of organized attempts to co-opt religion in the name of Christ" (McGuigan 1989).

The Corcoran Gallery in Washington, D.C., nervous over prospects for future funding, decided to cancel an exhibition of Robert Mapplethorpe photographs. Some of these photographs depicted homoeroticism and sadomasochism. Around the same time, viewers at the School of Art Institute in Chicago were invited to walk on an American flag as part of an art exhibit. The state legislature slashed the state's grant to the school from $70,000 to one dollar. In June 1989, after several members of Congress expressed outrage over the Serrano and Mapplethorpe exhibits, the subcommittee overseeing the NEA cut $45,000 (the amount given to those two exhibits) from its then $171 million budget. On July 26 of that same year, Senator Jesse Helms (R-NC) introduced an amendment which would prevent the NEA from funding "obscene or indecent" art work or to "promote, disseminate or produce obscene or indecent materials, including but not limited to depictions of sadomasochism, homoeroticism, the exploitation of children, or individuals engaged in sex acts; or materials which denigrate the objects or beliefs of the adherents of a particular religion or nonreligion" (Helms 1989). Furthermore, he stated that "[i]f senators want the federal government funding pornography, sadomasochism, or art for pedophiles, they should vote against the amendment." The amendment was passed by voice vote. The Senate proposed NEA budget banned for five years federal grants to the SECCA and the Institute for Contemporary Art at the University of Pennsylvania, the organizations that sponsored the programs featuring the Serrano and Mapplethorpe photographs. The art community and its advocates labelled this type of government action as censorship. Congress responded that this was not an attack on art works produced by the private sector, but rather on the use of public money. In addition, questions were raised time and again over "who defines art?"

The debate over federally funded art which ensued ran through the next year. In an effort to meet the requirements of the Helms amendment to its funding bill, which prohibited support of obscene work that does not meet high standards of artistic merit, the agency instituted an obscenity pledge. All grant recipients were required to certify in writing that they would not produce obscene work.[1] Protesting this action, several grant recipients refused to sign the pledge and hence, turned down their funding. John Frohnmayer, the Endowment chair, as well as Congress, had come under attack from the arts community. In July of 1990, the Chairman turned down the Solo Performance Advisory Panel recommendation of four artists whose acts dealt explicitly with sexual and political issues; three of the artists were homosexuals. At an August 5 meeting of the Council protestors stood outside shouting "We're here, we're queer, get used to it!" Later in the meeting when discussion turned to the four declined grants, activists began reading poetry by gay and lesbian artists including Shakespeare. When the activists were dragged away by police, the discussion was tabled to the next meeting.

On October 1, 1990 the House Appropriations Committee sent a bill to the floor that boosted funding for the NEA and the Kennedy Center and included no content restrictions on NEA-supported material. On October 11 the House voted 349-76 to reauthorize the NEA for three years. This legislation required that the NEA Chairman ensure that awarded grants take "into consideration general standards of decency and respect for the diverse beliefs and values of the American public" (*Washington Post* 1990 & provision) which replaced the more restrictive Helms language. The Agency was also required to have grant recipients repay their NEA funds if the works they created with the money were later found by a court to be obscene. The bill was sent to the Senate where it also passed. The Endowment immediately dropped its obscenity pledge.

Reciprocated Diatribes and World Views

This case represents one of many examples of incidents which have triggered the "reciprocated diatribes" discussed by Pearce and his colleagues (1989) between the new Christian Right and secular humanists (heretofore labelled orthodox and progressivists, respectively). Analyzing the dialogue between the two groups in the early 1980s, Pearce et al., argued that each side felt threatened by the other because they did not share a common vision of the ways in which people should come to decisions about the issues in question (1989, p. 158), for example, family and education: through secular authority or through God. The progressivists viewed the orthodox as foolish, and the orthodox viewed the progressivists as practicing "moral insanity" (p. 159). What both sides did share was the belief that there should be no ambiguity with regard to policies in these matters. In that effort, both sides sought resolution and clarity through public policy. Furthermore, the issues raised in public debate between the two sides were rarely the real issues at hand; they were simply symbolic of larger cultural differences. Those differences led to an inability of each side to see the other's viewpoint as reasonable or sufficient (1989, p. 159). The debates of the early eighties extended into the early nineties.

Why is this so? Hunter (in Pearce et al. 1989, p. 160) contends that the discourse stems from the evangelical politics of the right which do not observe the norms of civility as understood in contemporary society. In a secular world where emphasis is placed on the separation of church and state, such as the United States, it is deemed inappropriate for politicians or others to use their religious beliefs to influence policymaking, yet the religious right employs those beliefs in its battle for favorable policy positions. Even though progressivists do not invoke religion in their rhetoric, the fervor with which they argue their points makes the quality of their arguments religious. It is in this way that they can make explicit their world view. Cultural debates, then, are not simply about differences of opinion, but rather about "deeply rooted and fundamentally different understandings of being and purpose" (1991, p. 131). For example, multi-media artist David Wojnarowicz, in response to Wildmon's attempt to draw attention to the artist's controversial work known as his "sex series," stated that he created the work because he "felt the conservative climate had gotten so high ... that there was this call to deny sexuality itself" (Masters 1990, c1:1). Regarding the obscenity issue, he noted, "I can really approximate what it must have been to be a Jew during Hitler's rise to power—as a human being, as a homosexual, as a person with AIDS." To Wojnarocwicz and others on the progressivist side, it is much more than art that is criticized: it is one's identity, one's hope for what the nation claims and accepts as legitimate that is being attacked.

MOVEMENT ACTORS AND DATA

The movement in this conflict is the religious right, more specifically, Donald Wildmon's American Family Association (AFA), as they were the first to bring the attention of the Congress to the public funding issue. By way of background information, the American Family Association was founded in 1976 when the Reverend Donald Wildmon was unable to find "wholesome" programming on television. He describes the story this way,

> When we got into a program and there was a scene of adultery, we changed
> the channel; and we got into another program and somebody called somebody
> else an S.O.B., except they didn't use the initials; changed the channel again,
> got into a mystery program and then a scene came on, one man had another
> man tied down and was working him over with a hammer. I asked the children
> to turn the set off and decided I would do something about it (Solcraig 1990).

A pastor of a Methodist church in Southhaven, Mississippi at the
time, Wildmon asked his congregation to go without television for
one week. Within six months of that action he had left the ministry
and founded the National Federation for Decency (which became
the AFA in 1987). Wildmon's first boycott of advertisers came in
1978 when he informed Sears that NFD members would picket its
stores in 36 cities until it withdrew its sponsorship of *Three's
Company, Charlie's Angels*, and *All in the Family*. Sears canceled
its ads on two of the shows but denied its action had anything to
do with the Wildmon threat.

In late 1980, Wildmon met Jerry Falwell, then leader of the Moral
Majority, and convinced him to join forces to form the Coalition
for Better Television (CBTV). CBTV claimed the support of 200
organizations and announced that its 4000 members would begin
monitoring television content on the basis of "sex incidents per hour,"
scenes of violence and uses of profanity. During the 1980-1981
television season, Procter & Gamble withdrew advertising from 50
shows stating that the Wildmon group had something important to
say and they were going to listen.

CBTV disbanded a year after it was founded reportedly because
of a fallout between Wildmon and Falwell over boycott tactics.
Wildmon then began the Christian Leaders for Responsible
Television (CLEAR-TV). Past items on the agenda included, most
notably, a boycott of the Martin Scorcese film, *The Last Temptation
of Christ* and a successful campaign which convinced Pepsi to drop
Madonna from its television commercials. Other efforts included a
boycott of companies such as Coca-Cola and General Foods for
sponsoring such programming as *LA Law* and *Wiseguy*; and a
boycott of Holiday Inns for making pornographic movies available
to hotel guests.

For Wildmon, there is no group more maligned or unfairly
caricatured on television than Christians. Many of his efforts center
around this "anti-Christian bigotry," this is why he felt the need to do

something about the Serrano photograph. And he didn't stop there. Other agency grants that came under attack from Wildmon include the San Francisco Gay and Lesbian Film Festival, performance artist Karen Finley (who is known for smearing food over her body), and David Wojnarowicz, whose multimedia exhibit included some homoerotic scenes. Analyzed here are four American Family Association press releases, 3 *AFA Journal* articles, and one blanket commentary for use on editorial or op-ed pages of newspapers.

As for the AFA, what started out as a one-man operation out of Tupelo, Mississippi has now grown into a group which claims the support of 1600 religious leaders representing 70 denominations. Though Wildmon may have been the first social actor on the scene, he and his association did not stand alone. Another prominent figure for the Religious Right was Pat Robertson, President and Chief Executive Officer of the Christian Broadcasting Network (CBN), host of The *700 Club*, a 90-minute daily religious talk show, and head of the Christian Coalition. He created CBN in 1961. His network programming was patterned after the three major networks; what made CBN unique was that all sports, soap operas and news programming stemmed from a Christian perspective (Hadden and Swann 1981, p. 35).[2]

Wildmon has been characterized as "folksy," Robertson as more intellectually stimulating. A law graduate from Yale, Robertson exemplifies the upper middle class evangelist. The *700 Club* got its name from early fundraising efforts for Robertson's new television station (CBN). Robertson asked for 700 viewers willing to contribute ten dollars a month for the coming year. The telethon was called "The 700 Club." Early telecasts of the program revolved around the concept of a "Christian" talk show with two hosts, musical guests and others. After 1980 it changed to a magazine format. Stewart Hoover, in his analysis on mass media religion, notes,

> The *700 Club* embeds politics in its program in a variety of ways. Pat Robertson and the other hosts often comment on issues of the day, typically focusing on news events related to the "social agenda" of the new right.... The program has opposed abortion, and has favored prayer in the schools, capital punishment, banking reform, a strong defense policy, censorship of "pornographic" and violent media, and has opposed the women's movement on some key issues including the Equal Rights Amendment, and urged a more isolationist foreign policy. These political messages are purveyed in an evangelical and fundamentalist context but within a video setting that is unashamedly secular (1988, p. 77).

This description clearly places Robertson on the same side of the NEA debate as Wildmon. This analysis looks at thirteen transcripts from the *700 Club* in which the host speaks directly to the NEA issue from June 1989 through June 1990. Though Wildmon and Robertson are not the only actors for the movement, they represent the orthodox position regarding the arts issue during the period of analysis. I suggest that the Christian Action Network has joined the fray in more recent debates.

COUNTERMOVEMENT ACTORS AND DATA

Virtually all movements dedicated to effecting change are challenged by countermovements. And, generally speaking, the greater the mobilization of resources to effect change, the greater the countermobilization to prevent change (Etzioni 1968). As Zald and Useem argue, much of a movement's activity is aimed at "neutralizing, confronting, or discrediting its corresponding countermovements." Thus, the countermovement gains momentum by showing the harmful effects of the movement (in Zald and McCarthy 1987, p. 248), what Hunter would call showing the other side's "negative face" (1991, p. 144). The countermovement in this conflict is represented by those who sought to defend their position: the Endowment itself and People for the American Way.

People for the American Way was created by Norman Lear in 1980. PAW is comprised of religious leaders, magazine editors, businesspersons, members of Congress and members of presidential cabinets. The PAW came on the scene as a direct response to the new Christian Right's presence in the 1980 presidential election (Hadden and Swann 1981, p. 147). Today, PAW claims a national membership of over 285,000 and occupies a self-proclaimed "position of prominence in the struggle to defend and promote constitutional liberties." PAW's membership helps to sustain democratic ideals of the separation of church and state, the freedom to learn, an independent judiciary, and citizen participation in the democratic process.

One brochure put out by PAW describes the organization this way:

> Founded in 1980, People for the American Way has been a guiding voice in defense of the Constitution. Standing up to combat the intolerance of the Religious Right. Going to court to preserve our children's freedom to learn in the face of a growing censorship movement. Mounting a campaign to protect

civil rights and civil liberties. And in hundreds of other battles great and small in Congress, at school board meetings and on the evening news.... The People for the American Way are men and women of all walks of life, all religions, all races, all ethnic backgrounds, all lifestyles, who share a determination to keep aflame the torch of liberty.

Though action on the progressivist side of the arts debate was less publicized than the Reverend Wildmon's activities (so noted because of the lack of press material illustrating the contrary), PAW considers itself a major mobilizer of liberal sentiment over this issue. In addition to testifying before Congress on March 5, 1990, PAW's Action Fund was responsible for numerous legislative updates sent to its members, public service announcements, and one page advertisements urging people to "stand up for the right of freedom of expression." Material analyzed from this organization includes two "Action Fund" information sheets, one legislative alert, a list of talking points on the issue, a fact sheet on NEA grants, and one news release, one legislative update, and a statement before the Subcommittee on Post Secondary Education.

The National Endowment for the Arts was created by Congress in 1965. In 1991, the agency granted $175 million in federal funds. These funds are distributed at the discretion of a peer panel review. One-third of the funds go to individual artists while the other two-thirds go to arts organizations, theaters, art spaces, opera companies and the like. Since 1967, the Endowment has helped increase private support for the arts and humanities from $223 million to more than $4.6 billion. A panel of artists decides who is given grant money. Approximately 800 individuals each year come to Washington to review applications with the primary evaluation criteria being artistic excellence. Panels are composed of artists, arts administrators, critics, patrons, academicians and others with a recognized expertise in the particular art category on which they have been asked to make judgment. An advisory body made up of 26 private citizens, presidentially appointed who have made distinguished contributions to the arts reviews all panel recommendations at quarterly meetings. These members of the National Council on the Arts serve six-year terms, make recommendations on grants and advise the Chairman on policy matters. Finally, the Chairman of the NEA, who also chairs the council, makes the final determination on grants. Out of some

85,000 grants awarded in the last 25 years, fewer than 20 of them have come under public scrutiny, according to then NEA chairman John Frohnmayer. The photograph by Andres Serrano is one of those cases.

At a Newsmaker Breakfast at the National Press Club on September 17, 1990, Frohnmayer had this to say about the mission of the NEA as it related to an impending ceremony that afternoon:

> The children who attend these schools are lucky [elementary schools being honored by the Department of Education for outstanding programs in the arts]—they will be taught about wholeness, vision, creativity, imagination and innovation. This is what we're all about at the National Endowment for the Arts—a national intellectual commitment to creativity. It is signal proof of our truly humane society which does not ignore the arts; a truly civilized nation reveals its maturity by its government's commitment to enlarging the cultural opportunities for all its citizens. As the President said, the arts will continue to distinguish America as a world leader, rather than as merely a world power.

Materials analyzed from the National Endowment for the Arts include one open letter to the AFA, a list of talking points, and remarks by John Frohnmayer at the National Press Club.

Other actors in the countermovement, though not necessarily associated with formal organizations, also entered the fray. This analysis gavis attention to some individuals who were vocal about their position. Most are Hollywood celebrities or artists directly affected by the outcome of the NEA funding controversy, but also included are members of Congress. While Senator Jesse Helms (R-NC) and Representative Dana Rohrabacher (R-CA) represent the orthodox side of this debate, Senator Pat Williams (D-MT) and representative Sidney Yates (D-IL) represent the progressivist side. These comments are analyzed as well. Viewpoints were gathered from various sources: a videotape of the September 18, 1990 Phil Donahue show dealing with the NEA issue; print and radio media (quoted statements, sentiments regarding the issue; all materials dealing with the NEA controversy): eight newspaper articles, one magazine article and a two part "All Things Considered" piece from National Public Radio. Analyzing media pieces allowed me to examine how the debate was framed and covered, and how various statements were imbued with symbols.

Methodology

Wildmon and other actors in this movement became involved in a "symbolic crusade" (Gusfield 1986). As alluded to above, symbolic crusades are waged when one group, perceiving a threat from without, responds by getting public attention in order to legitimate or reaffirm its position of worth in society. Any victory is more than issue-oriented. It reaffirms the winner's prestige in society and acknowledges its style of life as proper.

To identify which "style of life" the movement was trying to preserve, as well as the "style of life" the countermovement was aiming to institute, I documented the frequency of particular symbols encompassed in the rhetoric of each side.[3] Movements use symbols to identify their position. Countermovements develop a parallel set of symbols to serve a similar function. Because most movements do not involve large proportions of the general population, movements and countermovements are mainly known to the public through their respective symbols. In the end, the effectiveness of a movement in the arena of public opinion rests in large part on the effectiveness of its symbols. Hence, these symbols develop the foundation for collective action.

The symbols most important to this debate fell under the categories of good, evil and legitimacy. Symbols of good were recorded when the phenomena were described in a positive, friendly or benign manner. Symbols of evil were recorded whenever phenomena were described in generally negative terms. Finally, symbols of legitimacy referred to explanations or justifications for the movement definitions of reality and goals (Cushman 1983, p. 34).

Attempting to identify universal materials for the movement and countermovement presented some difficulty. No archive existed from which a random sample could be drawn. While not random, there is no reason to assume the various materials under analysis were not representative of the positions outlined above. This study focused on the rhetoric of a specific movement regarding a specific issue. Thus, my data were a direct reflection of the most biased position statements of each side I could obtain.

A content analysis of the rhetoric of each side of this debate uncovered the symbols of evil, good, and legitimacy as defined by each side of the conflict. An examination of media coverage revealed the symbols that "carry over" to the public. Subsequently, how these symbols serve as barriers to communication are illustrated through examples of vilification of the opposition on both the movement and countermovement side.

This research consisted of a two-part analysis involving three readings of the data. The first part of the analysis uncovered actual symbols of the M/CM conflict as they were defined through the M/CM rhetoric itself. The frequency of each symbol was noted in an effort to establish whether or not a pattern existed (e.g., were there an overwhelming number of symbols of evil versus legitimacy). A definitive aggregation of each symbol would not be useful because there are disproportionate amounts of data from each side. The frequency of a particular symbol, however, may well represent central concerns of the movement. Thus, the first reading allowed for a simple recording of all symbols in the text and categorizing them under the appropriate heading.

The second part of my research involved an analysis of media coverage and examined whether or not the symbols used by the movement and countermovement were indeed the same symbols being transferred to the public.

The third part of my analysis pulled from both sources (M/CM propaganda and the media) those comments which were used to vilify the other side. Did the media use these comments in their coverage of events, perhaps serving to polarize the sides even more? Was the conflict characterized sympathetically, satirically or in some other fashion? Systematically I was looking for (a) how the debate was characterized, (b) what sources were used, and (c) what quotes the media chose from each side: did they include the prominent symbols as identified by the actors themselves?

My unit of analysis for the first two parts of the research was the single word or concept (e.g., freedom or freedom of expression would both be acceptable). Unlike analyzing sentences and paragraphs which can lead to double meanings, the smaller unit of analysis allowed definitive and easily detected meanings. I made two assumptions in this analysis. Utilizing frequency measures, I assumed that the frequency with which an attribute appeared in a message was a valid indicator of the focus of attention, value, and importance. Secondly, I assumed that each unit of analysis should be given equal weight which permitted aggregation or direct comparison (Holsti 1969, p. 122). Again, the purpose of a frequency count was not an effort to quantify symbols, per se, but rather to establish whether or not any pattern existed.[4] A criticism of content analysis is that it is not an accurate measure of the intensity of the communication (1969, p. 123). Given the brevity of the documents reviewed in this research and the short time span these documents cover, I am comfortable that the number of times a symbol occurred was an accurate measure of its intensity.

Results

What follows is a discussion of the general patterns which arose in my analysis of the rhetoric between the orthodox and progressivist activists in the cultural conflict.

Overall, the progressivist side of this debate used 154 symbols of evil which were mentioned 302 times; 122 symbols of good mentioned 464 times and 81 symbols of legitimacy mentioned 168 times. The right had 92 symbols of evil mentioned 299 times, 38 symbols of good mentioned 87 times and 35 symbols of legitimacy mentioned 152 times (36.2% of those dealt with tax dollars). Both sides employed symbols of evil more frequently than they did symbols of good. However, what is notable here is that the progressivists have over three times as many symbols of good than the orthodox side of this debate and twice as many symbols of legitimacy. Though the religious right has fewer legitimacy symbols, they use them nearly as often. What accounts for these differences? What do they tell us about the actors in this debate?

DEFINING "GOOD" AND "EVIL"

The religious right is waging battle within a secular society. Unable to convince a pluralistic culture that their values are good and right, their best ammunition lies in defining who the enemy is and noting why they are a threat to society. Consider what Robertson had to say about reaction to his impending Christian Coalition ad regarding the NEA:

> ... I think there will be a great deal of interest. But I do think if we don't take a stand, at this point, and those who stand for moral values and a moral consensus—now we've got flag burning; the funding of pornography and homosexuality, the sanctioning of this by the federal government; we've got the savings and loan mess; we've got other

things that these people are doing. If the Congress doesn't wake up to what is going on, I dare say there might be a switch of as many as fifty seats in the House of Representatives and a number of seats in the United States Senate. There could be a groundswell of people [who will] just say, 'Hey, enough. We've had enough' (transcript from "The 700 Club", June 20, 1990).

Convincing the general public and members of Congress that the old way is the best way is not a viable option for the religious right given the reaction of Congress to other issues (e.g., abortion). It becomes more potent, therefore, to concentrate on the banality of the opposition. The Federal government has allowed the flag to be burned as an expression of one's position. But only certain types of citizens burn the flag—those who are unpatriotic. These same people are sexually immoral. An ad from the Christian Coalition illustrates this: "These people" will use your money to "teach [your] sons to sodomize one another." That "these people" are evil is more than a matter of opinion. "These people" are undermining the very core of our society—our stance as a traditional Christian nation.

It is not ridiculous to suggest that the right sees very little remaining in society that is good. This is evidenced by the fact that symbols of good were used substantially less than symbols of evil. What is good? "Christian values," "children" and "America," to name the most prominent. Wildmon uses a couple of these symbols in the following response to the impending lawsuit filed by artist David Wojnarowicz:

The lawsuit is an attempt to win through the courts that which those who oppose us have not been able to win in the public arena—to blunt AFA's effectiveness, and, hopefully, to put us out of business. It is intended to silence those of us who fight for the rights of Christians and for traditional Christian values (AFA Journal 1990).

Typically the use of symbols are conflated so that good and evil are referred to in the same paragraph, and sometimes the same sentence. Consider the following from the same AFA Journal article:

Day after day there are groups trying to take away the rights of

Christians while promoting the "rights" of pornographers, atheists, child molesters, abortionists and homosexuals ....This is not happening in a democratic way, by people going to the polls and voting, but in the unelected courtrooms of America.

Christians are good, atheists are bad; democracy is good, courtrooms are evil. The debate is clearly broken down into mundane symbols.

The right has not cornered the market on symbolic warfare. Consider how the progressivist side is easily defined by its symbols as well. The progressivists represent the countermovement in this debate. As with most who find themselves on the defensive in any battle, it is just as important to protect and promote oneself, defend one's integrity, as it is to discredit the other side. This is done through symbols of good. The following is an excerpt from a list of talking points by the NEA for the National Press Club.

> It's not a question of the artists versus the public; it's a question of art not reaching the public as well as it could. Our mission, at least in part, is to rebuild the bridge between the arts and the public. We've already begun the process, and I'd like to highlight some initiatives and certain projects that demonstrate our commitment to that ideal. How do we best serve the American people? By opening doors to the diverse array of cultural experiences in this country .... Emphasize arts education. It empowers, teaches creativity, communication, self-esteem, the ability to make sense of chaos and provides building blocks for all future learning ... (September 17, 1990).

The very things the NEA advocates as "good"—creativity, diversity, and so on—are the very things that the religious right designates as bad. One group's symbols of evil become the other's symbols of good and vice versa.

The progressivists, as well as the orthodox, are quick to point out what is evil about the other side. Evil was conveyed through "(content) restrictions," "Donald Wildmon," "far right," and "censorship." Once again, symbols of good and evil share space in the paragraph below.

> This year, aided by numerous organizations from the Religious Right, Senator Helms and other extreme conservatives in Congress have put the future of the NEA and the National Endowment for the Humanities in jeopardy. The campaign against artistic expression is being orchestrated by far right groups including Rev. Donald Wildmon's American Family Association and Phyllis Schlafly's Eagle Forum. It is these right wing organizations who are putting the political pressure on Congress. These right wing groups are sending millions of direct mail letters charging members of Congress who support NEA with advocating pornography. They are touching off a flood of mail to Congress by citizens taken in by the Religious Right propaganda.[5]

The NEA is good, the far right is bad. And just as the far right accuses the left of flag burning and sexual promiscuity, the left charges the right with ruining the country as well.

> We have faced these same far right adversaries before in battles over public education, civil rights and the nomination of Robert Bork. Now they are turning their efforts toward suppressing all forms of creative expression through record labeling legislation, boycotts of television sponsors and this assault on the NEA.

A symbolic crusade is waged by each side in order to highlight "the good" and "the evil." Evil is indeed necessary, yet it is only useful in these debates if it can be recognized. It is recognized through the symbols that each side employs in defining the other and hence, defining the self.

Legitimating a Claim

Movements and countermovements can share the use of a symbol. This becomes most evident in an examination of legitimacy symbols. Both sides present themselves as defenders of institutions. For example, both use the government as a symbol of legitimacy. However, the right does this by invoking the use of "your tax dollars" to legitimate their position that it is indeed the public's money going to fund obscene art. The left highlights the fact that individuals do pay taxes to the federal government and that the government, as a legitimate institution has declared that it is worthwhile to fund the arts. Thus, if works receive money they must be "art."

Consider first how the orthodox side of this debate uses the term "tax dollars."

> ... It isn't just a little issue. Nor is it a matter of free speech. It's a matter of the government taking tax dollars to fund an assault on religion. That can't happen in America.

Now note how the left couches tax dollars within the language of "funding" and "government" appointed panels.

> It is citizens who come to this agency—over 800 of them each year—to do the government's business. These are citizens who are skilled in some area of the arts; occasionally they are lay people who are skilled in some area of

the arts. They get together and they function much like a jury functions in our system of law ....This is a citizen doing the government's business. But that's not the end of the citizen process because the federally appointed, the Presidentially appointed National Council on the Arts reviews the recommendations of these panels. Those are 26 of the most distinguished artists in our country. People such as Arthur Mitchell of the Dance Theatre of Harlem; Lloyd Richards of the Yale Drama School; Phyllis Curtain, famous opera singer; Helen Franenthaller, the painter. These people review the grants and make recommendations, and ultimately I, as the chair, decide what is funded on the basis of those recommendations.

Note here that the progressivist side is able to concretely identify those things which legitimate its position: its history, notable artists who make decisions about what art is and what art is funded. The Council on the Arts is presidentially appointed. The claims to legitimacy are several. As noted above, the number of legitimate symbols for the right is half those for the left. The orthodox side of this debate relies on the use of tax money as a euphemism for the abstract concept of morality. Not once in my examination was the Bible used as a symbol of legitimacy, even though it largely defines the world view of the religious right. Those on this side were more likely to use members of Congress or newspapers sympathetic to their position as symbols of legitimacy.

Vilifying the Opposition

As mentioned above, one side's symbols of good can be used against them when employed by the other side, making what once seemed "good" now appear evil, or at the very least questionable. In this debate, both sides used symbols of the other as ammunition and as a means of vilifying the opposition. Following are several examples:

David Wojnarowicz (artist): The American Family Association purports to want to instill *moral virtues in the American family* ...those virtues are made up of lies, distortion, mutilation, misrepresentation, innuendos, and half truths.

John Frohnmayer (then NEA chair): Does the American Family Association acknowledge that the arts are disciplines that require, for example, a ballet dancer to train for ten years, risk injury, face unemployment and perhaps, under the best of circumstances, to expect an average of $12,000 a year income? Is the kind of discipline, training and concentration required to create and perform all of the arts contrary to *family values*?

AFA Journal article: Many groups including Norman Lear's politically liberal People for the American Way have begun massive efforts to secure continued funding of pornographic and anti-Christian art by the NEA.

Pat Robertson: Ladies and gentlemen, in my estimation, this is an outrage. The liberals talk about *freedom, First Amendment freedom to speak out, to publish, we should be allowed to express ourselves on all points of view.* But when Alvin Felzinberg, senior deputy chairman of the NEA says you've gone too far taking taxpayer money to fund an assault on the deeply held religious views of the people of America ... with which they disagree is sinful and tyrannical .... It isn't

> just a little issue. Nor is it a
> matter of free speech. It's a
> matter of the government
> taking tax dollars to fund an
> assault on religion. That can't
> happen in America.

Each side's symbols of good are spat back at them with the sting
of cynicism and satire. Real conversation seems unlikely and
unwelcome. To show the least bit of understanding for the other is
to sleep with the enemy. Remaining true to one's own world view
is jeopardized.

SYMBOLS AND THE MEDIA

In analyzing the media's portrayal of the controversy over funding
the NEA, one image became clear: this was more than a controversy,
this was war. The debate was characterized as a "political imbroglio,"
a "renewed fight," and a "battle." There was a "furor over the NEA,"
and the climate was likened to a "hothouse." My examination of the
media also revealed that journalists selected quotes from actors of
the movement and countermovement which reflected the symbols as
they were identified in the rhetoric of each. "Other news sources"
(news magazines, radio) frequently relayed images of the movement
actors which were disparaging at best. Publications associated with
the left (the "liberal media") labelled the right as "the morals squad"
(*Newsweek*); publications associated with the right labelled the
opposition as "sickos" (*The Washington Times*). Even though
Wildmon and Robertson were known to be leaders on the right side
of this conflict, they were rarely quoted. Rather, Congressmen
sympathetic to their position were cited—most frequently Senator
Jesse Helms and Representative Dana Rohrabacher. While
legislators were a frequent source for the left as well, they were
matched by other sources—namely artists, art directors, gallery
owners, etc. Using sources in this way, the media further legitimated
the position of the left. The media reinforced the idea that the only
people who knew what art was were art people. The government was
a legitimate source. The arts community was a legitimate source. The
religious right? Apparently not. Excluding the outspoken
representatives of the far right further delegitimized its position in

society. Not only were the orthodox unable to define art, more
importantly, their opinions about what was moral or obscene didn't
appear to count for much either in the eyes of the media and therefore,
perhaps, society at large.

WHAT'S AT STAKE

It has been suggested by artists and others that art is merely an
expression of life, a reflection and perception of the reality in which
we live. If this is the case, it is not that homoerotic photographs are
bad, rather it is the acknowledgment that the homoerotic activity
actually taking place is. The depiction of homoeroticism in federally
funded art portrays the homosexual lifestyle as acceptable. It is here
that we return to Gusfield's notion of status politics, and Hunter's
concept of the culture war. What is at stake for the religious right
is nicely summed up by Pat Robertson.

> Well, you see, there's a little deeper issue here. I don't think people
> understand how the game is being played and what the issue is. It's
> not 40 or 50 thousand dollars. That's not the issue.... The issue is,
> is the legitimatization, I believe that's a word, of the homosexual
> lifestyle by the federal government and the undercutting of our laws
> on pornography.... So what this does is say we legitimatize the
> homosexual type of activity. So you have two men engaging in anal
> sex, big picture; the federal government is taking my money to pay
> for it; that's being set up in museums all across America. So people
> say, "Well, hey, the government is paying for that, so that legitimizes
> it" ("700 Club," June 14, 1990).

It is by invoking "America" in this statement and others that the right
emphasizes its fear for the nation at large. Through public art,
Americans have decided that homosexuals and atheists share the
fabric of this country. As Robertson says in an earlier quote, "We
can't let this happen in America." Why this can't happen is stated
pointedly by Donald Wildmon.

> What we are up against is not dirty words and dirty pictures. It is
> a philosophy of life which seeks to remove the influence of Christians
> and Christianity from our society. Pornography is not the disease, but
> merely a visible symptom. It springs from a moral cancer in our
> society, and it will lead us to destruction if we are unable to stop it.

In other words, it threatens to destroy a particular philosophy of life.

Hunter asserts (1991) that a culture war "emerges over fundamentally different conceptions of moral authority, over different ideas and beliefs about truth, the good, obligation to one another, the nature of community and so on" (1991, p. 49). Within the field of art and the controversy over federal funding, it would seem on the surface that the debate is over "what art *is*." Progressivists claim the work of Mapplethorpe and Serrano is "art." Those on the orthodox side claim it is not. And though these statements may represent a good portion of the public debate over the issue, it seems that there is something much more profound going on here than a controversy over the definition of art. The culture war over art has less to do with "what is art" than it does with what is the deeper public meaning that is given to it by the symbols of political debate. "Ultimately," Hunter states, "the battle over this symbolic territory reveals a conflict over world views—over what standards our communities and our nation will live by; over what we consider to be of 'of enduring value' in our communities; over what we consider a fair representation of our times" (p. 248).

> We're [the NEA] an easy target, after all. The arts are visible, and because *they often tap into the very issues that society is grappling with*, the arts can cause outrage, fear and anger. They're only doing their job—they can also cause peace, contentment and a feeling of the sublime."—Jane Alexander, present Chair of the NEA

Thus, like other specific skirmishes within the larger culture wars, the political debate over funding of the arts is actually an artifact of something much deeper—a conflict over the meaning of America. Though political solutions may bring temporary resolutions, the fundamentally disparate and strongly held world views resting just below the surface of the debate suggest that controversies over the arts, pornography, censorship, standards of decency, and the like will continue in some form or another for many years to come. The fight over the NEA following the Republican takeover of Congress in 1995 is just one example of how this particular conflict is far from being resolved.[6]

ACKNOWLEDGMENTS

I would like to thank Jeffrey K. Hadden and Sarah M. Corse for their comments on an earlier draft of this paper.

NOTES

1. This obscenity guideline was derived from the 1973 Miller v. California Supreme Court decision which labelled the following to be obscene: masturbation, activities related to excretory functions and simulated sex acts.

2. Robertson and the Christian Coalition have been prominent in politics as well: Robertson making a 1988 Presidential bid and Ralph Reed, the Executive Director of the Christian Coalition, mobilizing his members to support the "right" candidates in the 1994 mid-term elections.

3. My use and definition of symbols in social movements follows an outline prescribed by Thomas Cushman (1983) who used symbols to identify those important to the Moral Majority.

4. A criticism of content analysis is that it is not an accurate measure of the intensity of the communication (1969, p. 123). Given the brevity of the documents reviewed in this research and the short time span these documents cover, I am comfortable that the amount of the times a symbol occurred was an accurate measure of its intensity.

5. Testimony before the Subcommittee on Post-secondary Education. Given by Michael Hudson, Western Director of People for the American Way, March 5, 1990.

6. At the time of this writing, November 1995, reauthorization of the National Endowment for the Arts has been held up. The reappropriation of the agency is in process. Members of the House and Senate Interior Subcommittee have met and approved a budget of $99.5 million, an approproximate 40 percent cut to the Endowment's budget. When this conference agreement went to the floor for a vote it was not approved because of other measures related to Interior but not the NEA. The bill is back in conference and the process is not officially complete. Phase-out of federally funded art is uncertain, but perhaps not imminent.

REFERENCES

Cushman, T. O. 1983. *Symbols and Social Movements: The Case of the Moral Majority*. Master's Thesis. University of Virginia.

Dubin, S. C. 1992. *Arresting Images: Impolitic Art and Uncivil Actions*. New York: Routledge.

Etzioni, A. 1968. *The Active Society*. New York: Free Press.

Frohnmayer, J. 1990. Speech to the National Press Club, March 29.

_____. 1990. "Open Letter to the American Family Association," February.

"Group Claims NEA Endorses Pornography." 1993. *Washington Post*. September 10, G, 2:1.

Gusfield, J. R. 1986. *Symbolic Crusade: Status Politics and the American Temperance Movement.* Chicago, IL: University of Illinois Press.

Hadden J. K., and C. E. Swann. 1988. *Prime-Time Preachers.* Reading, MA: Addison-Wesley Publishing Company, Inc.

Helms, J. 1989. Quoted in *NY Times,* July 27.

Holsti, O. R. 1969. *Content Analysis for the Social Sciences and the Humanities.* Reading, MA: Addison-Wesley Publishing Company.

Hoover, S. M. 1988. *Mass Media Religion.* Newbury Park, CA: Sage Publications.

Hunter, J. D. 1991. *Culture Wars: The Struggle to Define America.* New York: Basic Books.

Kantor, E. 1989. "NEA and Clash of Symbols." *Washington Post.* September 26, A, 1:5.

Legislation. 1990. *The Washingon Post,* October 12.

Masters, K. 1990. "NEA Funded Art Exhibit Protested." *Washington Post.* April 21, C. 1:1.

Masters, K. 1990. Quote taken from a letter to President George Bush. Reprinted in "Stars Testify in Defense of NEA Funding."

McGuigan C. 1989. "When Taxes Pay for Art." *Newsweek 114:68, July 3.*

Pearce, W. B., S. W. Littlejohn, and A. Alexander. 1989. "The Quixotic Quest for Civility: Patterns of Interaction between the New Christian Right and Secular Humanists." In *Secularization and Fundamentalism Reconsidered,* edited by J. K. Hadden and A. Shupe. New York: Paragon House.

"Radical New York Homosexual Artist-Activist Sues AFA, Wildmon for 5,000,000," *AFA Journal,* July 1990, pp. 1, 23.

Robertson, P. 1990. The *700 Club,* June 4.

Solcraig, B. 1990. "Reverend Wildon's War on the Arts." *The New York Times Magazine,* September 2, pp. 22+.

Trescott, J. 1993. "Artists Add Voices on Decency." *Washington Post,* June 4, C, 10: 1.

————. 1994. "NEA Chief Endorses Artistic Freedom." October 12.

Washington Post, October 12, 1990.

Zald, M., and B. Useem. "Movement and Countermovement Interaction: Mobilization, Tactics and State Involvement." *Social Movements in Organizational Society.* New Brunswick, NJ: Transaction, Inc.

THE AMERICAN ABORTION DEBATE:
CULTURE WAR OR NORMAL DISCOURSE?

Michele Dillon

This paper investigates whether James Hunter's culture war thesis is an apt characterization of the American abortion debate. I focus on three arguments central to Hunter's analysis: (1) that the abortion debate involves two paradigmatically opposed world views; (2) that debate about abortion, since it involves moral discourse, is structurally different than other political debates, and (3) that the new alignments in abortion politics are culturally significant. Examining existing research in each of these three domains, I find that the debate over abortion is more complex than suggested by Hunter. World views of pro-life and pro-choice activists, for example, share a commitment to some overlapping values; the argumentative structure of abortion discourse has a pattern rather similar to that of political debate more generally, and new alignments on abortion, such as that between the Catholic Church and the Southern Baptist Convention, do not displace historically embedded differences in symbolic resources and cultural orientation. It may be more helpful, therefore, I suggest, to think of the abortion debate as an ongoing public conversation about America's cultural tradition and how it should be variously expressed in contemporary laws and practices.

This chapter investigates whether James Hunter's culture war thesis is supported by the debate over abortion in America. I focus, in particular, on three related points which form the core of Hunter's argument. First, and most crucially, Hunter argues that people who disagree on abortion and other controversial issues have fundamentally different conceptions of moral authority (pp. 43-51). The "culturally orthodox" is oriented to an external, definable, and transcendent authority. The "culturally progressive" view is based on a conception of truth which is processual, subjectivist, and rational (p. 44). I investigate this thesis by looking at the *world views* of activists and the general public on abortion.

The second point concerns *discourse*. Hunter argues that the contemporary cultural conflicts are about ultimate moral truths on which, unlike political matters, there can be no compromise (p. 46). I investigate whether, in fact, discourse on abortion is different than political discourse. Finally, I evaluate Hunter's argument that in the struggle for cultural domination, *new alliances* have emerged which supersede traditional religio-cultural divisions to constitute a new, and what Hunter deems, a culturally significant, alignment (p. 47).

COMPETING WORLD VIEWS

To what extent do studies of abortion activists and public opinion surveys on abortion support Hunter's contention that the culture war is between competing systems of moral understanding? I will address this question, first by discussing empirical studies of the values and world views of individual pro-life and pro-choice activists, and then by looking at the attitudes of the general American public.

Abortion Activists

If there are extremes in moral understanding on abortion, we should expect to find the clearest evidence of this among activists.

Unlike mainstream citizens, activists get involved in a political cause precisely because of the intensity of their commitment to the values at stake and their desire to see public policy reflect those values. As they try to convince others, including researchers, of the inherent truth of their views, we should not expect activists to acknowledge the reservations they may have in taking a monolithic view.

Studies by both Kristin Luker (1984) and Faye Ginsburg (1989) support the notion that there is a clear divergence of views between pro-life and pro-choice activists. It is evident, in particular, that the activists express very different understandings of sexual morality, and disagree as to whether motherhood and gender roles are natural or socially constructed. Luker's pro-life interviewees, for example, were motivated by what they perceived to be a widening gap in American public policy between what they tacitly assumed was commonly accepted, morally right behavior, and policy initiatives, most especially the Roe v. Wade decision, which challenged such assumptions. They viewed such changes, moreover, as legitimating and encouraging a set of values anathema to their understanding of the naturalness of motherhood for women.

Somewhat different from Luker's pro-life activists, the pro-life women in Ginsburg's study did not see motherhood and nurturance "as a natural moral quality, but one that is achieved" (p. 172). In other words, Ginsburg explains, in the historical context of legal abortion, women become mothers not automatically, but by effort (p. 195), an effort which demands that they transcend their own ambivalence about pregnancy and integrate it with changing ideas about women's roles. Pro-life activists thus oppose abortion because they see it, and pro-choice women, as "culturally male," that is, as rejecting the capacity for nurturance and motherhood which they regard as essential to womanliness (pp. 216-217).

Pro-choice activists have a quite different view of motherhood. They see it, not as natural and something which should necessarily take priority over other aspects of life, but as purposeful and voluntary. In Luker's study, pro-choice activists define motherhood as a social role whose material and emotional obligations should not be entered into without due consideration. Wanting motherhood to be a "real choice," they argue that, in the long run, abortion will enhance the quality of parenting by making it optional (p. 182).

Expressing a similar concern over the institutional context of motherhood, the pro-choice activists in Ginsburg's study expressed an understanding of nurturance that transcended biological reproduction. They argued for the cultural transmission of the nurturant values associated with the domestic sphere into the non-domestic spheres of work and politics, domains that they perceive as celebrating male-defined, materialistic and instrumental values. In the view of these pro-choice women, the greater diffusion of nurturant values in the public sphere would shift the boundaries between traditional female and male spheres of activity, thus enhancing women's interests and social justice as a whole (pp. 169-171).

The above differences between pro-life and pro-choice activists, however, should not obscure the similarities between them. A significant cultural commonality is that both groups value motherhood and the nurturant values associated with it. Ginsburg emphasizes that both pro-life and pro-choice interviewees "claimed nurturance as a source of moral authority" (p. 201). What they differed about was their practical interpretation of how it served their common goal of protecting women's interests (p. 140).

Similarly, pro-life and pro-choice activists shared many catalyzing experiences as women which led to their activism. Ginsburg (1989, p. 139), for example, argues that the convergences in the experiences and social backgrounds of her activists make it difficult to predict a priori who would become pro-life or pro-choice. Moreover, although the activism focused on divergent agendas, for both groups it was grounded in a concern with the status of women in society and the broader inequality which leads to a devaluing either of women as mothers or as participants in the public sphere.

It was also evident that despite the absoluteness of activists' commitment to either a pro-life or a pro-choice stance, for both groups, abortion presented moral complexities. Luker found, for example, that pro-life activists struggle with the need to accommodate their recognition of the occasional necessity of abortion within their framework of strict opposition to abortion (Luker 1984, pp. 175, 185). By the same token, pro-choice activists qualify their acceptance of abortion by denouncing its repeat use and its use as a method of birth control (pp. 179-180).

The nuances in activists' reasoning about abortion are also apparent in a national survey of members of the two premier abortion activist organizations, the National Abortion Rights Action League (NARAL) and the National Right to Life (NRLC) (Granberg 1981). As in Luker's and Ginsburg's (1989) studies, the survey found significant differences in the political attitudes and characteristics of pro-choice and pro-life activists. However, the study also highlighted areas of disagreement within each group. Three-quarters of NRLC members, for example, favored making abortion available to women whose life is endangered by the continuation of pregnancy. And only just over half of NARAL members approved of legal abortion as a method of sex selection (Granberg 1981, pp. 162-163).

These data indicate, therefore, that although there is indeed a clash between the political agendas on abortion pursued by pro-life and pro-choice activists, there are important contextual nuances which undermine the notion that these policy commitments are fired by absolutist world views. Both sides share basic value commitments as exemplified by their affirmation of motherhood, concern with women's social status, and sensitivity to the moral and practical implications of both pregnancy and abortion.

Public Opinion

Hunter emphasizes that "most Americans occupy a vast middle ground between the polarizing impulses in American culture" (1991, p. 43). He subsequently elaborates this point (1994, pp. 85-121) using data from a public ipinion survey conducted by Gallup for a project commissioned and underwritten by the pro-life American Life League (1994, p. 264). Hunter's analysis of the data leads him to express concern about he "depth of... mass legal illiteracy" (1994, p. 87) evident in respondents' knowledge of abortion policy. He states that: "Public ignorance about abortion law suggests that people are arguing with phantoms, not with each other, and certainly not over the facts of the legal dispute..." (1994, p. 89). If they were more knowledgeable, Hunter argues, "the majority of Americans would morally disapprove of the majority of abortions currently performed (1994, p. 98). In essence, Hunter is puzzled by what he calls the "muddled middle" (1994, p. 106), the ambivalences, nuances and moral contradictions expressed by the majority of Americans on abortion. He views this as "moral dissonance" (p. 106), and argues that "the disjuction between what most Americans approve of and what they are willing to allow is not easy to square" (1994, p. 98).

An alternative interpretation is that the majority of Americans are not "muddled," but are, in fact, quite clear about where they stand on abortion. National polls conducted since the Roe v. Wade decision document a steadfast trend indicating that the majority of Americans want abortion to be legal (Gallup Report 1989; Glenn 1987). Clearly, as Hunter (1994) and other studies show (Cook, Jelen, and Wilcox 1992), Americans have reservations about the morality of abortion. We should be surprised if they did not have ambivalences. It is also the case that Americans want abortion to be a legal option, allowing the woman to be the arbiter of her moral decision. Irrespective of the details of specific laws and policies, respect for the moral autonomy of individual conscience in regard to the law stands out as the hallmark of American public opinion on the abortion issue.

It is evident from the national data that Americans are not committed to a consistent pro-life ethic. They are particularly sympathetic to abortion in cases in which the mother's life (94%) or health (84%) is endangered, and if the pregnancy is coerced; for example, 85% approve of legal abortion in the case of rape. On the other hand, neither are Americans consistently pro-choice. While endorsing legal abortion in hard or coercive circumstances, less than half approve of abortion if the family cannot afford another child (46%) or if the woman is single and does not want to marry the father (42%) (Davis and Smith, 1993).

Reflecting these qualifications in attitudes toward abortion, Americans are uncomfortable with extremists on either side of the issue. For example, one-fifth of Americans have a very unfavorable opinion of people active in anti-abortion (27%) and abortion rights movements (23%). Although they regard activists as highly principled, they also see them as intolerant and extremist (The Gallup Poll 1993, pp. 76-81).

Several studies further elaborate the complexities and differentiation in Americans' views of abortion. Cook, Jelen, and Wilcox (1992), for example, demonstrate that most pro-choice citizens favor some restrictions on abortion, overwhelmingly reject abortion as a method of birth control, believe that there are too many abortions, and that many abortion decisions are made too hastily (1992, p. 145). Underscoring the moral challenge that abortion poses for those who are either consistently or situationally pro-choice, Cook et al. found a substantial proportion—around 40%—who, although believing that abortion is murder, also believe that it is ultimately a woman's decision (1992, pp. 145-149).

It is evident, therefore, that while expressing moral reservations about abortion, a majority of Americans lean toward supporting it as a woman's legal right. This is an ideological position that appears to be solidly rooted in Americans' sense of how the world should be. It is noteworthy, for instance, that 71 percent say that scientific evidence on fetal development does not influence their opinion on abortion, and 60% do not question whether their position on abortion is the right one (The Gallup Report, 1989, pp. 22-23).

Moreover, the sharpest shift in attitudes to abortion was recorded by Gallup in April 1990, when the proportion favoring unrestricted legal abortion increased from 24 percent to 31 percent, while the proportion holding the middle-ground position did not change substantially, remaining at 53 percent (Gallup and Newport, 1990, pp. 2-3). The increase in the percentage endorsing the most liberal position may have been a response to the Supreme Court's 1989 Webster decision which ruled in favor of pro-life demands and recognized states' rights to protect fetal rights. The heightened level of support for unrestricted legal abortion first observed in 1990 has remained within the 31 percent to 34 percent range since then (The Gallup Poll 1993, pp. 73-74).

Other studies also challenge Hunter's thesis that opinion on abortion is part of a broader, fundamentally different, moral understanding. Even among those who take either a strict pro-life or a strict pro-choice position, much empirical evidence documents a differentiation, not a constellation, of values. Using national data sets, Cook, Jelen, and Wilcox (1992) show that pro-life supporters are themselves deeply divided in their attitudes toward the death penalty, civil rights, feminism, and general societal equality (pp. 143-144). They conclude that the pro-life consensus is "quite fragile" and "any discussion of other political issues is likely to lead to disagreement" (p. 144). Rebecca Klatch's (1987) study similarly highlights ideological divisions among new-right women, especially with regard to classical liberal views of the individual and the role of the state.

The role of government in society is also a primary source of disagreement among pro-choice supporters. Those who take the most liberal position on abortion (that is, that it should be legal in all circumstances), are differentiated by liberal and libertarian tendencies, especially on economic issues (Cook et al. 1992, p. 147). It is also the case that a feminist orientation is not predictive of attitudes toward abortion (Tamney, Johnson, and Burton 1992, p. 43). Finally, situationalists, those who favor abortion in certain restricted circumstances, also do not comprise a cohesive attitudinal group (Cook et al. 1992, p. 155).

Similar to Cook, Jelen, and Wilcox's study (1992), Callahan and Callahan (1984) reinforce the profile of an American public that is morally and culturally complex. Based on focus group discussions with pro-life and pro-choice women, the Callahans suggest that the ideological and values differences between pro-life and pro-choice supporters are over stated, and that the relationship of abortion to deeper values is open to more flexible possibilities than is often apparent in the public debate (1984, p. 221).

In sum, whether we examine the abortion views of activists or the general public, we see evidence of moral nuance, complexity, and ambiguity. Nonetheless, the majority of Americans favor legal abortion, and even among those who take an extreme pro-life or pro-choice stance, their attitude toward abortion is not necessarily predictive of a coherent world view.

ABORTION AS A NON-NEGOTIABLE CULTURAL ISSUE?

The core of Hunter's thesis is the claim that current public controversies are cultural rather than political. The critical reason they are cultural, he maintains, is that while compromise is possible on political matters, it is not possible regarding questions of moral truth (1991, p. 46). Although Hunter acknowledges that "politics is, in large part, an expression of culture" (1991, p. 57), nonetheless, his sharp demarcation of political from cultural issues suggests a pre-Popperian positivist distinction between fact and theory (Popper 1934/1975). Hunter appears to be suggesting that politics operates in an ahistorical, context-less arena wherein differences over policy options are more readily negotiable than cultural disagreements which, for him, are interminable.

If we assume for the moment, following Hunter, that there is, indeed, such a sharp distinction between political and cultural issues, then people should argue differently about cultural than political questions. Is this the case? Is debate about abortion different than for example, how Republican and Democratic politicians debate domestic or foreign policy? Is it different from the kind of cognitive reasoning used by presidents when they address the nation or by Supreme Court justices debating points of legal interpretation?

In my own research (Dillon 1993, 1995a), I have applied the integrative complexity coding scheme to explore whether abortion discourse differs from arguments articulated in political and judicial debates. Integrative complexity is a quantitative coding schema that evaluates argumentative structure. It measures the number of dimensions or aspects of a problem that are taken into consideration, whether dogmatic, unidimensional positions are expressed, or whether account is taken of alternative interpretations, and also examines the extent to which conceptual connections are developed among the differentiated dimensions of judgment (Tetlock 1989, pp. 133-134).

I have found that, as a whole, abortion discourse is conducted at a fairly low level of integrative complexity. Rejecting the "rigidity of the right" thesis which argues that conservatives take a more dogmatic stance than their liberal counterparts, pro-life and pro-choice participants use arguments which follow a similarly simple structure (Dillon 1993). What does differentiate the structure of abortion-related statements, however, is whether they are issued by single-issue or multi-issue organizations. Thus, for example, multi-issue organizations such as the pro-life Catholic Church, and the pro-choice American Bar Association and American Medical Association, present more nuanced and equivocal arguments than do single-issue organizations either on the pro-life side, including the National Right to Life Committee, Operation Rescue, and the American Life League, or on the pro-choice side, including the National Abortion Rights Action League, Planned Parenthood, and the National Organization for Women.

Overall, however, the level of integrative complexity of abortion arguments is relatively similar to that observed in the realm of politics more generally. Philip Tetlock (1989) has found, for example, that in particular, conservative U.S. senators, ideologically conservative British parliamentarians, and liberal U.S. senators in an oppositional role, use integratively simple arguments in debating routine domestic and foreign policy issues. Tetlock also finds that the pre-election year speeches of American presidents in office are similarly low on integrative complexity. Likewise, Supreme Court justices, although more removed from the demands of articulating publicly persuasive arguments, present judicial opinions which fall within a low range of integrative complexity. This is especially true of justices who have a conservative voting record on civil liberties cases (Tetlock et al. 1985).

A second question that I have investigated is whether different abortion policy contexts impact on the sorts of argumentative strategies pursued by participants in the abortion debate. Specifically, I have examined the way in which the Catholic Church argues about abortion (Dillon 1995a). The Church's discourse presents an interesting test case of Hunter's thesis because Church opposition to abortion is grounded in the ultimacy of moral truth. If, as Hunter claims, compromise is off-limits when the moral truths at the root of today's culture war are being discussed, then we should expect no significant variation over time in how the Church publicly argues about abortion.

Analysis of the abortion statements issued by the U.S. bishops between 1973 and 1992, however, indicates that there is variation in the Church's argumentative strategy. It uses more integratively simple arguments during periods of actual or impending negative (pro-choice) shifts in abortion policy, such as after the 1973 Roe v. Wade decision, or regarding the 1992 proposed Freedom of Choice Act. By contrast, it articulates more integratively complex arguments during periods of actual or impending positive (pro-life) shifts in abortion policy, such as in response to the 1989 Webster decision, or arguing, in 1974, in favor of a constitutional pro-life amendment.

Once again, the variation in the level of complexity of the Church's abortion discourse parallels strategies used in political debate. In his time-series analyses of the integrative complexity of U.S.-Soviet diplomatic statements during the Cold War, Tetlock (1988), for example, found that the low points of complexity in American-Soviet communications coincided with periods of increased tension between the two superpowers, and that statements higher in complexity coincided with more cooperative periods. Despite the non-negotiable nature of the Church's moral opposition to abortion, therefore, it, nonetheless, employs argumentative strategies on abortion that parallel those used by nation states on national security.

In summary, while it is obviously difficult to test Hunter's thesis in any simple way, my research findings suggest that abortion is debated in the public arena in broadly the same way as are other political issues. Therefore, although many of us share Hunter's concern about the quality of political and public discourse, and the factual illiteracy and distortions that remain unexamined in such discussions, it is important to bear in mind that this is not a feature of moral discourse alone. Proponents in the abortion debate should not be singled out any more than members of Congress or local school board representatives, for example, for undermining the ideals of substantive democracy.

NEW CULTURAL ALIGNMENTS

Finally, I turn to Hunter's argument that the new cultural alignment has led to the formation of pragmatic alliances across faith traditions. Hunter argues that these new "institutional alliances are *culturally* significant for the simple reason that ideological and organizational associations are being generated among groups that have historically been antagonistic to one another" (1991, p. 47, emphasis in original).

It is true that the abortion conflict has given rise to new trans-denominational alliances. An interesting case in point is provided here by the unprecedented anti-abortion collaboration between the Catholic Church hierarchy (the National Conference of Catholic Bishops) and the Southern Baptist Convention. Although both have very different histories of abortion activism, and, historically, have had an antagonistic relationship toward one another, nonetheless, in 1992, they jointly filed an Amicus Curiae brief in the U.S. Supreme Court, Planned Parenthood of Southeastern Pennsylvania v. Casey case. What are we to make of this alliance? My research on the abortion discourses of the two organizations indicates that although they share a common pro-life stance, they remain embedded in very different cultural understandings (Dillon 1995b).

The natural law reasoning of the Catholic bishops in contrast to the importance of biblical authority for the Southern Baptists, different conceptions of church/state relations and of public/private morality, and the different cultural trajectories of the two organizations in American society, give rise to each religious organization arguing about abortion in significantly diverse ways. The Southern Baptists present sect-like, narrowly defined, biblically grounded arguments. They typically emphasize, for example, that "the Bible is replete in its teaching on the sanctity of life" (SBC pamphlet, "What the Bible teaches about abortion"). Quoting extensively from the Bible, the SBC argues that the "central truth that emerges from these Bible verses is that human life is sacred" (SBC pamphlet, "Is Life a Right?"). The Catholic bishops, in contrast, articulate broad based culturally open arguments which, in addition to Catholic doctrine, draw on science, and more especially, the

American political cultural tradition. They frame abortion as a deviation from the founding principles and moral and legal tradition of the American nation, arguing that the common good of American society can only be achieved if the fundamental right to life of the unborn is protected in law (see, for example, U.S. Bishops, Submission to Senate Subcommittee on Constitutional Amendments, 1974).

Looked at in their entirety, the Southern Baptist and Catholic discourses on abortion give clear voice to different cultural visions. Their common sharing of, and collaboration on a pro-life stance regarding abortion, therefore, contrary to Hunter's thesis, should not be seen as a transcendence of the deep cultural divisions that have been a feature of Catholic-Protestant world views since the Reformation. That these differences continue to have salience for public culture is underscored further by survey data demonstrating that the differing religious imaginations of Catholics and Southern Baptists lead them to express different public policy preferences on a range of social, economic, and political issues (Greeley 1989, 1993).

Just as Hunter overstates the cultural significance of new transdenominational alliances, he dismisses the significance of counter-paradigmatic cultural couplings. Hunter acknowledges that there are "counterintuitive developments" such as pro-life feminists (pp. 105-106). He rejects their significance for public culture, however, even though the political agendas articulated by formal groups representing these interests constitute the "middling positions" that, Hunter argues, are eclipsed in the public discourse (pp. 160-161).

By their organizational titles alone, "Feminists for Life of America" and "Catholics for a Free Choice," highlight the complexity of the abortion issue in American society. The existence of these organizations challenges the contention that at the root of the cultural tensions in American society is a clear and sharp divide between conservatives and liberals (Wuthnow 1988, pp. 222-223), or in Hunter's thesis (1991, pp. 43-46), between those who take an orthodox versus a progressivist approach to moral truth.

Established in 1973, "Catholics for a Free Choice" (CFFC), is a lay organization presenting a collective Catholic voice against the pro-life stance of the Catholic Church. CFFC newsletters, statements, and its quarterly journal *Conscience*, articulate arguments clearly underscoring that both pro-choice thinking and Catholic opinion are neither monolithic nor absolute. Unlike other pro-choice organizations such as NARAL, NOW and Planned Parenthood, CFFC rejects the claim that the abortion debate is fundamentally about a woman's right. They concur that "human reproduction is an intensely personal matter," but they are unequivocal, nonetheless, that it is one which is "also a fundamental social phenomenon" (CFFC, organizational literature). Along with other pro-choice organizations, CFFC supports public funding of abortions for poor women. They ground this claim within the Catholic social justice tradition even though they are advocating an abortion rights stance clearly at odds with Church teaching. Emphasizing that the "best choice" is when abortion is unnecessary (see, for example, a 1992 advertising campaign), CFFC denounces both the Catholic Church's opposition to abortion and artificial contraception, and the pro-choice movement's tendency to ignore the high incidence of abortion in American society.

In a parallel fashion, "Feminists for Life of America," (FLA), rejects narrow understandings of both feminism and a "pro-life" agenda. Founded in 1972, "Feminists for Life" challenges most obviously the commonly assumed belief that to be a feminist implies an endorsement of a pro-choice stance on abortion. Staking out an oppositional view, it argues that rather than liberating women, abortion "validates the patriarchal world view which holds that women, encumbered as they are by their reproductive capacity, are inferior to men" (FLA, organizational literature). It contends that feminism and opposition to abortion are "part of a larger philosophy that values all life."

"Feminists for Life" share with pro-choice feminists an acknowledgement of the link between women's reproductive status and the poverty and other social and economic problems confronted by women. They contend, however, that, rather than being a solution, "reliance on abortion diverts attention and effort away from seeking real, positive changes in women's lives" (FLA, organizational literature), that would, in part, allow them to be full participants in the public sphere. Thus, it is their framing of women's equality as orthogonal to abortion that sets "Feminists for Life" apart from other feminists, but it is their emphasis on the necessity to reject patriarchal structures which distinguishes them from other pro-life groups, many of whom affirm a traditional gender based division of labor.

The common focus by both "Catholics for a Free Choice" and "Feminists for Life" on the broader social and economic situation of women demonstrates that groups involved in the abortion debate, although adopting different policy stances, share overarching ideological commitments. It also shows the possibility of new, creative and unpredictable alliances, coalitions which can lead to the bridging of values rather than their polarization. Further evidence that moral bridges are possible is provided by the establishment of "Common Ground," a nationwide grassroots organization started in 1992 by abortion activists (see Kelly 1994). It organizes workshops and weekend retreats wherein pro-choice and pro-life advocates discuss their views and aim toward the articulation of a "common vision." Women who have attended these sessions testify to their new openness to, and understanding of opposing views on abortion (see, for example, "Common Ground," San Francisco, organizational literature), suggesting, contrary to Hunter, that abortion opponents do share a moral vocabulary. Hunter briefly acknowledges "Common Ground" and other local initiatives that seek to bridge the abortion divide (1994, pp. 232-234). In a book that purports, however, to be a "search for the common ground in American life where a more substantial and robust debate about the public good/goods can be engaged and sustained" (1994, p. 12), it is somewhat surprising the Hunter did not focus his study more on the efforts of such groups and of ordinary individuals—those whose voices, Hunter argues, are marginalized by the mass media—as they negotiate routinely the various dilemmas confronted by a commitment to the dual values of life and liberty.

SUMMARY

In this paper, I have drawn on empirical studies to assess the validity of three claims central to Hunter's culture war thesis: one, that abortion conflict is fueled by polarized systems of moral understanding, second, that discourse about abortion thus precludes compromise, and finally, that the conflict has led to the emergence of new, culturally significant, institutional alignments.

Although violent incidents characterize the abortion conflict and highlight its war-like extremes, empirical studies show that even among activists, where we would expect to find dichotomously opposed world views, there is evidence of a shared moral framework. Both pro-life and pro-choice advocates value motherhood, for example, even though they differ as to its conceptualization, and both sides express ambivalence about the absoluteness of their respective stances. The nuances in activists' views are more explicit in the attitudes of the general public. The consistent trend is that a majority of Americans express reservations about the availability of abortion but still lean toward its legalization. Importantly, views on abortion are not predictive of a cohesive world view that encompasses an individual's stance on a range of social and political questions.

The research reviewed here also highlights similarities between abortion discourse and political communication in general. The major organizational players in the debate present their abortion-related arguments in much the same way that individual politicians and nation states argue about domestic and foreign policy issues. Insofar then as negotiated compromise is possible in political debate, it would also seem to be possible in abortion policy.

Finally, the new pragmatic alliances which have coalesced over abortion are not necessarily indicative of a new cultural alignment. As underscored by the collaboration of the Catholic bishops and the Southern Baptist Convention, "amici curiae" does not translate into uniformity: significant differences continue to characterize the world views and cultural imaginations of the two religious organizations. By the same token, organizations which pursue different policy outcomes on abortion, nonetheless, share many ideological commitments, such as in the case of "Catholics for a Free Choice" and "Feminists for Life," a commitment to women's equality.

Overall, then, my review suggests that the public articulation of conflict over abortion does not constitute a non-negotiable or clear-cut cultural polarization. The evidence of a common cultural bedrock among opponents, whether they be individual activists and activist organizations, or mainstream citizens, and evidence of significant cultural differences among allies, challenges the assumption that two "mutually exclusive visions of the public good" (Hunter 1994, p. 15) are at issue over abortion. Abortion, clearly, is a divisive issue in American society. To argue, however, as Hunter does, that it constitutes a culture war over the meaning of America is to exaggerate the case. Hunter states that he does not make this observation lightly, but does so "because *culture wars always precede shooting wars* (1994, p. 4, emphasis in original). The author's intentions notwithstanding, in my opinion, this characterization, highlighted by the titles of Hunter's two companion books, *Culture Wars* and *Before the Shooting Begins*, contributes to the very polarization blamed by Hunter on, among other sources, the mass media (1991, pp. 225-230; 1994, pp. 154-168); activist organizations (1991, pp. 1355-158; 1994, pp. 45-82), and the politicization of churches (1994, pp. 182-188).

Debates over cultural values, while they are amplified in contemporary times due to the expansion in communication technology, have gone on for centuries. Such discourse is part of what constitutes culture and the "constant transformation" (Hall 1992, p. 225) of the meanings which structure our everyday reality. As the moral philosopher, Alasdair MacIntyre argues:

> ...when a tradition is in good order it is always partially constituted by an argument .... A living tradition then is an historically extended, socially embodied argument, and an argument precisely in part about the goods which constitute that tradition (1984, p. 222).

In my opinion, therefore, conflict over abortion can be understood better as one representation of American society's ongoing cultural conversation, rather than, as Hunter argues, a war which is *"ultimately about the struggle for domination"* (p. 52; emphasis in original). Cultural discourse, just as any other discourse, inevitably involves issues of reason, persuasion, and as argued by Foucault (1980), power and domination. I see nothing unique, therefore, about the American abortion debate that may distinguish it as a culture war. Further, the public conversation about abortion is neither confined nor unique to the United States. Conflict over abortion is a recurring theme in many other Western societies, most notably, in recent years, in Ireland and Poland (Dillon in press).

In sum, the overall picture which emerges from this review is that the ongoing conflict over abortion in America does not represent a culture war; it is not a "clash of absolutes" (Tribe 1990) or a clash of paradigms (Kuhn 1962) in which one must be overthrown by another. It is more akin to the reasoned, practical discourse that Jürgen Habermas (1975, p. 105) identifies as the cornerstone of participatory democracy. The arguments articulated, however inelegant and distorted, may well reflect the "discourse of elites" (Hunter 1991, p. 59), and the ambivalence of average citizens may, as Hunter argues, be "mind-boggling" and "remarkably superficial" (1994, p. 215). It seems, nonetheless, that although they are not

Plato's philosopher kings, Americans are, by and large, able to reason prudently about the values at stake without resort to coercive violence. Technical knowledge, after all, is not the sole engine driving social action.

REFERENCES

Callahan, S., and D. Callahan. 1984. "Abortion: Understanding Differences." *Family Planning Perspectives* 16: 219-221.

Cook, E., T. Jelen, and C. Wilcox. 1992. *Between Two Absolutes. Public Opinion and the Politics of Abortion.* Boulder: Westview Press.

Davis, J., and T. Smith. 1993. *The General Social Survey. Cumulative Codebook, 1972-1993.* Storrs, CT: Roper Center.

Dillon, M. 1993. "Argumentative Complexity of Abortion Discourse." *Public Opinion Quarterly* 57:305-314.

————. 1995a. "Institutional Legitimation and Abortion. Monitoring the Catholic Church's Discourse." *Journal for the Scientific Study of Religion* 34: 141-151.

————. 1995b. "Religion and Culture in Tension: The Abortion Discourses of the U.S. Catholic Bishops and the Southern Baptist Convention." *Religion and American Culture. A Journal of Interpretation* 5: 159-180.

————. In press. "Cultural Differences in the Abortion Discourse of the Catholic Church: Evidence from Four Countries." In *Sociology of Religion*, Vol. 57.

Foucault, M. 1980. *The History of Sexuality.* Vol. 1. New York: Vintage Books.

Gallup, G. 1994. *The Gallup Poll. Public Opinion 1993.* Wilmington, DE: Scholarly Resources Inc.

Gallup, G., and F. Newport. 1990. "Americans Shift Toward Pro-Choice Position." *The Gallup Poll Monthly* April, No. 295: 2-4.

Gallup Report. 1989. "Attitudes on Abortion Little Changed Since Supreme Court Ruling." *The Gallup Report* February, No. 281: 16-23.

Ginsburg, F. 1989. *Contested Lives. The Abortion Debate in an American Community.* Berkeley: University of California Press.

Glenn, N. 1987. "Social Trends in the United States: Evidence from Sample Surveys." *Public Opinion Quarterly* 51: S109-S126.

Granberg, D. 1981. "The Abortion Activists." *Family Planning Perspectives* 13: 157-163.

Greeley, A. 1989. *Religious Change in America.* Cambridge: Harvard University Press.

Greeley, A. 1993. "The Continuing Reformation: Catholics and Southern Baptists in the United States." University of Chicago, unpublished manuscript.

Habermas, J. 1975. *Legitimation Crisis.* Boston: Beacon Press.

Hall, S. 1992. "Cultural Identity and Diaspora." Pp. 222-237 in *Identity: Community, Culture, Difference*, edited by J. Rutherford. London: Lawrence and Wishart.

Hunter, J. 1991. *Culture Wars.* New York: Basic Books.

Hunter, J. 1994. *Before the Shooting Begins. Searching for Democracy in America's Culture War.* New York: Free Press.

Kelly, J. 1994. "A Dispatch from The Abortion Wars. Reflections on 'Common Ground'." *America* 171: 8-13.

Klatch, R. 1987. *Women of the New Right*. Philadelphia: Temple University Press.

Kuhn, T. 1962. *The Structure of Scientific Revolutions*. Chicago: University of Chicago Press.

Luker, K. 1984. *Abortion and the Politics of Motherhood*. Berkeley: University of California Press.

MacIntyre, A. 1984. *After Virtue. A Study in Moral Theory*, 2nd ed. Notre Dame, IN: University of Notre Dame Press.

Popper, K. 1975[1934]. *The Logic of Scientific Discovery*. London: Hutchinson.

Tamney, J., S. Johnson, and R. Burton. 1992. "The Abortion Controversy: Conflicting Beliefs and Values in American Society." *Journal for the Scientific Study of Religion* 31: 32-46.

Tetlock, P. 1988. "Monitoring the Integrative Complexity of American and Soviet Policy Rhetoric: What Can be Learned?" *Journal of Social Issues* 44: 101-131.

Tetlock, P. 1989. "Structure and Function in Political Belief Systems." Pp. 129-151 in *Attitude, Structure and Function*, edited by A. R. Pratkanis, S. J. Beckler, and A. G. Greenwald. Hillsdale, NJ: Erlbaum.

Tetlock, P., J. Bernzweig, and J. Gallant. 1985. "Supreme Court Decision Making: Cognitive Style as a Predictor of Ideological Consistency of Voting." *Journal of Personality and Social Psychology* 48: 1227-1239.

Tribe, L. 1990. *Abortion. The Clash of Absolutes*. New York: W.W. Norton.

Wuthnow, R. 1988. *The Restructuring of American Religion*. Princeton: Princeton University Press.

SAME SEX POLITICS:

THE LEGAL STRUGGLE OVER HOMOSEXUALITY

J. David Woodard

This chapter examines the struggle over the status of homosexuality through an analysis of Colorado Amendment Two (1992-1993) and Cincinnati Issue Three (1993-1994) legal contests. Popularly enacted initiatives overturned "human rights" ordinances which granted gay, lesbian and bisexuals protected legal status. The incendiary legal contests which followed these initiatives centered on such matters as whether homosexuals are a "demonstrably powerless group." Below the surface of these legal questions, however, were deeper cultural disagreements over the moral boundaries of human relationships and the definition of what constitutes normal sexuality. A status politics theoretical approach is employed to help make sense of the way the deeper cultural divide manifests itself in legal and political disputes.

Whether measured by the pitch of the national emotion it stirs, the number of books and articles it inspires or the volume of press reports it generates, the debate over gay and lesbian rights has become a hotly contested issue in American politics. Just as the political issues of black Americans dominated the 1960s, women the 1970s, and abortion the 1980s, gay and lesbian rights are likely to become the commanding partisan issue of the 1990s.

Few subjects in the American culture wars are more emotional than questions of what constitutes normal sexuality and acceptable family life. There is little agreement today as to what attitudes people should have about homosexuals, and any societal consensus—if it ever existed—has vanished. In the 1992 elections Bill Clinton was the first Presidential candidate openly to support homosexual rights. The acrimony of the subsequent debate over lifting the ban on gays in the military surprised many in the Clinton administration.

The gay rights controversy has intensified focus on traditional "family values" as a theme of American electoral politics. In July of 1992, then Vice-President Dan Quayle said George Bush was "willing to stand up for basic values, rather than to treat all life-style choices as morally equivalent" (Quayle 1992). In contrast, Bill Clinton became the first American President not only to court the gay vote, but to mention gays in his acceptance speech at the Democratic national convention, to invite a gay man with AIDS and a lesbian to address the convention, and to work to remove the ban against homosexuals serving in the military.

In the 1990s, gay activists have adopted the classic civil-rights strategy of demanding legislation that would add homosexuals to the list of groups granted legally protected status. Two local controversies over homosexual rights garnered national attention and have become emblematic of similar conflicts taking place in many suburbs and cities throughout the United States First came the clash over the legal status of homosexuals in Colorado in 1992-1993, and then the battle over homosexual rights in Cincinnati in 1993-1994. Ultimately, the Colorado controversy reverberated into a national boycott of the state while the Cincinnati case became the focus of interest groups across the nation. Due to the increasingly influential role of the media today, it is possible for a community dispute over a gay pride march, or a protest against a homosexual firing, to become a national issue overnight.

STATUS POLITICS

How is it that something as private as one's sexual orientation has become the focus of open political controversy? The answer lies in the new nature of politics in America. Political conflict today is rooted in two different systems of moral understanding and authority. As depicted in James Hunter's work, it is a division between the "orthodox" and "progressivist" tendencies in American culture (Hunter 1991). The orthodox "are committed to a transcendent foundation for moral judgment." For them, certain moral "truths" are non-negotiable. For the progressivists, on the other hand, "moral authority is based ... in the resymbolization of historic faiths and philosophical traditions." Moral truth, rather than being fixed or stagnant, "is perpetually unfolding." As Hunter explains further, progressivists hold to a "form of moral understanding that is uniquely shaped by and oriented toward legitimating the prevailing zeitgeist or spirit of the age."

Though it may not on the surface appear as such, these conflictual tendencies are at the root of the legal controversy over homosexuality. The orthodox, guided as they are by the authority of certain unchanging truths, believe that the moral boundaries for human sexual relationships have been naturally and divinely mandated. Legitimate human sexuality, according to the orthodox, should be realized only within a marital relationship between a male and a female. "Homosexuality, therefore, is a perversion of the natural or created order." The progressivists, in contrast, believe that the norms guiding relationships between and among the different genders are socially constructed. The legitimacy of certain forms of sexuality rests not in the authority of certain externally derived mandates, but in the "positive and caring" nature of the relationship. Thus, homosexuality "does not represent an absolute and fundamental perversion of nature but simply one way in which nature can evolve and be expressed."

As this cultural fissure plays itself out in the legal realm, it assumes a form of discourse depicted in social scientific literature as "status politics." Groups vying for social acceptance use legal means to legitimize their efforts. Therefore, their political and legal struggles have less to do with economics and more to do with recognition and status. Richard Hofstadter and Daniel Bell, writing in 1955, contended that the material prosperity in post-war America would lead to a new type of political conflict among groups striving not for financial gain, but to improve their social standing in society (Bell 1955). In the culture wars over homosexuality, we have the politics of social status writ large. Each side in this debate employs particular legal strategies in order to legitimize its view of the world. This is more obvious on the progressivist side, where pro-gay activists argue that homosexuals are a beleaguered group in need of government protection. Less obvious, but no less determinative, is the orthodox concern with the social devaluing of their understanding of the world—an understanding that is directly challenged by the social acceptance of the homosexual lifestyle. Interestingly, and in keeping with a status politics theoretical perspective, the focus of the legal conflict over this issue centers on the social status of the homosexual community.

Homosexual activism, in the contemporary context, can be understood as an effort by a particular group to gain acceptance in the larger society by using the arguments, symbols, and policy proposals of a politically vulnerable minority. At issue in Colorado, and later in Cincinnati, was the question of whether homosexuals are discriminated against as a class. The federal courts were asked to rule on whether gays and lesbians deserved special protection under the Fourteenth Amendment which forbids the state from denying "to any person within its jurisdiction the equal protection of the laws."

Attorneys representing the concerns of gays and lesbians argued in court that homosexuals are an oppressed *class* of persons requiring a unique sort of public protection. In the Colorado case, for example, one expert witness testified, "Gay people are a minority group for whom the political processes ordinarily relied upon to protect minorities from the majoritarian political process typically fail" (Sherrill 1991).

In general, the cultural wars of status politics arise when the prestige accorded one group is perceived to be less than what was expected. Increased AIDS funding, the passage of a "human rights amendment" with special provisions for "sexual orientation," and admission of gays into the military are not at base economic victories but rather signals that the majority culture recognizes homosexuality as a viable alternative lifestyle. Thus, the political controversy over homosexuality is more attitudinal than material. Proponents of gay rights are interested in vague goals, such as "acceptance," while opponents are intent on withholding such social approval. Whether or not a legally sanctioned endorsement of homosexuality is granted symbolizes the public's acceptance or rejection of a particular understanding of the world. It is the symbolic significance of these legal battles which motivates both sides of the culture war to engage in the conflict.

COLORADO

The conflict in Colorado began in February, 1991, when a homeschool parent read about public hearings on an "Ethnic Harassment Bill," then winding its way through the state legislature. The proposal was to give homosexual "orientation" a legal standing equal to that given to racial minorities. Moreover, it would have made verbal criticism of homosexuals a possible felony offense. The cities of Denver, Boulder, and Aspen had already passed ordinances prohibiting discrimination on the basis of sexual orientation. Governor Roy Romer had previously issued an executive order to the same effect, and the Colorado General Assembly had enacted a statute prohibiting health insurance companies from determining insurability based on sexual orientation (Bransford 1994).

The addition of "sexual preference" as a protected category (in the same way that age, race, and gender are protected by the 1964 Civil Rights Law) was given little play by the press. From the perspective of the homeschool parent mentioned earlier, and others in Colorado, the legislation would have given special rights—not equal rights—to homosexuals. Opponents of the legislation were familiar with the enforcement provisions of the "Ethnic Harassment Bill," and knew that similar ordinances in cities like Aspen and Denver had expanded the entitlement claims of homosexuals for public jobs and had authorized substantial legal damages in cases of bias. After working to defeat the legislation in chambers, a group calling itself "Colorado for Family Values" (CFV) was formed in order to amend the state constitution to prevent special class considerations for homosexuals.

Lawyers for CFV drafted a state-wide initiative to be voted on in the 1992 general election. The title of the amendment read: "No protected status based on homosexual, lesbian or bisexual orientation." Initial reaction to the proposed amendment was tepid. Advocates soliciting signatures discovered that few people understood the significance of the proposed amendment and found that most had no opinion on the matter. To put the proposal on the ballot in November, however, backers in the state needed 49,279 signatures.

Supporters of the amendment approached popular Colorado football coach Bill McCartney, whose publicly articulated views on family issues puts him on the orthodox side of the cultural divide. McCartney called a press conference to declare that he had no choice but to take a stand against homosexuality and in favor of the amendment. "It's a responsibility," he said, "It's inherent in the Christian faith." McCartney's comment sparked a firestorm of criticism, but it also had the desired effect of eliciting wider support for the amendment. In the next month, supporters of Amendment Two gathered a total of 84,445 names, more than enough to put the proposal on the ballot.

Prominent Colorado politicians either remained neutral on the issue or decried the amendment as discriminatory. Governor Roy Romer, Congresswoman Pat Schroeder, and Senator Ben Nighthorse Campbell all spoke out against the adoption of Amendment Two. A Denver radio station even refused to run advertising by Colorado for Family Values. Meanwhile, backers of the amendment received unexpected support from six of Colorado's top civil rights activists, including a sitting and past president of the State Civil Rights Commission. Two prominent black civil rights activists stepped forward to urge minorities to vote for the amendment. And a number of Christian radio stations were also supportive (Rocky Mountain News 1992).

Proponents of the amendment attracted media attention with the charge that gays and lesbians wanted "special rights." Opponents of Amendment two—who, interestingly, included a large number of Denver pastors, rabbis, and other representatives of Jewish and Christian organizations—responded to this charge by calling CFV's motives immoral. Though arguments in opposition to Amendment Two were numerous, the argument which was apparently most salient to Colorado citizens was the assertion that Amendment Two legalized discrimination against homosexuals (*Colorado Gazette Telegraph* 1992).

Throughout the campaign, polls indicated that Amendment Two was failing. A statewide survey in October 1992 found 52 percent of Colorado residents against the measure, 39 percent in favor, and

9 percent undecided (*Colorado Daily Sentinel* 1992). In the weeks before the election, both sides bought prime television commercial time to make last minute appeals. Papers filed after the vote show that opponents of Amendment Two spent nearly twice as much as supporters; Colorado for Family Values spent $378,792 while Equality Colorado, an organization which opposed the Amendment, raised and spent $681,485.

The outcome of the vote was a surprise to many. As reported in the Denver Post the morning after the election: "Gay-Rights Ban Narrowly Winning: Amendment Two Opponents Stunned." (*The Denver Post* 1992). Foes of Amendment Two had taken confidence in the polls, but the voters had either not told pollsters their true feelings or had changed their minds in the voting booth. Final election totals showed a fairly comfortable margin of victory, 53.3 percent voting in favor of the amendment and 46.7 percent against it. An analysis of the results reveals that support for Amendment Two was especially strong in Colorado Springs—where there were twice as many proponents as opponents of the measure—and in Denver, which had previously voted in favor of a local ordinance supporting gay rights. Although Bill Clinton carried the state on election night, favorable votes for Amendment Two outnumbered votes cast for Clinton by more than 13 percent (*Colorado Gazette Telegraph* 1992). Apparently, many Democratic voters, generally sympathetic to liberal causes, were also in favor of Amendment Two.

The day after the vote, Governor Roy Romer and Denver Mayor Webb marched to the state capitol with approximately 400 homosexual activists to protest the amendment. Gay and lesbian groups immediately called for a boycott of Colorado during the lucrative winter ski season. Barbara Streisand, record mogul David Geffin, and other prominent Hollywood entertainers asked that celebrities cancel their traditional holiday vacations to places like Aspen and Vail. The Atlanta city council, New York City mayor David Dinkins, and officials in five other cities banned all official spending and travel in Colorado (*Rocky Mountain News* 1992).

Press conferences held in New York, Los Angeles, Philadelphia, and Washington, D.C. labeled Colorado the "Hate State." Elected state officials in Colorado appeared on national television to promote winter tourism and to express their own opposition to the Amendment Two vote. Another example of national resistance to the Amendment Two decision came when a New York gay group threatened to throw packages of Colorado-based Celestial Seasons Tea into the East River to protest the referendum outcome. Though no such "Tea Party" took place, the threat attracted national media attention. In the end, however, the boycott of Colorado was dropped when favorable ski conditions proved a stronger draw than a lengthy protest. The December 21, 1992 headline in the *Rocky Mountain News*—"Aspen Booked Solid for the Holidays"—is just one indication of the ban's ultimate lack of success.

Court Pleadings

Within a week of the Amendment Two outcome, a lawsuit was filed in Denver District Court challenging Colorado's unprecedented electoral approval of a rule prohibiting state or local laws against discrimination based on sexual orientation (*Evans vs. Romer* 1993). Gay and lesbian activists contended that the referendum was blatantly unconstitutional and motivated by a religiously inspired antipathy toward homosexuals. Plaintiffs' lawyers said Amendment Two would chill speech, limit advocacy, and coerce people to "adhere to a single, state-approved belief respecting gay, lesbian or bisexual orientation" (*Evans vs. Romer* 1993). Defenders of the referendum claimed that the Amendment Two outcome merely affirmed the generally held belief that gays and lesbians should not be granted special legal protection. They welcomed the court challenge and noted that "every time the U.S. Supreme Court has been given the opportunity to grant civil rights statutes based on sexual behavior, it has said 'no'" (*Colorado Daily* 1992).

If amendment opponents could demonstrate that Amendment Two had a sinister intent, denying homosexuals equal protection under the law, they could then argue that passage of the initiative was evidence that they were disadvantaged and deserving of a protected legal status. The federal government has three main tests, or criteria, to decide who will be added to the list of specially protected classes. To win in Colorado, the gay, lesbian, and bisexual plaintiffs had to prove that homosexuals as a group:

1.   exhibited obvious, innate, or immutable distinguishing characteristics similar to race, gender, handicap or national origin.

2. evidenced a lack of ability to obtain average, mean economic income, education, or cultural opportunity.
3. are a demonstrably powerless group.

One way of illustrating the significance of these criteria is to consider their application to African Americans. As a group, blacks clearly have an immutable skin trait, as well as a history of discrimination and political powerlessness. Gay plaintiffs were challenged to show that homosexuals had similar handicaps. A nationwide association of homosexual organizations stood ready to help in this endeavor.

At the time of the Amendment Two vote there were over ninety nationally based homosexual organizations, with more than 150,000 regular donors and a combined mailing list of about a half a million. In the decade of the 1980s, eight states, more than 119 cities and counties in 25 states, and 65 universities had adopted anti-discrimination laws with respect to "sexual orientation" (Woodard 1993). The Colorado court case became the first national test for the basis of legal protection of homosexual behavior.

Initial court testimony in Denver centered on the "immutable characteristics" of homosexuality (i.e., whether or not same sex attraction is genetic or acquired). Experts confronted one another on the familiar "nurture" versus "nature" controversy. The stage was set for extended testimony on issues like the difference between homosexuality and bisexuality, sex change operations, and the academic merits of the *Journal of Pedophilia*.

Plaintiffs argued that sexuality was not a conscious choice for most people. Plaintiff experts testified that the origins of sexual orientation, though not well understood, were not the result of choice. Moreover, they argued that no scientific evidence demonstrating the effectiveness of conversion efforts (to turn individuals from homosexuality) exist. Based upon this evidence, they argued that the court should conclude that sexual orientation was inborn. State experts countered that scientific evidence could not establish homosexuality as an immutable trait and that incidents of conversion from the gay lifestyle were an everyday occurrence. It was reasonable to conclude, they held, that homosexuality was a choice and was thus not entitled to special protection.

In the next phase of testimony the plaintiffs presented evidence contending that homosexuals were "disadvantaged economically" relative to others in society. In this regard, plaintiffs argued that gays and lesbians were invisible in the society and unable to form a group identity and find group cohesion. Research presented by amendment opponents showed that 76 percent of lesbians and gays had experienced some form of discrimination, resulting in rejection by friends, family or a church/synagogue with attendant loss of job or career setback (Gay & Lesbian Community Action Council). Plaintiffs also argued that homosexuals regularly suffered isolation, discrimination and attack by the majority "straight" culture, which made them chronically unemployed and unable to reach even an average income.

State experts produced surveys asserting that homosexuals were among the most economically successful groups in the country, and argued that their lack of family responsibilities implied they had large discretionary incomes. Information gathered by Simmons Market Research Bureau in 1991 and presented at the trial, showed the average household income of homosexuals to be $55,430, compared to the national average of $32,144. It was further asserted that nearly 60 percent of homosexuals are college graduates compared to 18 percent nationally, and nearly half are in professional managerial positions compared with about sixteen percent nationally (*The Simmons Report* 1990). Plaintiff lawyers countered that such data was invalid because of the impossibility of locating homosexuals socially as an identifiable economic group.

The third phase of the plaintiff's argument focused on the political power of homosexuals. The courtroom opponents of Amendment Two argued that the failures of the homosexual lobby on issues such as gays in the military and the 1987 Helms amendment (which limited federal spending on AIDS education), confirmed that homosexuals are politically powerless. One expert produced data from a University of Michigan survey which asked respondents about their feelings toward various groups of people, including homosexuals. The "Feeling Thermometer" used for this measurement ranged on a scale from zero to 100 degrees, with zero representing the coldest possible feeling toward a group, 100 the warmest. Fully 61.5 percent of the Michigan sample in 1984 placed their feelings toward gay men and lesbians *below* 50 degrees, with 30.5 percent at zero degrees (Sherrill 1989).

Clearly, the plaintiffs attorneys argued, gays and lesbians are among the most disliked groups in the national survey. According to one expert witness, their plight is worse than African Americans: "Americans were more than five times as likely to have negative feelings toward gay people than towards black people, and over 17 times as likely to hold the coldest possible feelings toward gay people as toward black people" (Sherrill 1991). Indications of such antipathy were presented to demonstrate the powerlessness of gays and lesbians.

State experts countered by arguing that gay, lesbian, and bisexual interest groups are an effective and powerful lobbying force. Data from the Federal Election Commission was presented to show that homosexuals are among the fastest growing and best financed lobbies in the country. According to state experts, in 1993 the top six gay groups raised more than $12.5 million for operating and political purposes. Five years earlier the same six groups had combined budgets of only $3.2 million. State experts argued further that The Human Rights Campaign Fund (HRCF), the leading homosexual political action group, ranks in the top 50 of more than 4700 Political Action Committees on the 1992 Federal Election Commission report. Contributions to HRCF were up 136 percent over donations in the previous reporting cycle. HRCF is reported to have given $3.5 million to the Clinton campaign in the last Presidential election and to have contributed to 190 Senate and House candidates in 1992 with an 85 percent success ratio (Federal Election Commission Press Office 1993). In close contests where the homosexual lobby contributed between $7000 and $10000, HRCF candidates won 21 of 28 times (Woodard 1993). State of Colorado attorneys argued that such success contradicts homosexuals' claim of powerlessness.

In Colorado ten attorneys from groups as diverse as the Lambda Legal Defense and Education Fund, the American Civil Liberties Union, and the Cities of Aspen and Boulder handled the plaintiffs' litigation. Amendment Two supporters were defended by the State of Colorado. Colorado Attorney General Gale Norton, leading the state's defense, attempted to show that the state had "a compelling interest" in establishing the law by a referendum. Legal experts for the plaintiffs stated that such a standard was difficult to meet, and was certainly not met in the Colorado decision.

Ultimately, the Federal Court of Colorado reached a decision. It sustained the homosexual plaintiffs' contention that Amendment Two should be set aside, because the state had no compelling interest for such a law. At the same time, the judge in the case ruled that homosexuals as a group did not meet the

criteria to qualify as a "suspect class" under federal law. Oral
arguments in the Colorado case were heard in October, 1995. The
State of Colorado asked in its appeal whether a popularly enacted
state constitutional amendment, which curbs special state or local
protection for homosexuals, violates any fundamental rights
given that gays, lesbians, and bisexuals are not a "suspect class."
In short, since homosexuals aren't a victim class, why not
implement the referendum?

CINCINNATI

One year after the Colorado election, on November 2, 1993, the voters
of Cincinnati passed an amendment to the city charter which read:
"No special class status may be granted based upon sexual
orientation, conduct or relationships." Again, the issue in Cincinnati
was triggered by a controversial city "human rights" ordinance which
gave protection to homosexuals for their "sexual preference." And
again the popular vote margin was decisive, with 62 percent
supporting the amendment to the city charter. In response to the vote,
the city of Cincinnati was sued by gay and lesbian groups who
maintained that the charter amendment, labeled Issue Three, was
discriminatory. The arguments in federal court had a familiar, if more
local, ring. Gay rights advocates claimed that the passage of the
charter amendment rescinded the constitutional rights of gays,
lesbians, and bisexuals. "What Issue Three did was make it impossible
for the Cincinnati City Council to pass any law, adopt any policy,
take any action whatsoever that would benefit gays and lesbians,"
said John Burlew of the Ohio Civil Rights Commission (*Cincinnati
Enquirer* 1994). Attorneys for Cincinnati said homosexuals should
not have special privileges, and that the vote imposed nothing more
than a neutrality upon city government. "We're just trying to
vindicate the democratic choices of the people of Cincinnati," said
Michael Carvin, the Washington, D.C. lawyer who handled the case
for the group, Equal Rights-Not Special Rights.

In June of 1994 the case went to trial. The trial lasted one week,
and a decision was rendered two months later. In its decision the
court concluded that the amendment to the city charter infringed
upon the fundamental rights of homosexuals to the political process
and was therefore set aside. Unlike the Colorado case, the judge in

Cincinnati went on to find that gays, lesbians, and bisexuals are a "quasi-suspect" category and entitled to "heightened scrutiny" under the law (Equality Foundation 1994). The court ruling in the Cincinnati case remains on appeal.

Political Tactics

The similarities in Cincinnati and Colorado are striking: in both cases discontented, amateur citizen activists unexpectedly succeeded in challenging a political establishment sympathetic to the requests of homosexuals. In both cases, the popular vote was solidly in favor of denying homosexuals special distinction as a group which has been discriminated against. In both instances the federal courts ruled in favor of the homosexual plaintiffs.

The courtroom battles in the two legal cases are a microcosm of the larger cultural struggle to define what constitutes social normalcy in regard to human sexuality. The arguments and litigation of those court cases were not merely abstract legal discussions, but rather were representative of yet another fissure in the civil dispute over the government's role in the definition and protection of the family. Several tactics of the homosexual groups and their opponents deserve special explanation.

Efforts to measure the influence of interest groups often begin with the a priori assumption that what really matters is money and size. Lewis Froman, however, argued in the early 1960s that these resources are less important than they first appear: "How intense people are in their preferences often determines the distribution of outcomes in a dispute" (Froman 1962). Froman illustrates this "intensity preference" factor by arguing that, "whenever there is a minority with strong preferences and a majority with weak preferences...the result will be a decision in favor of the minority." In sum, a small but intense minority can be very effective in gaining access to, and rewards from, the political system.

Much of the testimony in both Colorado and Cincinnati focused on the size of the homosexual population. Plaintiffs argued that homosexuality is invisible and widespread, while defendants contended that homosexual practice is limited and irregular. The pioneering work of Alfred Kinsey in the 1940s held that 10 percent of the population is homosexual. For homosexual activists the Kinsey figure is sacrosanct. Subsequent research has raised questions about the reliability of the Kinsey study, contending that researchers trusted data gleaned from criminals—including sex offenders—and erroneously extrapolated the sample findings to the general population. Recent research estimates are that little more than 1.0 percent of the population is actively homosexual (Reisman and Eichel).

If the one percent figure is accurate, the question remains: Why are gay, lesbian, and bisexual groups so successful in their political objectives? Based upon Froman's "intensity preference" factor, homosexual groups are influential because their membership feels strongly about a narrow range of interests to the virtual exclusion of all other issues. These political convictions are deeply held, and the homosexual groups' complaints are loud and persistent. Richard Goldstein writes that gay liberation's "entry point is an experience that fuses the personal and the political" (Goldstein 1980). For politically active homosexuals, their lives and sexuality become forceful political statements.

In response to the political activism of homosexuals, elected leaders and officials have been particularly accommodating. This is because elected officials always strive to limit criticism by placating active groups whenever possible. Such policies of appeasement explain the astounding success of homosexual groups which continue to make political progress while the majority of the public—and even the decision-makers themselves—hold private judgments that are opposed to these gains. The most effective way to restrain the impulse of politicians to appease vocal minorities is through use of the ballot box. In Colorado and Cincinnati, voters used their ballots to stop what they perceived as favoritism, under the guise of the protection of homosexual activity in their state and local communities.

Though Froman's "intensity preference" factor is useful in explaining the fervor with which homosexuals engage in and effectively influence the political process, it does not account for the enormous hostility between non-gay proponents and non-gay opponents of homosexual rights. Here again, the larger cultural division between the orthodox and progressivist tendencies in American culture is illuminating. The translation of these tendencies into legal discourse, however, necessarily involves changing the substance of the arguments.

For example, proponents of legislation that would limit the "sexual preference" language in laws applicable to homosexuality are most successful when they use the "equal rights not special rights" approach with voters. Graphic descriptions of homosexual activity or religious arguments which label homosexuality an "abomination" only serve to hurt amendment campaigns. Though many on the orthodox side of the cultural divide have initiated amendment campaigns based on the conviction that a rising tide of homosexual activism is morally harmful to the culture, they recognize that religious rhetoric serves mainly to convince undecided voters that the amendment is fueled by intolerance. Recognizing this, anti-gay activists choose instead to invoke the more plausible "rights" based language. In terms of the larger culture wars thesis, however, it is important to understand that it is the activists' moral understanding that drives them to become involved in the anti-gay rights legal struggle.

Homosexual groups engage in the debate by drawing on a similar genre of rights-based language. Gay activists hold that the widespread referendum campaigns are evidence of rampant anti-gay prejudice and are a flagrant denial of the civil rights of homosexual citizens. Moreover, homosexual activists argue that a lack of funding for AIDS research and the sequence of aforementioned political defeats are confirmation of anti-gay prejudice in the majority culture. Typically, gay groups link their special preference demands to an increase in funding for AIDS education, research, and patient care. The platform of the 1993 March on Washington for Lesbian, Gay and Bi Equal Rights called for universal access to health care and an increase in funding for AIDS research (*Washington Post* 1993).

Recent research by those opposing homosexual demands for increased AIDS funding shows that AIDS is not an equal-opportunity ailment. When Michael Fumento argued that AIDS "was a disease essentially of homosexual men and intravenous drug abusers and their partners" his comments brought a firestorm of criticism from the media and homosexual activists (Fumento 1987). Recently Gabriel Rotello, gay columnist of New York Newsday, wrote that it was time to tell the truth, "Up to 50 percent of gay men and IV users are infected with HIV, while just a tiny fraction of 1 percent of middle-class straights are" (Leo 1994). Regardless of how many HIV infected Americans are or are not homosexual, the general public perception remains, rightly or wrongly, that AIDS is a gay male disease.

In political parlance, AIDS is the "wedge issue" for homosexuals, meaning it divides the opposition while galvanizing a majority in favor of the homosexual community. Gay and lesbian activists characterize opposition to their rights agenda as the political equivalent of bigotry and support for the scourge of AIDS. To be against the Lesbian, Gay, Bisexual, and Transgender civil rights bill is, they argue, to say that prejudice and disease should continue unabated. Attention given the AIDS crisis has provided homosexual activists a platform to stress their special needs and particular political problems.

For Amendment Two (Colorado) and Issue Three (Cincinnati) proponents, these initiatives imposed nothing more on the government than a position of neutrality regarding homosexuality. For the homosexual plaintiffs, the voter referendum confirmed what they already believed, that is, that they are a discriminated minority group in need of governmental protection. The sentiment among the majority of voters was that gay activists were asking for recognition as a fully protected minority class with status and privileges based solely upon their divergent sexual behavior.

FUTURE PROSPECTS

The court decisions in Ohio and Colorado have given little comfort to either side in this dispute. Amendment supporters in these two venues resent their democratic votes being overturned by a capricious judiciary antagonistic to their sensibilities. Homosexual rights advocates believe they deserve, and were denied, suspect class status. The issue is such that neither side is likely to be placated even by a decision rendered by the Supreme Court.

Moreover, both factors resent their portrayal in the media. Gay and lesbian groups complain that white America is "homophobic," intolerant, and hostile. Typifying their frustration with the media was the testimony of one expert for the plaintiffs in the Colorado case: "People with access to the means of mass communication ... seek to capitalize on the public's hostility toward gay people [and] may well reinforce and encourage such hostility" (Sherrill 1991).

Amendment proponents were equally disappointed in the media. According to amendment supporters, the media framed the issue of homosexuality in terms of compassion, a bias, they argued, that created sympathy for gays as a minority. Consider, for example, the examination of media coverage conducted by the conservative

Christian organization, Focus on the Family. This organization, headed by James Dobson and headquartered in Colorado Springs, reportedly found in a content analysis of 571 newspaper articles—totaling 8700 paragraphs—a distinct bias in favor of the homosexual side of the controversy. As reported by the organization, the press carried more comments from amendment opponents than amendment supporters. According to the report, news accounts cited negative comments from 271 different sources, but positive comments about the amendment from only 43 news sources (Focus on the Family 1993).

Both sides, then, are concerned about the potential bias of the press. In addition, both sides are anxious about the social status of the homosexual community. For progressivists, governmental protection of "sexual preference" signifies a welcome elevation in the social status of homosexuals. It also gives greater legitimacy to the homosexual lifestyle. For the orthodox, the legal protection of sexual orientation represents a threat to their cultural hegemony, waning though it may be. Interestingly, both sides consider themselves to be the object of bias and discrimination. Proponents of Amendment Two, as mentioned above, believe the media was unfairly biased against them; opponents based their case on the position that homosexuals are a powerless group. Ironically, then, efforts to secure greater social status for homosexuals were pursued by trying to prove that homosexuals occupied an inferior social position. What makes this debate particularly incendiary, however, is not just the issue of social status, but how the elevation or reduction of the social status of homosexuals is interpreted by the divergent camps within America's culture war.

Conflict over the legal sanctioning of homosexuality is ultimately rooted in the more basic struggle over the legitimation of one world view over another. The elevation of homosexuality to the status of a protected class represents an affront to the orthodox understanding of the nature of the family and acceptable expressions of sexuality. It challenges their moral understanding of the world. In the same way, popular approval of the Colorado and Cincinnati amendments, from the progressivist perspective, represented hostility towards the homosexual community and its views of human sexuality nearly becoming institutionalized. In both cases, changes in social status were either resisted or supported based on their perceived justification or delegitimation of a particular world view. The crux of the struggle over social status was thus rooted in divergent definitions of the "good."

It is this foundation of the conflict that makes the debate over the legal status of homosexuals so controversial. James Hunter writes, "Perhaps with the exception of abortion, few issues in the contemporary culture war generate more raw emotion than the issue of homosexuality" (Hunter 1991). Concerns about homosexuality go to the very definition of what constitutes a family, indeed of what constitutes the sacred. Because of the deeper cultural roots that these judicial battles signify, it is unlikely that a legal remedy will make the controversy go away any time soon.

The upcoming Supreme Court decision in the Colorado case has all the trappings of becoming a decision, like *Roe v. Wade*, which will stand as a lightening rod of cultural protest and debate. While the legal verdict will center on whether gays, lesbians, and bisexuals are a suspect class entitled to protected governmental status, the larger cultural debate over the legitimation of world views will remain just below the surface, at once complicating and inflaming legal discussions. And, just as the *Roe v. Wade* decision did nothing to pacify the cultural conflict over abortion, a Supreme Court ruling on Amendment Two is likely only to intensify the debate over homosexuality.

As it plays itself out in legal discussions, progressivists will argue that majority laws restricting homosexuality are evidence of discrimination and prejudice. The orthodox will counter with statements that homosexuals should be free to pursue their lifestyle but without special government protection. In the years ahead, issues like the AIDS epidemic and its associated health care costs are likely to fuel the battle over whether or not homosexuality is an acceptable lifestyle. The American public will continue to confront the issue of homosexuality in the areas of health (AIDS funding and expanded health care), educational curricula (determining what books regarding homosexuality are appropriate for school libraries), and local marriage and property laws (whether heterosexual rules ought to apply to same-sex marriages). No decision by the Supreme Court can prevent expanded homosexual claims in a myriad of venues.

Opponents of gay, lesbian and bisexual rights see portento of a future where the government mandates affirmative action policies directed toward the protection of homosexual rights. They pose a number of questions about what this might mean. Will day care operators be able to deny employment to people who openly practice homosexuality? Will school teachers and administrators be required to hire gays and lesbians? Will they be ordered to instruct children that homosexuality is both a normal and attractive lifestyle? Will employers, business owners, and the military be regulated by a handbook of pro-gay bureaucratic rules? Will landlords be required to rent to same-sex couples?

Attempts to answer these questions will foster significant conflict. The controversy over gays in the military which flared up in the first months of the Clinton administration, the discussion surrounding the 1993 March on Washington for Lesbian, Gay and Bi Equal Rights, the political fights over participation of homosexuals in New York parades, and the two legal cases considered in this study all suggest that the public acceptance of homosexuality will remain a matter that deeply divides Americans.

As we saw in the Colorado and Cincinnati cases, legal questions centered on the issue of the social legitimacy of homosexuality. Consistent with a status politics theoretical paradigm, the legal struggle focused on the social status of homosexuals. Ironically, plaintiff efforts to gain legitimacy were pursued by portraying homosexuals as a powerless group, while defendant efforts to limit government protection of homosexuals were attempted by portraying homosexuals as a well-funded and increasingly influential political lobby.

Also consistent with a status politics understanding of political conflict was the apparent basis of the controversy in non-material rather than economic concerns. The fervor with which activists on both sides of the divide participated in the struggle can be explained further by understanding the sources of moral authority that participants brought to the debate. Recognition of the chasm that divides American culture helps us to interpret the controversies over the social status of homosexuals. The legal elevation of the status of homosexuals gives legitimacy to a progressivist world view. Denying this status reaffirms an orthodox world view. In either case a particular definition of reality is either legally sanctioned or legally denied. The root of these legal controversies are rooted in a deeper cultural division portends that future struggles will persist.

REFERENCES

Bell, D. 1955. "The New American Right." In *The New American Right*, edited by D. Bell. New York: Criterion.

Bransford, S 1994. *Gay Politics vs. Colorado*. Cascade, CO: Sardis Publishing.

Cincinnati Enquirer, June 20, 21, 1994.

Colorado Gazette Telegraph, November 5, December 3, 1992.

Colorado Daily Sentinel, October 18, November 5, 1992.

The Denver Post, November 4, 20, 21, 27, 1992.

Equality Foundation of Greater Cincinnati, Inc. et al. vs. The City of Cincinnati (1994) U.S. District Court, Southern District of Ohio, Western Division, C-1-93-773.

Evans vs. Romer, 1992-1993. Opening Brief, pp. 14-15. Colorado: Attorney General's Office.

Federal Election Commission Press Office. 1993.

Focus on the Family. 1993. *Citizen: Feeding Frenzy*, August.

Froman, L. 1962. *People and Politics*. Englewood Cliffs, NJ: Prentice Hall.

Fumento, M. 1987. "AIDS: Are Heterosexuals at Risk?" *Commentary*, November.

————. 1993. *The Myth of Heterosexual Aids*. Washington DC: Regnary Gateway.

Gay & Lesbian Community Action Council. "Northstar Projects: Out and Counted," December, 1987.

Goldstein, R. "The Politics of Liberation." *Village Voice*, June 25-July 1.

Hofstadter, R. (1955). "The Pseudo-Conservative Revolt." In *The New American Right*, edited by D. Bell. New York: Criterion.

Hunter, J. D. 1991. *Culture Wars*. New York: Basic Books.

Leo, J. 1992. "Framing the Wrong Picture." *U.S. News and World Report*, Quayle, D. *Time*, August 3.

Maslow, A. and J. Sakoda. "Volunteer Error in the Kinsey Study." *Journal of Abnormal and Social Psychology* 47.

Reisman, J. and E. Eichel. 1990. *Kinsey, Sex and Fraud*. Lafayett, LA: Huntington Howe.

The Simmons Report. September, 1990. Privately printed.

Sherrill, K. 1989. "Homosexuality and Civil Liberty." A paper prepared for delivery at the annual meeting of the American Political Science Association, August 30-September 3, 1989, Atlanta, Georgia.

————. 1991. "Half Empty: Gay Power and Gay Powerlessness in American Politics." A paper prepared for the 1991 Annual Meeting of the American Political Science Association. Washington, DC, August 28-September 1, 1991.

Washingon Post, April 18, 1993.

Woodard, J. D. "Same Sex Politics." *World*, February.

————. 1993. Testimony in *Evans vs. Romer*.

PART II

THE CULTURE WARS AND BEYOND

CONTRASTING STYLES OF POLITICAL DISCOURSE IN AMERICA'S PAST AND PRESENT CULTURE WARS

James L. Nolan, Jr.

The cultural conflict between orthodox and progressivist impulses in American society as depicted in James Hunter's *Culture Wars*, clearly manifested itself in the various cultural skirmishes of the 1992 Presidential election. Both sides of the cultural divide, however, employed a conspicuously therapeutic form of discourse. Using the Lincoln-Douglas debates of the mid-nineteenth century as a historical comparison to the 1992 Presidential debates, I show the ways in which traditional sources of legitimation have been replaced by more therapeutic ones. I suggest that use of the therapeutic source of legitimization may have an important bearing on the ultimate outcome of the contemporary culture wars, in that it substantively undermines the traditional moral understandings to which the orthodox appeal.

At the 1992 Republican National Convention in Houston, Pat
Buchanan declared that America was in the midst of a "cultural war,"
"a religious war," "a struggle for the soul of America" (Buchanan
1992, p. 2543). Buchanan's assessment of cultural conflict in
contemporary society conformed to James Hunter's definition of the
American "Culture Wars." However, Buchanan used what was meant
as an analytical tool as a war cry, calling on conservatives to more
self-consciously, indeed more vindictively, engage the battle. Though
others from across the political and cultural spectrum were less
explicit about enlisting themselves in the battle, they were no less
involved in the conflict. While Buchanan's use of the term "culture
wars" in the 1992 campaign was primarily for political purposes,
cultural divisions in America are, in fact, pre-political.

As conceived in Hunter's work, divisions in contemporary
American culture are rooted in the fundamentally disparate world
views out of which Americans operate. On one side are the orthodox
whose commitments are derived from "an external, definable, and
transcendent authority." On the other side are the progressivists
whose tendencies are "to resymbolize historic faiths according to the
prevailing assumptions of contemporary life" (Hunter 1991, pp. 44-
45). The fault line between these two tendencies is so pronounced
that it supersedes the historical divisions between Christians and Jews
and between Protestants and Catholics. One's tendency toward
orthodoxy or progressivism is now a more likely determinant of one's
cultural alliances than are denominational or even political party
affiliations. While this cultural divide is pre-political, it clearly has
political ramifications, as evidenced by debates over the meaning of
America, in the 1992 campaign.

In political campaigns, the electorate associates each candidate
with certain symbols—symbols which represent the varying moral
impulses in American culture. As the campaigns progress, the
candidates themselves become symbols of our national life. This
certainly happened in the political discourse surrounding the 1992
elections. In this setting, political debate reflected the deep-seated
conflict existing in American culture, a conflict which emanates from
two starkly contrasting definitions of what America is all about. As
much as the politicians and pundits tried to assert during the 1992
campaign that cultural issues served only to divert attention from
the "real" issues of the economy (e.g., the Clinton campaign slogan,
"It's the Economy Stupid"), cultural conflicts flared up during both

parties' conventions and raged throughout the campaign. Debates over abortion, "family values," feminism and the role of women, gays in the military, pornography, and school choice all emanated from the deep fissure that exists just below the surface of political dialogue.

To contrast the substance of contemporary political discourse with that of the past, I compare in this article the Presidential debates of the 1992 elections with the famous Lincoln-Douglas debates of 1858. The latter is a particularly relevant comparison in that the 1858 contest also took place in a time of deep cultural division, a divide not unlike the one existing in the contemporary context. I find that while the rhetoric of the 1858 debates relied on traditional codes of moral understanding to legitimate various positions, the 1992 presidential debates drew instead upon what could be called a more "therapeutic" form of discourse. In the last part of the paper I argue that use of the therapeutic form of dialogue may have an important bearing on the ultimate outcome of the contemporary culture wars. But first how did the culture war, as understood in Hunter's work, play itself out in the 1992 electoral contest?

THE CULTURAL DIVIDE IN THE 1992 CAMPAIGN

The 1992 campaign evidenced the fundamental differences between the orthodox and progressivist visions for America's future. For example, Sylvia Hellman, a Dallas member of the Christian Coalition and attendee at the Republican convention, was clearly operating within an orthodox frame of reference, when she stated the following in an interview with the *Washington Post:*

> Our perspective is that the world was made by a Creator, and that He loves us very much, and that in loving us He gave us a guidebook, and that's the Bible. And in the guidebook, which conservative Christians take literally, there are rules to live by. Sometimes, the rules demand that we do things that don't make sense to us, but we find out later they are best (Von Drehle 1992, p. A15).

In the same article, Ed Tarpley, a Republican convention delegate from Colfax, Louisiana, is reported to have stated: "Our values derive from the Scriptures and from Judeo-Christian values 2,000 years old...Our values are not governed by the changing events of the world."

Progressivists, on the other hand, demonstrate a willingness to adjust their values to the prevailing *zeitgeist*. Truth is not fixed, but is derived from one's ongoing knowledge of and encounter with the world. Thus, Clinton's appeal to "change" fits well with the progressivist inclination, as does his reported belief that "the approach to specific moral issues in a democracy should change as popular opinion changes" (Yancey 1994, p. 29). The progressivist world view demands that we change with the times. This perspective was evident in Barbara Jordan's speech at the 1992 Democratic National Convention when she asserted that we must, "change in order to satisfy the present, in order to satisfy the future..." (Jordan 1992, p. A27).

These two foundational and deeply held beliefs, one embracing change and the other aligning itself with traditions of the past, fueled a host of debates which—sometimes heatedly—monopolized the 1992 presidential elections.

The Areas of Conflict

One important source of contention in the 1992 election was the uproar over "family values." Then-Vice President Dan Quayle's criticism of the television character, Murphy Brown, and her decision to bear a child out of wedlock set off a firestorm. The reactions to Quayle's speech by journalists, politicians, and even the fictional television characters, Murphy Brown and Bart Simpson, demonstrated the deep conflict over the nature and structure of the American family. The orthodox ideal is a two-parent, nuclear family with the mother at home caring for the children. Marilyn Quayle appealed to this notion of the family in her speech at the Republican Convention. "Watching and helping my children as they grow into good and loving teenagers is a source of daily joy for me. There aren't many women who would have it any other way." "Not everyone," Quayle argued later in the speech, "believed that the family was so oppressive that women could only thrive apart from it" (Quayle 1992, A34). First Lady Barbara Bush also discussed family values during the 1992 Republican convention and was joined on the platform by her children and grandchildren. She argued that her husband's ultimate measure of success was not his many political victories, but his close ties to his children.

Tipping his hat to the more inclusive definition of the family bolstered by the progressivist world view, Clinton stated in his acceptance speech that he was "fed up with politicians in Washington lecturing the rest of us about family values."

> Our families have values. But our government doesn't. I want an America where family values live in our actions, not just in our speeches. An America that includes every family. Every traditional family and every extended family. Every two-parent family, every single-parent family, and every foster family. Every family (Clinton 1992, A14).

Closely related to the "family values" debate was the controversy over the proper role of women in society. On the progressivist side, Hillary Rodham Clinton, who pursued a law career while her husband was governor of Arkansas, is now famous for her sarcastic quip about "staying home and baking cookies." Mrs. Clinton, in her role as the President's wife and closest advisor, quickly became a symbol for the progressivist assault on traditional views of women's roles. As *Time* magazine reported, "Hillary, who personifies many of the advances made by a cutting-edge generation of women, finds herself held up against what is probably the most tradition-bound and antiquated model of American womanhood: the institution of the First Lady" (Carlson 1992, p. 31).

If Hillary Clinton challenged the traditional role of the First Lady, then Marilyn Quayle and Barbara Bush essentially affirmed it. At the Republican convention they were held up "as paragons of stay-at-home motherhood." Barbara Bush gently reminisced about driving carpools, attending Little League games, and leading Cub Scouts. Marilyn Quayle, in a more strident tone, opined that feminists are disappointed with the outcome of the feminist movement "because most women do not wish to be liberated from their essential natures as women" (Quayle 1992, A34). In response to Marilyn Quayle's affirmation of the traditional role of women, Congresswomen Constance A. Morella of Maryland, said the speech reminded her of the discredited opinion of Justice Joseph P. Bradley written in 1872—"The paramount destiny and mission of women are to fulfill the noble and benign offices of wife and mother—this is the law of the Creator" (Stanley 1992, A1).

A third source of conflict revolved around the matter of homosexuality. In short, the culturally orthodox consider homosexuality to be an immoral aberration—contrary to the laws of God. Progressivists view homosexuality as a viable alternative lifestyle, deserving of our tolerance, acceptance, and respect. Clinton was the first Presidential candidate in history publicly to embrace the homosexual community as a legitimate voting block. That a gay campaign worker with AIDS spoke at the Democratic convention is just one example of this candidate's accepting posture toward the gay community.

While Clinton was making these overtures to the homosexual lobby, Buchanan was busy lamenting the prospect that if "Clinton and Clinton" were elected they would impose "homosexual rights" on all Americans. Moreover, Buchanan urged his supporters to stand with President Bush "against the amoral idea that gay and lesbian couples should have the same standing in law as married men and women." Andrew Sullivan, the gay editor of the *New Republic*, observing the debate over homosexuality in the 1992 election ominously noted that the battle lines were drawn: "We may be at a watershed," Sullivan said. "This battle is finally joined.... The test is whether you can publicly denounce people for something they cannot help" (Jordan 1992, A27).

So it went, issue after issue, candidates and activists appealing to passions on one side of the cultural divide or the other. Indeed, the cultural battle was waged over a host of issues: funding for the arts, educational reform, church-state relations, abortion and so on.[1]

THE CULTURAL ECLIPSE OF PARTY LOYALTIES

It is important to note that the culture wars, as they were played out in the 1992 election, were not a battle between Republicans and Democrats, as though all Republicans were orthodox and all Democrats progressive. In fact, cultural skirmishes flared up during both parties' conventions. For example, a considerable amount of media attention was given to the Democratic party's denial of a convention speaking role to Democratic Pennsylvania Governor Robert Casey because of his pro-life views on abortion. Instead, convention organizers invited five pro-choice Republicans to the Democratic convention stage.

Clinton, being the adept politician that he is, was certainly cognizant of these contrasting impulses in American culture. This in no small measure explains why Hillary Clinton assumed a quieter and more docile image after the earlier campaign fracas over her "radical feminist" views and her initial more forthright involvement in speeches and press encounters. During the campaign Clinton was often photographed exiting Baptist churches with Bible in hand. During his acceptance speech he invoked the biblical imagery of a New Covenant and made a number of references to family members, including his wife, mother, and the grandfather who taught him that all are equal "in the eyes of the Lord." Moreover, he spoke of daughter Chelsea's birth, and how he was "overcome with the thought that God had given [him] a blessing" his father never knew (Clinton 1992, A14). He even referred to abortion as something he wanted to make "safe, legal and rare." This "new Democrat" was new in that he had the political savvy not to allow himself to be labeled a "radical liberal" as were Dukakis and Mondale before him. All these gestures were arguably directed toward appeasing those with orthodox impulses in American culture.

The tensions of the culture wars were also evident at the Republican National Convention. Many delegates were disturbed at the religious nature of the Republican platform. Some prominent Republicans, including Barry Goldwater and California Governor Pete Wilson, spoke out against the platform's strong anti-abortion language. Massachusetts Governor Christopher Weld was seen wearing a "Pro-Bush, Pro-Choice" button on the convention floor. Even First Lady Barbara Bush made public for the first time her decidedly pro-choice beliefs. Moreover, a pro-choice woman, Secretary of Labor Lynn Martin, introduced Bush at the convention. The Republicans even asked Mary Fisher, a female AIDS victim, to speak at the convention, and though not gay herself, she pleaded for compassion for all with the AIDS disease, including homosexuals. These overtures, however, did not stop Republicans from arguing over the official Republican platform, nor did it stop demonstrators outside the Astrodome from protesting against the Bush administration's efforts (or lack thereof) to combat AIDS. Journalists noticed the tension within the ranks of the Republican party. David Gergen, for example, described in *Newsweek* magazine the "fight for the soul of the party," and a *New York Times* article, alluding to a previous cultural division in America, posed the question: "Is G.O.P. a House Divided?" (Gergen 1992, p. 58; Stanley 1992, A1).

In response to these contrasting impulses candidates sought to ingratiate themselves to each side of the culture war. Because of the incommensurable nature of the world views behind the various public conflicts, candidates seeking to appease both sides often appeared disingenuous. Overshadowing this politically motivated appeasement, however, were the statements made by activists who chose to portray the opposition as "extreme," "radical," and marginal to the mainstream norms of American society.

The Vilification of the Other

According to Hunter, the nature of discourse within the American culture wars is typically hostile, negative, and intolerant. Each side discredits the opposition by portraying it as radical and un-American. This leads to a political discourse which seeks only to vilify the enemy rather than engage in constructive debate (Hunter 1991, pp. 135-138). Both sides of the cultural divide employed this type of incendiary language during the 1992 election.

The culturally orthodox, for example, depicted the Clintons as advocates of "homosexual marriages," as "radical feminists," "hedonistic," "immoral," "anti-family," "godless," and "un-Christian." This effort to discredit the Clintons was self-conscious. During the Houston convention, for example, a Republican strategist stated:

> Our purpose is to define George Bush and the Republican Party as the proponent of fundamental social norms in terms of the family, in terms of sexual behavior and in terms of reward for work. Conversely, we intend to define Clinton and the Democrats as advocates of individual fulfillment, without regard to generally held values and beliefs (Edsall 1992, p. A1).

This strategy manifested itself in numerous ways. Congressman Newt Gingrich accused the Democrats of promoting "a multicultural, nihilistic hedonism that is inherently destructive of a healthy society" (Apple 1992, A 13:4). Richard Bond, Chairman of the Republican National Committee, caricatured Hillary Clinton as a "lawsuit-mongering feminist who likened marriage to slavery and encouraged children to sue their parents" (Carlson 1992, p. 31). Bond stated further that if Clinton were elected, Jane Fonda would be at the White House as "guest of honor at a state dinner for Fidel

Castro" (Lewis 1992, L A25). Pat Robertson claimed that the Clintons were devising "a radical plan to destroy the traditional family" (Will 1992, C7). Pat Buchanan derided the Democrats for letting "a militant leader of the homosexual rights movement" speak at their convention (Buchanan 1992, p. 2543). Marilyn Quayle strongly implied that the Clintons and their supporters were marginal to the mainstream of American values when she declared that "not everyone joined the counterculture, not everyone demonstrated, dropped out, took drugs, joined the sexual revolution, or dodged the draft" (Blumenthal 1993, p. 20).

Those on the progressivist side of the cultural divide were just as likely to demonize their opponents. Cultural progressivists depicted the culturally orthodox as "hate-mongers," "fear-mongers," "bigots," "Nazis," "McCarthyites," "right-wing radicals," "extremists," "homophobes," and the like. George Stephanopoulos, for example, characterized Pat Buchanan's convention speech as "Cape Fear," while Colbert I. King compared Buchanan to David Duke (King 1992). Mario Cuomo reportedly likened Buchanan's culture wars speech to the rhetoric of the Third Reich: "What do you mean by culture?.... That's the word they used in Nazi Germany" (Bethel 1993, p. 16). Even more explicitly, Carl Rowan said that "Buchanan's remarks were the closest he had ever heard to a Nazi address." That Bush gave the convention over to the "radical right-wing of Phyllis Schlafly, Pat Buchanan, and Pat Robertson" became a mantra of sorts for Clinton during the rest of the campaign.

In his speech during the Democratic convention Jesse Jackson compared Dan Quayle to King Herod of the New Testament: "It was Herod, the Quayle of his day, who put no value on the family" (Jackson 1992, A12). In a *New York Times* editorial, Anthony Lewis likened the Republican convention to McCarthyism. "I remember Joe McCarthy. I have been going to national political conventions since his day, and I do not recall one as mean in spirit as this one" (Lewis 1992, L A25). The Republican convention was described by various journalists, a group typically sympathetic to a progressivist world view, as "Rot on the Right" (Barrett 1992, p. 25), "A Feast of Hate and Fear" (Ivins 1992, p. 32), a "Thick Soup of Values-Blather" (Will 1992, C7), as "Pandering and Pandemonium" (McGrory 1992, C1), where "Merchants of Hate" (Lewi 1992, C7), flirted with "the Dangers of Negativism," immersed themselves in "Gay-Bashing" (Jordan 1992, A27), and revealed "Conservatism's Ugly Face" (Lind 1992, August 19).

In the face of this type of rhetoric it is no surprise that public debate becomes irreconcilably polarized. Discourse that vilifies the enemy necessarily results in an embattled "we vs. they" mentality, which serves to preclude the possibility for constructive dialogue and overshadows the voices of reason.

The media consistently ignored the so-called "muddled middle" during the election. The nuanced and often more complicated views of those in the middle don't fit within the sound-bite long quips of contemporary news accounts and are not as interesting as the more inflammatory statements by the extremists. In August of 1992, Republican Christine Todd Whitman, who was at the time running for (and would eventually win) the governorship of New Jersey, wrote an op-ed in the *New York Times* which exemplified the more middle-of-the-road, and arguably more typical, views that are less often reported by the media. Though pro-choice she believed there were areas where both sides of the cultural divide could work together.

> We all should support better sex education to prevent unwanted pregnancies and programs that reduce the need for abortion. We should also back organizations that assist women who choose to bring their pregnancies to term—whether these groups help with parenting skills or adoption placement or financial aid (Whitman 1992).

Again, Todd's words were the exception to the rule. Those views that earned the most press coverage were generally more harsh, polarized, and less interested in pursuing common ground. The picture of political discourse in the 1992 Presidential election, then, generally supports the formula laid out by Hunter regarding the nature of cultural conflict in contemporary America. There was, however, another important aspect of the 1992 campaign that may have significant implications for the future of cultural conflict in the U.S.—namely, the increasingly therapeutic nature of public debate.

THERAPEUTIC DISCOURSE

Another defining, though less discussed, aspect of the 1992 elections was the reliance upon more therapeutic forms of political discourse. A *New York Times* account of the Democratic National Convention, observed that if Clinton were to win, he would "be the first post-therapy President ever to inhabit the White House" (*New York Times* July 15, 1992, A7). The article titled, "I'm in Therapy, You're in Therapy: A Much-Analyzed Candidate Offers a 12-Step Plan to Democrats Anonymous," reported that both the Clintons and the Gores had been involved in counseling; the former to work through marital problems and issues related to Roger Clinton's drug addiction and Clinton's stepfather's alcoholism and the latter to work through difficulties surrounding the injuries their son received in a car accident. Both talked publicly about these matters.

Clinton's proclivity to "sprinkle his interviews with the trendy language of co-dependency" set the tone for a convention that in some ways resembled the atmosphere of a 12-step group meeting. Pilar Perez, a Jerry Brown delegate from California, for example, observed that "everyone in the state's delegation was comparing the convention to group therapy" (*New York Times*, July 15, 1992, A7). Elements of America's increasingly therapeutic culture—the elevation of the self as a source of moral authority, the greater emphasis on emotions for understanding oneself and one's relations with others, the victim mindset, and the self-referential practice of "sharing" or displaying publicly one's internal workings[2] (*New York Times* July 17, 1992, A15)—were evident in a number of the speeches given at the Democratic convention. Al Gore, for example, shared this about his son's accident during his acceptance speech: "I want to tell you this straight from my heart: that experience changed me forever." Likewise, Jesse Jackson identified with the pain of Americans: "Across the globe, we feel the pain that comes with new birth. Here in our country pain abounds." New York Mayor Dinkins observed in his welcoming address that by walking the streets of New York, one can "feel the pain of an entire nation."

Identifying specifically with the pain of single-parent children, Clinton offered these empathetic words:

And I want to say to every child in America tonight who's out there trying to grow up without a father or a mother; I know how you feel. You're special, too. You matter to America. And don't you ever let anybody tell you you can't become whatever you want to be. And if other politicians make you feel like you're not a part of their family, come on and be part of ours.

But Clinton and the Democrats were not the only politicians employing the sentimentalized and emotive language of therapy. In New Hampshire President Bush feebly attempted to reassure voters that he was in touch with their felt needs: "Message, I care..." Even the fire breathing Buchanan, in his convention speech, tried to connect with those hurt by hard times. "We need to reconnect with them. We need to let them know we know how bad they're hurting. They don't expect miracles, but they need to know we care" (*Congressional Quarterly*, August 22, 1995, p. 2543).

What is the significance of this therapeutic form of rhetoric? How does it differ from what politicians have said in previous political campaigns? I will attempt to answer the former question by first considering the latter. To do this I will compare the substance of discourse in the 1992 Presidential debates between Bill Clinton, George Bush, and Ross Perot to the 1858 debates between Abraham Lincoln and Stephen Douglas. The Lincoln-Douglas debates provide an interesting comparison because they were the most widely followed political debate in America's last culture war. As Hunter explains, "the last time this country 'debated' the issues of human life, personhood, liberty, and the rights of citizenship all together, the result was the bloodiest war ever to take place on this continent, the Civil War" (Hunter 1993, pp. 4-5).

David Zerefsky also notes the similarities in the cultural conflicts of these two time periods in a recently published documentation of the 1858 campaign, observing that the issue of slavery "occupied a position not unlike that of the abortion controversy in the late twentieth century." Moreover, he observes that in "an age in which moral disputes, such as abortion, medical ethics, creation sciences, gay rights, or capital punishment, seem to reflect incommensurable premises the Lincoln-Douglas debates are worthy of study..." (Angle 1991, pp. xvi-xvii). Following this recommendation, I use the Lincoln Douglas debates as a historical comparison to the 1992 debates.

An analysis of the Lincoln-Douglas debates reveals, however, that instead of appealing to a therapeutic ethos, these two candidates drew upon more traditional codes of moral understanding to legitimate their positions on slavery. In both their situation and ours, the candidates discussed cultural issues that deeply divided American society. In the contemporary case, however, therapeutic language was employed to justify one's position, while in the mid-nineteenth century the candidates drew upon the ideals of civic republicanism and biblical Protestantism to justify their views. A careful review of the type of rhetoric used in both instances helps us understand how the therapeutic form of language used today may affect the outcome of the contemporary culture wars.

THE LINCOLN-DOUGLAS DEBATES

Though the Kennedy-Nixon debates in 1960 were actually the first presidential debates where candidates from the two major parties faced each other in person for the sake of political deliberation, the Lincoln-Douglas debates (which was a race for a U.S. Senate seat) rest in American folklore as the place where two likely contenders for the Presidency first stood on a platform and faced each other in a debate format. For most of America's political history, face to face debates between Presidential contenders (and, for that matter, contenders for other national offices) were regarded as a violation of protocol and an affront to political propriety. More common were the campaigning efforts of surrogates who typically stumped on behalf of their party's nominees.

The famous 1858 Lincoln-Douglas debates, though a contest for an Illinois Senate seat, were by nineteenth century standards very unusual. As a *New York Evening Post* correspondent reported in 1858, "The present political canvass in Illinois is a singular one, and I think, without a parallel in the history of electioneering campaigns in this country."[3] Though Douglas was to win the Illinois Senate seat, the contest addressed the important and divisive issue of slavery and provided Lincoln with the national exposure he needed to win the Presidency two years later, when he again faced Douglas.

The 1858 debates, however, hurt Douglas' chances for the Presidency because of the arguments he advanced in support of the doctrine of popular sovereignty (a position favorable neither to Northern abolitionists nor to proslavery Southerners). In fact, Douglas' alienation from Southern Democrats resulted in the nomination of two Democratic candidates for the 1860 Presidential race. Northern Democrats supported Douglas while Southern Democrats supported John Breckinridge, a split which helped Lincoln secure victory in 1860. The 1858 debates, then, were directly relevant to the outcome of the 1860 election. Thus, prior to 1960 the Lincoln-Douglas debates came the closest to a Presidential debate between two major party candidates, and are often considered within the literature as the historical antecedents to the modern presidential debates.[4]

Though there were similarities between the 1858 debates and the modern-day Presidential debates in terms of the presence of two candidates from the major parties facing each other on the platform, the discussion of national issues, and the focus of widespread national attention on the contests, there were also some major differences. The most obvious, of course, are the differences in technology. Every Presidential debate since, including the Nixon-Kennedy debates, has been televised. Though the Lincoln-Douglas debates had huge audiences (there were as many as 15,000 in attendance at some), and the debates were printed for an even wider circulation in the major newspapers of the day, there is still no comparison to the enormous audiences reached by live national television today.

In terms of format there were also significant differences. The Lincoln-Douglas debates lasted three hours. In each of the seven total debates, the first candidate was allowed an hour to open the debate. The second would speak for an hour and a half. Then the first candidate would be given an additional half hour to respond. The structure of the time was such that it allowed for the advancement of complex, syllogistic arguments. Also, because there were no moderators in these debates, Lincoln and Douglas could respond directly and often somewhat caustically to the accusations and arguments of the other.

The Centrality of Logos

The long and often complex arguments advanced by both Abraham Lincoln and Stephen Douglas during the debates clearly demonstrate an emphasis on the place of reason. Such an emphasis was in keeping with a classical style of political rhetoric. According to Aristotle, traditional legal and political discourse necessarily involved the portrayal of ethical character (ethos) and the appeal to logical reasoning (logos). Moreover, in Aristotle's classical treatise, *Rhetoric*, emotional appeals (pathos) were understood to be more typical of ceremonial or eulogistic than political or legal oratory.

Appeals to reason were central to the 1858 debates. Lincoln and Douglas spoke to audiences that were apparently able and willing to listen to long arguments which built upon previous points, and which presupposed a familiarity with other speeches and government documents. On several occasions, Douglas reminded the audience to restrain their enthusiasm and applause, and listen to the logic of his arguments. For example, in Ottawa, the first of the seven debates, Douglas opened, "I desire to address myself to your judgment, your understanding, and your consciences, and not to your passions or your enthusiasm."[5] In Quincy, the sixth debate, Douglas pleaded with the crowd in a similar way. "I desire to be heard rather than to be applauded. I wish to address myself to your reason, your judgment, your sense of justice, and not to your passion."

It was on the basis of his reasonableness not upon passion or sentiment that Douglas wanted to be judged. "I wish to be judged by my principles, by those great public measures and constitutional principles upon which the peace, the happiness and the perpetuity of this republic now rest."

Lincoln also strongly employed logical reasoning in his counter arguments to Douglas. Consider the following statement offered by Lincoln in the Galesburg debate.

Judge Douglas declares that if any community want slavery they have a right to have it. He can say that logically, if he says that there is no wrong in slavery; but if you admit that there is a wrong in it, he cannot logically say that anybody has a right to do wrong. He insists that, upon the score of equality, the owners of slaves and owners of property—of horses and every other sort of property— should be alike and hold them alike in a new territory. That is perfectly logical, if the two species of property are alike and are equally founded in right. But if you admit that one of them is wrong, you cannot institute any equality between right and wrong. And from this difference of sentiment—the belief on the part of one that the institution is wrong, and a policy springing from the belief which looks to the arrest of the enlargement of that wrong; and this other sentiment, that it is no wrong, and a policy sprung from that sentiment which will tolerate no idea of preventing that wrong from growing larger, and looks to there never being an end of it through all the existence of things,—arises the real difference between Judge Douglas and his friends, on the one hand, and the Republicans on the other. Now, I confess myself as belonging to that class in the country who contemplate slavery as a moral, social and political evil, having due regard for its actual existence amongst us and the difficulties of getting rid of it in any satisfactory way, and to all the constitutional obligations which have been thrown about it; but, nevertheless, desire a policy that looks to the prevention of it as a wrong, and looks hopefully to the time when as a wrong it may come to an end.

The contemporary appetite for sound-bite long appeals would have no patience for such a musing argument. And this excerpt represents what was only a two or three minute portion of a 90-minute statement. Evident in the above remarks is not only Lincoln's penchant for logically based discourse, but a deep concern with right and wrong. Lincoln, particularly in the final debate, spoke at length about "right" and "wrong." To him it was a central matter for determining appropriate state action. Important to our analysis here, however, is understanding what provided the basis for distinguishing right from wrong. In other words, from what type of code of moral understanding did candidates draw to justify or legitimate their positions? It becomes clear in studying the Lincoln-Douglas debates that both candidates relied on traditional sources of legitimation.

"A House Divided"

Both Lincoln and Douglas supported their positions on the slavery issue with references to traditional religious ideals and symbols. Consider, for example, Lincoln's famous biblical metaphor, "a house divided against itself cannot stand." There was much discussion in the debates about this metaphor.

> A house divided against itself cannot stand. I believe this government cannot endure permanently half slave and half free. I do not expect the house to fall— but I do expect it will cease to be divided. It will become all one thing, or all the other. Either the opponents of slavery will arrest the further spread of it, and place it where the public mind shall rest in the belief that it is in the course of ultimate extinction, or its advocates will push it forward till it shall become alike lawful in all the states—old as well as new, North as well as South.

Douglas criticized Lincoln's use of this metaphor in a Springfield speech, to which Lincoln offered the following retort in the Ottawa debate.

> He has read from my speech in Springfield, in which I say that 'a house divided against itself cannot stand.' Does the Judge say it can stand? I don't know whether he does or not. The Judge does not seem to be attending to me just now, but I would like to know if it is his opinion that a house divided against itself can stand. If he does, then there is a question of veracity, not between him and me, but between the Judge and an authority of a somewhat higher character. Now, my friends, I ask your attention to this matter for the purpose

of saying something seriously. I know that the Judge may readily enough agree with me that the maxim which was put forth by the Savior is true, but he may allege that I misapply it...

Lincoln justified using the metaphor by appealing to the cultural system from which it was derived. Douglas responded to Lincoln's challenge, but he did so on the basis that Lincoln himself suggested, that is, on the applicability of the passage, not the veracity of the quote or its source.

In the Galesburg debate, Douglas cleverly applied this metaphor to Lincoln's own party, where there was likewise division over the slavery issue—an interesting parallel to the noted division within the present day Republican party over the abortion issue.

If it be true, as I have shown it is, that the whole Republican party in the northern part of the state stands committed to the doctrine of no more slave states, and that this same doctrine is repudiated by the Republicans in the other part of the state, I wonder whether Mr. Lincoln and his party do not present the case which he cited from the Scriptures, of a house divided against itself which cannot stand.[6]

Douglas also tried to show how Lincoln's use of the metaphor was a misapplication when the Democratic candidate argued that the framers of the Constitution established a government which contained both free and slave states from its outset.

Is this sectional warfare to be waged between Northern states and Southern states until they all shall become uniform in their local and domestic institutions merely because Mr. Lincoln says that a house divided against itself cannot stand, and pretends that this scriptural quotation, this language of our Lord and Master, is applicable to the American Union and the American Constitution? Washington and his compeers in the convention that framed the Constitution, made this government divided into free and slave states. It was composed then of thirteen sovereign and independent states, each having sovereign authority over its local and domestic institutions, and all bound together by the federal Constitution. Mr. Lincoln likens that bond of the federal Constitution joining free and slave states together to a house divided against itself. And says that it is contrary to the law of God and cannot stand. When did he learn, and by what authority does he proclaim that this government is contrary to the law of God and cannot stand. It has stood thus divided into free and slave states from its organization up to this day.

In both instances Douglas took issue with Lincoln not for using the metaphor or for taking it from a religious source, but for misapplying it. For Douglas the problem was one of application. According to the "Little Giant," if Lincoln were to be consistent, he needed to offer a reason for the differences within his own party and the existence of both free and slave states since the nation's origin.

Pro-Slavery Legitimations

That Douglas' contention with the "house divided" metaphor was not with its source but with its application was underscored by the fact that Douglas himself drew heavily upon religious imagery to support his own positions. He claimed, for example, that principle compelled him and his party "always [to] do right, and trust the consequences to God and the people." Likewise, he claimed that his resistance to the urgings of President Buchanan that he change his position on the Kansas-Missouri Compromise while in the Senate were based on the belief that he "was accountable to Illinois, as [his] constituency, and to God, but not to the President or to any other power on earth." Consider Douglas' resolve as expressed during the Freeport Debate:

> I have stood by my principles in fair weather and in foul, in the sunshine and in the rain. I have defended the great principles of self-government here among you when Northern sentiment ran in a torrent against me. And I have defended that same great principle when Southern sentiment came down like an avalanche upon me. I was not afraid of any test they put to me. I knew I was right—I knew my principles were sound—I knew that the people would see in the end that I had done right, and I knew that the God of Heaven would smile upon me if I was faithful in the performance of my duty.

Similarly, in the Jonesboro debate, Douglas sought to provide additional religious legitimacy to his position regarding slavery when he claimed, "I do not believe that the Almighty made the negro capable of self-government." In the same speech he argued that the founders were surely directed by divine guidance when they chose not to put "their negroes on equality with themselves." Instead of establishing such equality, claimed Douglas, the founders "with uplifted eyes to Heaven...implored the Divine blessing upon them...never dreaming that they were violating divine law by still holding the negroes in bondage and depriving them equality."

Douglas also questioned whether Lincoln's antislavery statements could possibly be Christian when they would starve the slaves to a point of extinction. During the Quincy debate, for example, Douglas argued that Lincoln's support for the prohibition of slavery in the new U.S. territories would "smother slavery out," and that subsequently slavery would be eliminated "only by extinguishing the Negro race, for his policy would drive them to starvation." Douglas then added sardonically, "This is the humane and Christian remedy that he proposes for the great crime of slavery." In the final debate in Alton, Douglas took issue with Lincoln in a similar fashion when he argued that Lincoln's policies would "extinguish slavery by...starving [slaves] out of existence as you smoke a fox out of his hole." What was so apparently appalling to Douglas about this position was the fact that Lincoln erroneously justified his actions based upon religious precepts. "And he intends to do that in the name of humanity and Christianity ... Mr. Lincoln makes out that line of policy, and appeals to the moral sense of justice, and the Christian feeling of the community to sustain him."

Douglas' comments highlight the fact that there was some general "Christian feeling" to be appealed to within the culture. His point of contention was not that appealing to such a sentiment was wrong or that the sentiment itself was wrong, but that Lincoln was somehow acting disingenuously or at least ignorantly by aligning his positions with that sentiment. To be sure, both candidates aligned themselves with a religious ethos, indicating the extent to which this source of legitimation prevailed within the culture and provided a basis for the justification of state policies.

Abolitionist Legitimations

Lincoln would often argue in favor of the eventual abolition of slavery by citing the Declaration of Independence which guaranteed the equality of freedom for all men. As Douglas himself observed:

> Mr. Lincoln, following the example and lead of all the little Abolition orators, who go around and lecture in the basements of schools and churches, reads from the Declaration of Independence, that all men were created equal, and then asks how can you deprive a negro of that equality which God and the Declaration of Independence awards to him. He and they maintain that negro equality is guaranteed by the laws of God, and that it is asserted in the Declaration of Independence.

Douglas took issue with this argument, calling it a "monstrous heresy." He reminded the audience that Thomas Jefferson, the author of the document, was an owner of many slaves and remained so until his death. "Did he intend to say in the Declaration that his negro slaves, which he held and treated as property, were created his equals by Divine law, and that he was violating the law of God every day of his life by holding them as slaves?"

Lincoln responded to this question by once again appealing to a religious ethos, and his retort suggests that Jefferson himself was haunted by the prevailing power of the same.

> And I will remind Judge Douglas and this audience, that while Mr. Jefferson was the owner of slaves, as undoubtedly he was, in speaking upon this very subject, he used the strong language that 'he trembled for his country when he remembered that God was just;' and I will offer the highest premium in my power to Judge Douglas if he will show that he, in all his life, ever uttered a sentiment at all akin to that of Jefferson.

Lincoln also appealed to religious ideals when he likened Douglas' opposition to anti-slavery arguments to that of Satan warring against the Bible. Moreover, he mocked Douglas' commitment to the legal authority of the Dred Scott decision, arguing that Douglas' deference approximated that of submission to a religious declaration. "He did not commit himself on account of the merit or demerit of the decision, but it is a 'Thus saith the Lord.' The next decision, as much as this, will be a 'Thus saith the Lord.'"

Vision for America

The slavery issue was not the only topic which motivated appeals to traditional sources of legitimation. Douglas, for example, invoked moral language in reference to Illinois' state debt. Traditional religious symbols were also employed in discussions about America's identity and destiny. Indeed, when defining America and making declarations about America's future, both candidates drew heavily upon religious images to validate their respective visions. Douglas, for example, declared that during America's entire history, "Divine Providence has smiled upon us, and showered upon our nation richer and more abundant blessings than have ever been conferred upon any other."

In the first debate Douglas similarly spoke of America's divine and manifest destiny when he stated, "We have crossed the Allegheny mountains and filled up the whole North West, turning the prairie into a garden, and building up churches and schools, thus spreading civilization and Christianity where before there was nothing but savage-barbarism." Because of its divine mission, Douglas believed that America would increase in territory, in power, and in strength and would be a guide for freedom throughout the civilized world. Lincoln, likewise, spoke of America's future with reference to Providence, when he predicted that slavery would ultimately become extinct. "I do not suppose that in the most peaceful way ultimate extinction would occur in less than a hundred years at the least; but that it will occur in the best way for both races in God's own good time, I have no doubt."

Such justifications for America's identity and for state policies during this period were not unique to the Lincoln-Douglas debates. It was reported, for example, that in the Pryne-Bromlow debates of the same year the contestants argued about the legitimacy of slavery through a chapter and verse exegesis of relevant scriptural passages. (Jamieson and Birdsell, p. 82). Such references to traditional religious sources of legitimation, however, were less explicit in the 1992 debates, the second period of cultural division considered here. Again, the common feature of each set of debates was that they both took place in times of intense cultural conflict. In the 1992 debates, however, therapeutic appeals predominated over religious appeals.

CLINTON-BUSH-PEROT DEBATES

It has not been unusual for candidates in Presidential contests to focus on the issue of character. An important point of discussion in the Kennedy-Nixon debates, for example, was the issue of Kennedy's age and experience. In the classical rhetoric sense, the Clinton-Bush-Perot debates demonstrated a lack of emphasis on syllogistic logic (Aristotelian *logos*) and departed, as well, from traditional understandings of *ethos*. Instead the greater emphasis was on *pathos* (the speaker's appeal to the emotional sentiments of the audience), the type of persuasion in the Aristotelian sense most typical in ceremonial or eulogistic rather than political oratory.

Such a movement toward pathos was evident, for example, in the debate over the so-called "character" issue. Clinton, in particular, was able to shift the discussion away from traditional understandings of character and argue instead that the candidate most suited for office was the candidate who most cared for the people. When asked specifically about the issue of experience, for example, Clinton answered with the following.

> Experience is important, yes. I've gotten a lot of experience in dealing with ordinary people over the last year, month. I've touched more people's lives and seen more heartbreak and hope, more pain and promise than anybody else who's run for president this year.[7]

With this assertion Clinton made the standard for Presidential qualification the degree to which a candidate could empathize with the pain of the American people. Such a standard is novel in the sense that it cannot be objectively measured or quantified, obviously departing from previous standards where greater emphasis was placed on such things as expertise, years in office, not to mention moral character.

Clinton's effectiveness in de-emphasizing ethos as a viable criteria for evaluating a candidate was apparent in the second debate when a questioner pleaded with the candidates to stop talking about the character issue. "Can we focus on the issues and not the personalities and the mud?" One of the character issues that dogged Clinton throughout the campaign was his draft record and his participation in demonstrations against the Vietnam War while a Rhodes Scholar at Oxford, something Marilyn Quayle referred to in her convention speech. Bush attempted to raise this issue during the debates, but interestingly did so by appealing to his feelings.

> My argument with Governor Clinton—you can call it mud wrestling, but I think it's fair to put in focus—is I am deeply troubled by someone who demonstrates and organizes demonstrations in a foreign land when his country's at war. Probably a lot of kids here disagree with me. But that's what I feel. That's what I feel passionately about. I'm thinking of Ross Perot's running mate sitting in the jail [in Vietnam]. How would he feel about it? But maybe that's generational. I don't know.

Bush raised the issue of Clinton's demonstrations in Europe, but did so without appealing to a cultural ethos that might give meaning to such ideals as honor, national loyalty, or courage. Instead he asserted that this was a matter about which he felt very strongly, and even conceded that others might feel differently. He claimed to be deeply troubled by it, not because it was wrong, but because it was something he felt passionately about. He even suggested that Ross Perot's running mate, Admiral Stokdale, might not feel very good about it. Clinton, for his part, defended this accusation by also appealing to feelings. "I was opposed to the war. I couldn't help that. I felt very strongly about it, and I didn't want to go at the time."

The Therapeutic Compulsion

One of the interesting things about the 1992 debates was the extent to which Bush and Perot likewise employed a therapeutic mode of discourse. One would not consider either George Bush (the aristocratic prototype) or Ross Perot (the managerial prototype) the most likely personalities to be inclined toward this style of discourse. Nevertheless, on a number of occasions both resorted to therapeutic language in discussing various matters. Consider, for example, Bush's response to a question about the AIDS epidemic.

> I think that we're showing the proper compassion and concern...I am very much concerned about AIDS and I believe that we've got the best researchers in the world out there at NIH working the problem. We're funding them—I wish there was more money—but we're funding them far more than any time in the past, and we're going to keep on doing that...Mary Fisher...electrified the Republican convention by talking about the compassion and the concern that we feel. It was a beautiful moment...So I think the appeal is yes, we care.

As if for a moment to express what he really thought about the matter of AIDS he slipped into a seemingly "uncaring" posture.

> And the other thing is part of AIDS—it's one of the few diseases where behavior matters. And I once called on somebody, "Well, change your behavior. Is the behavior you're using prone to cause AIDS? Change the behavior." Next thing I know, one of these ACT-Up groups is out saying, 'Bush ought to change his behavior." You can't talk about it rationally. The extremes are hurting the AIDS cause. To go into

> a Catholic mass in a beautiful cathedral in New York under the cause
> of helping in AIDS and start throwing condoms around in the mass,
> I'm sorry, I think it sets back the cause.

Then, as though correcting himself, he moved back into a more
empathetic mode.

> We cannot move to the extreme. We've got to care. We've got to
> continue everything we can at the federal and the local level. Barbara
> I think is doing a superb job in destroying the myth about AIDS. And
> all of us are in this fight together, all of us care.

It appears that Bush, in these comments about AIDS, was appealing
to both sides of the cultural divide, but sprinkled throughout were
the emotional appeals of a therapeutic perspective.

Ross Perot likewise defended his views with therapeutic rationales.
Consider his pontification about racial divisiveness, "But let me just
say to all of America: if you hate people, I don't want your vote.
That's how strongly I feel about it." Once again, racial division was
not decried on a moral basis, but on the basis that Perot felt strongly
about it. Speaking to the same issue, Perot encouraged Americans
to "love one another," and in his closing remarks he told Americans
that he was running for President because, as he put it, "I love you."
Responding to a question about America's posture toward
developments in Bosnia, Perot inserted the following: "Certainly we
care about the people, we care about the children, we care about the
tragedy." The statement, however, was offered in the context of
arguing for European, rather than U.S., responsibility for the region.

Perot also expressed strong feelings toward those who volunteered
themselves for military service. In discussing this affection he unveiled
the prototype of therapeutic discourse.

> There's another group that I feel very close to, and these are the men
> and women who fought on the battlefield, the children—the families—
> of the ones who died and the people who left parts of their bodies
> over there. I'd never ask you to do anything for me, but I owe you
> this, and I'm doing it for you. And I can't tell you what it means to
> me at these rallies when I see you and you come up and the look in
> your eyes—and I know how you feel and you know how I feel.

Thus, Perot pointed to the quintessential therapeutic dialogue: a complete conversation, even without words, on the basis of feelings.

All three candidates used therapeutic language when discussing children and the American family. Bush stated that when Barbara Bush "holds an AIDS baby, she's showing a certain compassion for the family; when she reads to children, the same thing." He affirmed her public demonstration of empathy. Clinton defined the family as, in part, a place where children "know they're the most important people in the world," and Ross Perot, drawing heavily, though perhaps unwittingly, upon developmental psychology, claimed, "A little child before they're 18 months learns to think well of himself or herself—or poorly. They develop a positive or negative self-image."

The Talk-Show Debate

The language employed by the candidates was not the only thing resembling the therapeutic model in these debates. Indeed, the very structure of the second debate, which was held in Richmond, Virginia on October 15, 1992 more closely resembled a day-time television talk show than a typical Presidential debate. Moderator Carole Simpson, of ABC News, assumed the role of a Phil Donahue or Oprah Winfrey as she roamed the studio with a microphone and took questions from the audience. This was the first time in the history of the Presidential debates that citizens other than prominent members of the national media were allowed to directly ask the candidates questions. The questions themselves were thick on the emotive and reminiscent of the type of discourse typical in the day-time talk shows. Consider for example, this interchange between an audience member and the candidates.

> Questioner: Forgive the notes here, but I'm shy on camera. The focus of my work as a domestic mediator is meeting the needs of the children that I work with, by way of their parents, and not the wants of their parents. And I ask the three of you, how can we, as symbolically the children of the future president, expect the two of you, the three of you to meet our needs, the need in housing and in crime and you name it, as opposed to the wants of your political spin doctors and your political parties?

Moderator: So your question is?

Questioner: Can we focus on the issues and not the personalities and the mud? I think there's a need, if we could take a poll here with the folks from Gallup perhaps, I think there's a real need here to focus at this point on the needs.

Clinton: I agree with him.

Bush: Let's do it.

Moderator: President Bush?

Bush: Let's do it. Let's talk about programs for children. Questioner: Could we cross our hearts? It sounds silly here, but could we make a commitment? You know, we're not under oath at this point, but could you make a commitment to the citizens of the United States to meet our needs, and we have many, and not yours again? I repeat that. It's a real need, I think, that we all have.

Bush: I think it depends how you define it. I mean, I think in general let's talk about these issues, let's talk about the programs. But in the Presidency, a lot goes into it. Caring goes into it. That's not particularly specific. Strength goes into it. That's not particularly specific. Standing up against aggression. That's not specific in terms of a program. This is what a President has to do. So in principle, though, I'll take your point and think we ought to discuss child care or whatever else it is.

It seems that the questioner was not deeply interested in the specific issues or in knowing what the candidates thought about them. Instead he seemed more concerned with having the candidates "cross their hearts" and swear to show compassion for the "real needs" of the people. Bush's attempt to empathize by inserting the phrase "caring goes into" the Presidency had the appearance of being wholly disingenuous. Bush's inability to empathize with the audience in this fashion was even more pronounced in another exchange during the Richmond debate. The following question was first asked by a member of the audience, and led to contrasting responses from the candidates.

Questioner: How has the national debt personally affected each of your lives? And if it hasn't, how can you honestly find a cure for the economic problems of the common people if you have no experience in what's ailing them?

After Ross Perot offered a brief response, the question was put to President Bush.

Bush:	Well, I think the national debt affects everybody.
Moderator:	You personally.
Bush:	Obviously it has a lot to do with interest rates—
Moderator:	She's saying, "you personally." You, on a personal basis. How has it affected you? Has it affected you personally?
Bush:	I'm sure it has. I love my grandchildren—
Moderator:	How?
Bush:	I want to think that they're going to be able to afford an education. I think that that's an important part of being a parent. If the question—maybe I—get it wrong. Are you suggesting that if somebody has means that the national debt doesn't affect them?
Questioner:	What I'm saying is—
Bush:	I'm not sure I get—help me with the question and I'll try to answer it.
Questioner:	Well, I've had friends that have been laid off from jobs.
Bush:	Yeah.
Questioner:	I know people who cannot afford to pay the mortgage on their homes, their car payment. I have personal problems with the national debt. But how has it affected you, and if you have no experience in it, how can you help us, if you don't know what we're feeling?
Moderator:	I think she means more the recession—the economic problems today the country faces rather than the deficit.
Bush:	Well, listen, you ought to be in the White House for a day and hear what I hear and see what I see and read the mail I read and touch the people that I touch from time to time. I was in the Lomax AME Church. It's a black church just outside of Washington, D.C. And I read the bulletin about teenage pregnancies, about the difficulties that families are having to make ends meet. I talk to parents. I mean, you've got to care. Everybody cares if people aren't doing well. But I don't think it's fair to say, you haven't had cancer. Therefore, you don't know what it's like. I don't think it's fair to say, you know, whatever it is, that if you haven't been hit by it personally. But everybody's affected by the debt because of the tremendous interest that goes into paying on that debt everything's more expensive. Everything comes out of your pocket and my pocket. So it's that. But I think

in terms of the recession, of course you feel it when you're President of the United States. And that's why I'm trying to do something about it by stimulating the export, vesting more, better education systems. Thank you. I'm glad you clarified it.

The questioner was not interested in Bush's policy position regarding the national debt nor his proposals for reducing the deficit. Her concern was not really even with the recession and any ideas Bush might have for resolving it. Instead what she was really concerned about was Bush's personal experience with the economic woes faced by Americans. If he did not have personal experience then how could he know what she was "feeling." By definition then, what the questioner was looking for was a therapeutic response. Bush first tried to address the question based upon the literal words that were asked. After the moderator clarified what the audience participant was really asking, Bush unsuccessfully attempted a empathetic response, but failed to connect with the questioner.

Clinton, on the other hand, handled the question with great ease when it was directed to him. He took several strides into the audience and directly engaged the questioner.

> Clinton: Tell me how it's affected you again.
> Questioner: um—
> Clinton: You know people who've lost their jobs and lost their homes?
> Questioner: Well, yeah, uh-huh.
> Clinton: Well, I've been governor of a small state for 12 years. I'll tell you how it's affected me. Every year Congress and the President sign laws that make us do more things and give us less money to do it with. I see people in my state, middle-class people—their taxes have gone up in Washington and their services have gone down while the wealthy have gotten tax cuts. I have seen what's happened in this last four years when—in my state, when people lose their jobs there's a good chance I'll know them by their names. When a factory closes, I know the people who ran it. When the businesses go bankrupt, I know them. And I've been out here for 13 months meeting in meetings just like this ever since October, with people like you all over America, people that have lost their jobs, lost their livelihood, lost their health insurance...

Clinton responded empathetically by discussing how the country's economic woes had directly affected him and those with whom he had personal contact. In word and in style he connected with the questioner. He showed that he cared. Clinton's ability in this regard was really no surprise. It was the Clinton campaign that recommended the Richmond format, a setup that closely resembled in style the electronic town meetings Clinton had been conducting throughout the campaign. In fact, at the end of the Richmond debate he took credit for the format and expressed his appreciation to the audience for making it a "positive experience."

> Thank you, Carole, and thank you ladies and gentlemen. Since I suggested this format I hope it's been good for all of you. I really tried to be faithful to your request that we answer the questions specifically and pointedly. I thought I owed that to you and I respect you for being here and for the impact you've had on making this a more positive experience.

CONCLUSION

One wonders whether Lincoln and Douglas were likewise concerned that their audiences enjoyed a "positive experience." The record suggests that they probably were not. In any respect, both sets of candidates were engaged in debate during times of intense cultural division in American society. Both sets of candidates also drew upon the meaning systems which prevailed within the culture at their time in history. What may be a bit counter intuitive is that both Lincoln and Douglas drew upon traditional, particularly religious, sources of meaning to legitimate their positions; and both Bush and Perot in addition to Clinton drew upon a therapeutic ethos. Many think of Lincoln as the classic embodiment of what Robert Bellah and others have described as American civil religion.[8] A conspicuously religious orientation, however, is not so commonly associated with Stephen Douglas. That he drew upon it so freely speaks to the salience with which a religious world view remained a part of the larger culture at that time in history. At the same time, Bush and Perot are not individuals typically accused of being therapeutic in orientation. Nevertheless, they drew upon this system of meaning to justify and explain their positions. Again, that they were so compelled indicates the strength of this orientation in the cultural fabric of contemporary American society.

That the national debate over slavery was significantly influenced by the cultural orientation which determined the parameters of discourse is perhaps obvious. Lincoln's arguments, heavily steeped as they were in logic and moral reasonings, would simply be implausible in a different cultural context. They were only persuasive in as much as they resonated with the sentiments of the society. In the same way, today's prevailing systems of moral understanding affect the substance of debate and the plausibility of certain orientations.

If this is the case, then what does the evident use of therapeutic language by politicians on both sides of the cultural divide mean for the American culture wars? I would propose that it portends the eventual demise of orthodoxy and the ultimate victory of progressivism. Therapeutic discourse, just like religious language, is not neutral. Its words and symbols represent a certain understanding of the world, of human nature, and of the basis of moral authority. The meaning system represented within a therapeutic frame of reference better fits within a progressivist orientation with its more relative, subjective, and changing understanding of truth. But the emotive, self-referential orientation of the therapeutic perspective undermines an orthodox world view.

For example, when Pat Buchanan says, "George Bush is a defender of the right to life and a champion of the Judeo-Christian values and beliefs upon which this America was founded," he makes Bush a symbol of an orthodox world view; an orientation which considers truth to be fixed, objective, historically rooted, and derived from a transcendent, external-to-the-self source. But when Bush defends patriotism and loyalty to one's country on the basis that it is what he "feels passionately about," admitting that others may feel differently and that maybe it's just a "generational" thing, he uses a form of language that is more relative, more subjective, more self-referential. Theoretically and practically, the therapeutic perspective is antithetical to an orthodox orientation.

Nonetheless, as we saw in the rhetoric of the 1992 election generally and in the Presidential debates specifically, those on the orthodox side of the cultural divide are just as likely to use it as are those on the progressivist side of the divide. Continued use of this type of language among the orthodox will increasingly make unpalatable and implausible a form of public discourse which refers to unchanging standards of truth, to tradition, and to sources of moral authority outside of the self. Thus, though the culture wars rage on, as various conflicts in the 1992 election indicate, the progressivists can take solace in the influence of the therapeutic ethos on the orthodox side of the cultural divide. The use of therapeutic language by the orthodox ultimately undermines the traditional codes of moral understanding to which they appeal.

NOTES

1. Take, for example, the battle over funding for the arts. Progressivists argued for freedom and decried censorship while the orthodox insisted that some art violates certain standards of decency and should not be funded by the government. The orthodox view on this issue was put forth by William Bennet, former Drug Czar and Secretary of Education. "On our side of the cultural dividing line," he said, "we believe that the government should not subsidize pornography and obscenity." Bennet likewise spoke to the conflicts in the area of education when he stated further that "we believe that our nation's public schools should not be doing things like handing out condoms to our children. Educators should not be allowed to usurp the authority from parents in this and other sensitive areas" (from transcription of William Bennett's Republican National Convention speech, "Bennett Renominates Quayle for Vice President," *Congressional Quarterly*, August 22, 1992, p. 2554). Perhaps the most inflammatory issue raised during the 1992 campaign was the conflict over abortion. The Republicans took a strong pro-life stand in their party platform, while Clinton declared in his acceptance speech, "I am pro-choice, strongly. I believe this difficult and painful decision should be left to the women of America" (from transcription of Bill Clinton's July 16, 1992 Democratic Convention speech in the *New York Times*, "Transcript of Speech by Clinton Accepting Democratic Nomination, July 17, 1992, A 14). In response to Clinton, Pat Buchanan once again made dire predictions about the future of America. He forewarned that part of the "Clinton and Clinton" agenda was to impose an "abortion on demand" policy in the United States (from transcription of Pat Buchanan's August 17, 1992 Republican National Convention Speech, "Buchanan Urges His Brigades to Stand Beside the President," *Congressional Quarterly*, August 22, 1992, p. 2543).

2. What Philip Rieff has termed the "triumph of the therapeutic" ethos in American culture has several defining features. Included among these is the elevation of the self as the "touchstone of cultural judgment" (Bell 1976); the greater emphasis on emotions for understanding oneself and one's relations with others (MacIntyre 1984); the rise of a new priesthood of psychologists and psychiatrists (Zilbergeld 1983); the "pathologization of human behavior," (Rice 1992); and the victim mindset (Sykes 1992).

3. As cited in Kathleen Hall Jamiesen and David S. Birdsell, *Presidential Debates: The Challenge of Creating an Informed Electorate* (Oxford: Oxford University Press, 1988), p. 7, *New York Evening Post*, October 21, 1858.

4. Consider, for example, Sidney Kraus, *The Great Debates: Background–Perspective–Effects*, (Bloomington: Indiana University Press, 1962), pp. 56-57; and Jamieson and Birdsell (1988), pp. 7-10 and 35-83.

5. All citations for the Lincoln-Douglas Debates, which from here on will not be footnoted, were taken from Paul M. Angle's printing of the speeches in *The Complete Lincoln-Douglas Debates of 1858*, Chicago: University of Chicago Press, 1991, pp. 102-176, 189-275, and 285-402. There were seven debates in all: The Ottawa Debate, The Freeport Debate, The Jonesboro Debate, The Charleston Debate, the Galesburg Debate, and the Alton Debate. For most quotes I name the debate where the statement was made.

6. Angle, p. 318. Three weeks earlier Douglas had offered the same basic point at the Charleston debate. "And here let me recall to Mr. Lincoln the scriptural quotation which he has applied to the federal government, that a house divided against itself cannot stand, and ask him how does he expect this Abolition party to stand when in one-half of the state it advocates a set of principles which it has repudiated in the other half."

7. All citations from the Clinton-Bush-Perot debates were taken from the day-after transcriptions of the debates printed in the *Washington Post*, October 12, 1992, A16-A19; October 16, 1992, A33-A36; and October 20, 1992, A22-A25.

8. See, for example, Robert Bellah and Phillip E. Hammond, *Varieties of Civil Religion* (New York: Harper and Row, 1980), p. 12.

REFERENCES

Angle, P. 1991. *The Complete Lincoln-Douglas Debates of 1858*. Chicago: University of Chicago Press.

Apple, R. W. 1992. "GOP Is Flirting With the Dangers of Negativism." *New York Times*, August 19, A13:4.

Aristotle. 1954. *The Rhetoric and Poetics of Aristotle*. Introduction by Edward P.J. Corbett. Translation by W. Rhys Roberts. New York: Modern Library.

Barrett, L. 1992. "Rot on the Right." *Time*, August 24, p. 28.

Bellah, R., R. Madsen, W. Sullivan, A. Swidler, and S. M. Tipton. 1985. *Habits of the Heart: Individualism and Commitment in American Life*. Berkeley: University of California Press.

Bellah, R., and P. Hammond. 1980. *Varieties of Civil Religion*. New York: Harper and Row.

Bethel, T. 1993. "Culture War II," *The American Spectator*, July, p. 16.

Blumenthal, S. 1992/1993. "All the President's Wars." *The New Yorker*, December 28/January 4, p. 20.

Buchanan, P. 1992. Republican National Convention Speech, *Congressional Quarterly*, August 22, p. 2543.

Carlson, M. 1992. "All Eyes on Hillary." *Time*, September 14, 1992, p. 31.

Clinton, B. 1992. Democratic Convention Speeches. *New York Times*, July 16, 17, A14.

Congressional Quarterly, August 22, 1995, p. 2543.

Gergen, D. 1992. "A Fight for the Soul of the Party." *Newsweek*, August 31/September 7, p. 58.

Gore, A. 1992. Democratic National Convention Speech. *New York Times*, July 15, A12.

Habermas, J. 1973. *Legitimation Crisis.* Boston: Beacon Press.

Hunter, J. 1991. *Culture Wars: The Struggle to Define America.* New York: Basic Books.

—————. 1993. *Before the Shooting Begins: Searching for Democracy in America's Culture Wars.* New York: Free Press.

"I'm in Therapy, You're in Therapy: A Much-Analyzed Candidate Offers a 12-Step Plan to Democrats Anonymous." *New York Times,* July 15, A7.

Ivins, M. 1992. "A Feast of Fear and Hate." *Newsweek,* August 31, p. 32.

Jackson, J. 1992. Democratic National Convention Speech. *New York Times,* July 15, A12.

Jamieson, K. and D. Birdsell. 1988. *Presidential Debates: The Challenge of Creating an Informed Electorate.* Oxford: Oxford University Press.

Jordan, M. 1992. "Voters Decry GOP 'Gay Bashing." *Washington Post,* August 21, A27.

King, C. 1992. "Once This Was the Party of Frederick Douglas." *The Washington Post,* August.

Kraus, S. 1962. *The Great Debates: Background–Perspective–Effects.* Bloomington: Indiana University Press.

Lewis, A. 1992. "Merchants of Hate." *New York Times,* August 21, LA25.

Lind, M. 1992. "Buchanan, Conservatism's Ugly Face." *New York Times,* August 17.

MacIntyre, A. 1984. *After Virtue. A Study in Moral Theory.* Notre Dame, IN: University of Notre Dame Press.

McGrory, M. 1992. "Houston: Pandering and Pandemonium," *Washington Post,* August 23, C1.

New York Times, July 15, 1992, A7.

New York Times, July 17, 1992, K18.

Quayle, M. 1992. Republican Convention Speech. *Washington Post,* August 20, A34.

Rice, J. 1992. *A Disease of One's Own: Psychotherapy, Addiction, and the Emergence of "Co-Dependency."* A dissertation presented at the University of Virginia, Department of Sociology. May, 1992.

Rieff, P. 1966. *The Triumph of the Therapeutic.* Chicago: University of Chicago Press.

Stanley, A. 1992. "Family Values and Women: Is GOP a House Divided?" *New York Times,* August 20, A1.

Sykes, C. 1992. *A Nation of Victims: The Decay of the American Character.* New York: St. Martin's Press.

Toner, R. "Appeal for Trust." *New York Times,* July 14, 1992, A1.

Von Drehle, D. 1992. "A Celebration of Religious Right as Platform Panel Sees the Light." *Washington Post,* August 18, 1992, p. A15.

Whitman, C. T. 1992. "How to Be Pro-Choice and Pro-Bush." *The New York Times,* August 21, p. A25:1.

Will, G. F. 1992. "This Thick Soup of Values-Blather." *Washington Post,* August 23, C7.

Wuthnow, R. 1988. *The Restructuring of American Religion.* Princeton, NJ: Princeton University Press.

Zilbergeld, B. 1983. *The Shrinking of America.* Boston: Little, Brown and Company.
Yancey, P. 1994. "The Riddle of Bill Clinton's Faith." *Christianity Today*, April
    25, p. 29.

CROSSING CULTURAL DIVIDES:
MORAL CONFLICT AND
THE CAIRO POPULATION CONFERENCE

Joseph E. Davis

The moral/cultural issues that have generated heated conflict at the national level cut across the boundaries of nation states and even broader civilizational divides. The highly publicized debate that erupted over the 1994 U.N. Population Conference in Cairo provides a window on the cross-cultural engagement of such issues. The Cairo program was a reorientation of international population control efforts through a new focus on cultural change. Rather than North/South or religious/secular, it is argued, the public conflict over the Cairo program is best seen as a moral argument between holders of different world views, each occupying different social locations. The contestants, the issues and the tactics are analyzed. The question of cross-cultural moral conflicts in the future is also considered.

In a widely discussed 1993 article, "The Clash of Civilizations?," Samuel Huntington argued that with the end of the Cold War, "international politics moves out of its Western phase" (Huntington 1993, p. 23). This phase was characterized by conflicts between princes, nation states and ideologies. In the coming world order, the "clash of civilizations will dominate global politics. The fault lines between civilizations will be the battle lines of the future" (p. 22). Civilizations, in Huntington's definition, are broad cultural entities of common history, institutions and subjective self-identification. The differences between them are of the most basic kind:

> The people of different civilizations have different views on the relations between God and man, the individual and the group, the citizen and the state, parents and children, husband and wife, as well as differing views of the relative importance of rights and responsibilities, liberty and authority, equality and hierarchy (Huntington 1993, p. 25).

He identifies seven, perhaps eight major civilizations in the world today: Western, Confucian, Japanese, Islamic, Hindu, Slavic-Orthodox, Latin American, and "possibly African civilization" (Huntington 1993, p. 25).

The strength of this paradigm is the emphasis Huntington places on culture and the role of culture in the post-Cold War world. In an important sense, as one scholar argues, "all clashes have been of civilizations, with political and economic ideologies being mere by-products of civilizations" (Saba 1994). Yet these "by-products" often dominate the discussion of international affairs, while cultural differences remain at the periphery. Huntington moves culture back to the center.

In drawing the boundaries of civilizations and arguing for their significance, Huntington is concerned with political, security and economic outcomes. Within his "civilizations," however, conflict is being waged over precisely the cultural elements that he argues holds them together. Moreover, cross-cultural alliances have formed that bridge these elements. In order to better understand the cultural clash that moves along this other set of fault lines, this paper considers the public conflict over the United Nations International Conference on Population and Development, held September 5-13, 1994 in Cairo, Egypt. The struggle over that event suggests dividing lines that are moral in nature, and that run through and across "civilizations."

BACKGROUND

Population control has meant several different things during the course of the twentieth century. In each of its phases it has rested on the notion that fertility is not just a family matter.[1] In its first phase in this century, the eugenics movement, as it was then called, sought social control over the fertility of those considered "unfit" out of a concern for social decline brought about by the deterioration of the genetic stock. Between 1907 and 1931, for example, thirty states in the United States passed eugenic statutes providing for the sterilization of the "unfit" (Shapiro 1985).

Discredited by the Nazi experiment and advances in genetic science, social efforts at fertility control after World War II focused on a more general concern with overpopulation. Declining infant mortality rates and longer lifespans were leading to a rapidly expanding population worldwide. The movement, enhanced by the new science of demography, pressed the view that population growth must be curbed. The watershed year for this new development was 1952 when both the Population Council and the International Planned Parenthood Federation were founded (in part by activists from the eugenics movement[2]). Under the influence of these two organizations, and a growing number of others, new concerns about demographic expansion, what later would be called the "population explosion," were met with increasing efforts to foster fertility control. These efforts focused on the underdeveloped countries, the birth rates having fallen steadily in the developed (many of which are now below net replacement fertility). Governments were called upon to actively involve themselves in regulating national population growth.

The United Nations has long been a major player in promoting population control initiatives. Its decennial population conferences are a major part of this leadership role. The final document signed at Cairo was built in part on the World Population Plan of Action adopted at the World Population Conference held in Bucharest, Romania, in 1974. The Plan of Action focused on making birth control technology available, promoting family planning and encouraging governments to set goals for reducing birth rates. It called for the developed countries to provide the funding necessary to reach demographic objectives. At the Bucharest meeting, underdeveloped countries clashed with developed over the rich countries' disproportional use of natural resources, imposition of population control, and failure to provide adequate economic development aid. The 1984 International Conference on Population in Mexico City worked within the framework of the Plan and produced a set of recommendations aimed at fostering its realization. Again, nations were encouraged to create policy and set goals at the national level to slow population expansion. In contrast to Bucharest, the governments of underdeveloped countries had largely come on board with the developed in viewing their populations as growing too fast.[3] Talk of population control as "genocide," heard at Bucharest, grew muted.

In the years since Mexico City, an increasing number of governments have adopted population policies. Some seventy nations now have one (Eberstadt 1994). But even in the absence of explicit population targets, a large percentage of governments are involved in family-planning programs.[4] According to a U.N. report, in 1993, 89 percent of governments were providing direct or indirect support to such programs (U.N. Secretary General 1994, para. 129). Many governments also use the media—increasingly available even in the poorest areas—to aggressively promote population agendas.[5] These efforts have had an effect. In a 1991 report marking its first twenty years, the United Nations Population Fund (UNFPA) noted that in just one generation population control efforts "have already helped to produce a world population that is well over 400 million smaller than it otherwise would have been" (Sadik 1991, p. 1).

In that same report, the Fund described population programs as aimed at "providing couples with the information and means required to freely exercise their human right to determine the number and the spacing of their children ... " (Sadik 1991, p. 1). This description is indicative of the general rationale that animated the Bucharest and Mexico City conferences, namely, that population control programs are designed to give people more choice in family planning. While governmental incentive and disincentive schemes were allowed under the World Population Plan of Action, they were not to violate this freedom of choice (U.N. 1974, para. 34).[6] At Cairo, the notion of free choice was taken a step further. Out of a concern that population programs can become coercive, there was a movement, albeit tentative and inconsistent, away from target-driven demographic goals.[7] Indeed, the term "control" in population control was replaced with "stabilization." As the British Minister for Overseas Development described the "new approach": "population stabilisation through sustainable development, not population control" (Chalker 1994).

But what happens when people make the wrong choice? As scholars have noted, availability of contraception does not automatically revolutionize people's view of family size (Katz and Stern 1980; Eberstadt 1994). Even among those in underdeveloped countries who have chosen to use birth control, the aim is not necessarily to have fewer children. As Kingsley Davis argued more than 25 years ago, the "population problem" is the result of *wanted* births (Davis 1967). Providing contraception can reduce unwanted pregnancies, but it does not necessarily yield population stabilization. Thus, if birth rates are to be lowered across the board something additional is needed. What Bucharest and Mexico City didn't do, according to Nafis Sadik, director of the UNFPA and secretary general of the Cairo conference, "was establish an enabling environment in which people could make the *right* decisions" (Conners 1994, p. M3, emphasis added). The issues of "sustainable development," "empowerment of the individual," and "gender equality" were seen, according to Sadik, as key to providing this environment. They played a defining role in the Draft Programme of Action for the Cairo conference (U.N. 1994a). While not entirely absent from the Bucharest and Mexico City planks, at Cairo these issues were grafted onto international population policy in a new way. The intense public controversy that surrounded the conference centered on implications of these new elements.[8]

THE PUBLIC CONFLICT OVER CAIRO

By the time the delegates of 174 U.N. member countries (and 6 non-member countries) and more than 2000 representatives of non-governmental organizations (NGOs) had gathered in Cairo for the U.N. conference and its parallel NGO Forum '94, the outpouring of commentary on the conference was already massive. Much of the coverage of the conflict in the English language press, both in the United States and elsewhere, cast the discord in terms of a few rearguard traditionalists interrupting the march toward a new and important international consensus. Indeed, this is how the organizers of the conference and certain prominent government representatives, such as Timothy Wirth of the United States, and many of the non-governmental organizations involved with the conference tended to characterize the issues (see, e.g., Catholics Speak Out 1994; (IWHC) International Women's Health Coalition 1994; views quoted in (NPR) National Public Radio 1994; Rensberger and Lancaster 1994; Kirschten 1994). However, a closer reading of the concerns being expressed suggests a different interpretation, raising doubts about the emerging "consensus" and how it was achieved.

The Draft Programme was the result of three preliminary drafting conferences. On March 18, 1994, prior to the third meeting, Pope John Paul II addressed a letter to Nafis Sadik raising serious objections to the draft program then in circulation:

> The draft final document ... is a cause of grave concern to me.... Indeed, certain basic ethical principles are contradicted by its proposals. Political or ideological considerations cannot be, by themselves, the basis on which essential decisions for the future of our society are founded (Pope John Paul II 1994, p. 2).

The third conference, held in April, did not allay these concerns. Objections raised by the Vatican and a few other countries to the 113-page final Draft Programme of Action led to certain phrases and sentences being put in brackets for further discussion at the two-day preliminary conference in Cairo and the conference itself. After April "an unprecedented contest of moral values" (Lancaster and Rensberger 1994, p. A12) on an international plane took place.

The Parties to the Conflict

In order to get a picture of the parties to the conflict, an initial task is to consider whom the public contest was *not* between. First, the divide was not simply between the developed countries and the underdeveloped, or, to borrow a phrase from Kishore Mahbubani, between "the West and the Rest" (Mahbubani 1992). As will be suggested below, there were issues that ran along this fault line. They were not, however, central elements of the *public* debate. In the public forum some argued that the Cairo program was largely a Western, and even specifically United States plan (see, e.g., Taheri 1994a; activists quoted in Waldman 1994, p. 10).[9] But this is not entirely accurate. Although the United States was a significant force behind the Programme of Action, a large number of women's organizations from the developed countries took part in its drafting (Rensberger 1994), as did a wide variety of developing country private and governmental family planning groups.[10] Further, the U.N. bureaucracy responsible for the conference and the national delegations who participated at all stages were primarily non-Western nationals (the conference general secretary was a Pakistani). Admittedly, these non-Westerners were elites and not necessarily representative of their compatriots.[11] But this fact only further emphasizes the need to draw finer lines of distinction.

Second, contrary to the arguments of some (e.g., Rosenfeld 1994a), this was not simply a fight between those who take a "religious" and those who take a "secular" approach to life. A "multi-religious consultation" held before the conference issued a widely publicized joint statement that was critical of many aspects of the Draft Programme. The accompanying papers by scholars representing Hinduism, Buddhism, Orthodoxy, Catholicism, Protestantism (Southern Baptist), Islam, Baha'i and Judaism, however, show some important differences across religious traditions (World Conference on Religion and Peace 1994). Clearly, the women's movement cuts through religious communities, and this includes the Muslim. The same is true on the specific matter of abortion, so hotly contested at Cairo. Catholics for a Free Choice, a small, pro-choice Catholic group, for instance, was constantly quoted by the media challenging the Vatican position and was among a group of progressive religious organizations that placed a full-page ad in the *New York Times* insisting that the Vatican was wrong about fertility control (Catholics Speak Out 1994). The examples could be multiplied.

Rather than North/South or religious/secular, the public conflict over Cairo is best seen as a cultural conflict between the holders of different world views, world views rooted in different systems of moral understanding. Very broadly speaking, following Hunter (1991), we might distinguish between the "orthodox" on one side and the "progressives" on the other. Central to the orthodox world view is a commitment to an "external, definable and transcendent [moral] authority" (Hunter 1991, p. 44). At Cairo, the orthodox spoke what William Vendley of the non-sectarian World Conference on Religion and Peace described as a language of moral norms rooted in some larger vision of the common good (Steinfels 1994). The adherents of this moral perspective were represented at Cairo by the Vatican, some Muslim imams, other religious leaders, a small array of NGOs, several governmental delegations and some individual members of governmental delegations.[12] Additionally, various orthodox citizens and groups publicly commented on the Cairo proceedings (e.g., International Institute for Culture 1994), including Islam's most prestigious scholarly voice, the Al-Azhar Islamic University in Egypt (Reuters News Service 1994). A Catholic-church led demonstration in Manila drew 200,000 participants (Dikkenberg 1994).[13]

In the progressive world view, according to Hunter (1991), "moral authority tends to reside in personal experience or scientific rationality, or either of these in conversation with particular religious or cultural traditions" (p. 45). At Cairo, the progressives spoke what Vendley described as the language of specific situations, hard cases— i.e., rape, no or unsafe medical care—that are seen to contest the applicability of existing moral norms. Or they spoke the language of demography and public health, a language of numbers and instrumental problem-solving (Steinfels 1994). The progressives were the dominant force at the conference, including many governmental delegations and their members,[14] many NGOs, including feminist, population control and some religious groups, and the U.N. population bureaucracy itself. The alliance of these groups spoke, for the most part, through the Draft Programme itself. Many additional progressive individuals and groups also contributed to the conversation on population and development from afar.

When seen as a clash of moral communities, the alliances that took sides in the public conflict over Cairo take on new intelligibility. The befuddlement and consternation in some quarters that greeted Muslim support for Vatican positions regarding the Draft Programme are a case in point (Stanford 1994; activists quoted in Stackhouse 1994). In fact relations between the Vatican and Muslim governments have frequently been tense in recent years as the Vatican has sought to defend the human rights of Christian minorities in Islamic lands. However, both the Vatican and much of Islam share opposition to many practices seen as morally objectionable, including abortion, homosexuality, and sexual promiscuity, all of which were prominent at Cairo. Both question the moral foundations of the West and are alienated from Western and Westernized elites. Both fear that the West is using international organizations in an attempt to destroy the traditional ways of life with which they identify. A pragmatic alliance between them on such issues has a moral logic, their other differences notwithstanding. As the Vatican spokesman, Joaquin Navarro-Valls, observed with respect to this development: "It's not strange in any way if representatives of other religions might have felt a confluence with the Holy See" (quoted in Drozdiak 1994, p. A19).

On the progressive side, the joining of the women's movement to the population control movement also follows a certain logic. In the developed countries, the feminist movement has placed its stress on reproductive choice and access to reproductive services as a necessary condition for equality and personal autonomy. In general, the movement has aggressively supported any development that will free women from their biology and render motherhood an individual and voluntary option. The result has been a feminist-family planning alliance that makes some parts of both movements virtually indistinguishable. Internationally, this alliance has been gaining momentum among elites since at least the 1985 U.N. Conference on Women in Nairobi. That meeting, according to a prominent NGO director, "was a transforming meeting for the women's movement." At Cairo, she argued, "what you [will] see is 10 years of political and financial maturity in the women's movement" (Kirschten 1994, p. 1017). The key role that "advancing gender equity" and "empowerment of women" play in the Programme of Action is testimony to this development. "The population debate," in the words of one observer, "has become a showcase for the internationalization of what used to be called the feminist movement" (Kirschten 1994, p. 1017; cf. Associated Press 1994; Elliott and Dickey 1994, p. 22; Murphy 1994). This alliance makes no secret of the fact that it sees orthodox groups as major stumbling blocks to the promotion of its agenda.

The Contested Issues

The issues that dominated the public discussion over Cairo were fundamentally moral in nature. These issues cluster into three levels of public conflict: on the surface, a conflict over language; beneath that a conflict over human rights; and, finally, deeper yet, a conflict over the shape of the future.

The Conflict Over Language

As noted above, after the third preliminary meeting in April 1994, certain phrases and sentences in the final Draft Programme of Action were put into brackets for further discussion at Cairo. The majority of these bracketed portions captured what the orthodox saw as code language for unacceptable moral positions on certain key issues. In each case, except concerning development and migration, the progressives maintained that the orthodox were reading ideas into the document that simply were not there.

Abortion. Abortion was treated in the Draft Programme from a health point of view. Phrases in the Draft Programme, such as "reproductive rights," "reproductive health care," "fertility regulation," and "safe motherhood," were challenged by the orthodox as promoting the acceptance of abortion (see, e.g., European Catholic Bishops 1994; College of Cardinals 1994). The United States, which had sought to promote abortion rights at Cairo (Novak 1994), backed off in the days before the conference began, with U.S. Vice President Gore insisting on several occasions that "the United States has not sought, does not seek and will not seek to establish any international right to an abortion" (quoted in Branigin 1994). Nafis Sadik argued that contrary to what some were saying the Draft Programme "does not advocate or promote abortion" (quoted in AP 1994).

Marriage/Family. The orthodox found the lack of any reference to the institution of marriage in the Programme, and the use of phrases such as "the family in all its forms" to be expressions of a denigration of the traditional family. Progressives insisted that the Programme was simply acknowledging the fact that there are many single parents in the world.

Promiscuity/Adultery. The orthodox saw these behaviors promoted by Draft Programme references to the rights of individuals to "sexual health" and in references to providing adolescents with sex education outside the family and reproductive and sexual health care in a confidential manner. Some Islamic leaders even saw this advice as promoting the conditions for greater prostitution (RNS 1994). In a joint statement, the Catholic Bishops of the United States argued that the Draft Programme "treats all sexual behavior as acceptable, even for unmarried adolescents" (U.S. Bishops 1994). The progressives denied a hidden agenda in the Programme language, but emphasized that in the "real world" of AIDS and teen sexual activity, what people actually do sexually must not be glossed over with ideals.

Homosexuality. Islamic groups especially saw homosexuality in Programme references urging an end to discrimination against "other unions" besides marriage. Progressives countered that the "other unions" are common-law marriages which are quite common in some countries, such as those of the Caribbean.

Development/Migration. Not all the bracketed language in the Draft Programme represented orthodox concerns. Several phrases put in brackets by the developed countries dealt with issues of development aid to the underdeveloped. An additional phrase dealt with a "right to family reunification," that is, where families have become separated by migration of some members to another country a right to reunite the family through migration of the remaining family members would be recognized. While these questions had a more clearly North-South dimension, they also had a moral dimension that was raised in the public debate by the orthodox. First, the concern was expressed that the developed countries were solely interested in population control and not development. Second, the right of family reunification was argued as a matter of basic justice and recognition of the family as the core unit of society.

The Conflict Over Human Rights

Below the specific conflicts over the Draft Programme language, a deeper level of conflict over different conceptions of human rights can be seen. This conflict played itself out along three dimensions:

Health rights vs. non-medicalized moral norms. Here the clash of a morality of general moral norms with a morality of specific situations is most apparent. For progressives, the large number of maternal deaths and complications arising from unsafe abortions, AIDS and sexually transmitted diseases, and teen births must be urgently addressed. Condoms, reproductive health services, education in sexual health and the like address, in order to alleviate, specific crises. They do not promote these problems. In treating abortion and some matters of sexuality in a health framework, the Draft Programme, in the orthodox view, obscured "objective moral criteria." For the orthodox, the moral norms are clear; specific hard cases do not invalidate them. Rather, they bespeak the need to address the cultural forces that promote them. Handling problem pregnancies, AIDS and adolescent sexuality require means that are consistent with basic human dignity, including protecting the rights of the unborn, and cannot be resolved with "technological fixes."

Individual rights vs. family rights. The progressive response at Cairo to the larger questions of sexuality, fertility and population growth centered on promotion of gender equity and the empowerment of women as individuals to make decisions. The Draft Programme included extensive discussion of fostering women's involvement in all levels of decision making, from the family to the shape and nature of society; greater and more equal workforce participation; greater educational opportunities; more equal roles in parenting and with household tasks; and ready access to the means of fertility control. The problem for the orthodox hinged on definitions of women's rights that are individualistic in their focus and that pit women against the family. Not the individual but "the family should make decisions about the family," as one Catholic activist put it (quoted in Elliott and Dickey 1994, p. 24). In the orthodox view, gender roles are conceived within a religiously grounded paradigm of natural complimentarity within the family, not of an equality understood as sameness. They saw their view of women's "rights" trumped by the Draft Programme's feminist viewpoint (Navarro-Valls 1994). Further, the family is seen as the cornerstone of society and its rights to "responsible parenthood" transcend those of the state. Population programs that empower individuals at the expense of institutions, such as the family, remove an important check on the power of the state. Additionally, given that the rights of the family transcend those of the state, family reunification should be recognized.

"Sustainable development" vs. "integral development." For the progressives, the long-term good of persons requires "sustainable development." Genuine improvements in human welfare cannot be made or sustained, regardless of economic aid, when the number of those to feed, house and educate keeps growing. Thus, funding population control is an important, even essential, form of development assistance. Nafis Sadik told the third drafting conference that population issues must be joined to economic development strategies so that they are "not viewed as an optional extra, something that can be discarded or treated with benign neglect in response to perceived sensitivities of any type" (quoted in Kirschten 1994, p. 1019). The good of the human family and individual families requires putting population control on this new and more secure footing.

The Vatican criticized the Draft Programme because it contained so little discussion of development. According to Archbishop Renato Martino, chief Vatican representative to the United Nations: "Only several out of 113 pages deal with development. That fact alone tells you something about the priorities of the rich Western countries" (quoted in Drozdiak 1994, p. A19). The key concern is that rather than fighting poverty with reductions in trade barriers, debt relief, and other economic means, the developed countries are using birth control funding to avoid their social justice responsibilities. Moreover, true development is not just an economic matter, it must be "directed to the true good of every person and of the whole person" (Pope John Paul II 1994, p. 2). Among other things, this "integral development," requires respect for cultural heritages and the freedom of persons to be "active agents of their own development."

The Conflict Over the Future

Beneath the human rights debate lay a larger set of concerns over who shapes the future and in what image. Both sides saw Cairo as an historic turning point that will have far-reaching and long-term cultural and demographic consequences. According to Pope John Paul II: "What is at stake is the very future of humanity" (Pope John Paul II 1994, p. 2). A progressive columnist in the United States described the conference as "the international embrace of the largest calculated act of social engineering in history" (Rosenfeld 1994b).

What the conference might mean for the future, however, is perceived differently. For the progressives, Cairo came none too soon. Although population programs have had real success, the global growth rate remains high and a new and major effort must be made to slow it. Environmental preservation, economic progress, political stability and everyone's quality of life are at stake. The shift to a developmental approach that emphasizes women's health and empowerment taps "into sources of spontaneous motivation among the programs' intended beneficiaries and agents" (Rosenfeld 1994b) and is a dignified and non-coercive way to change fertility rates. Shifting away from governmental population targets and increasing the role of NGOs at all levels of policy and implementation will further harness and reduce coercive approaches.[15] More generally, modern progress, especially with regard to women's education and freedom and gender equality, is a good that should be shared everywhere (see activist's views cited in Goodstein 1994). New funding for the women's movement will continue the momentum gained since the 1985 conference in Nairobi. Despite disturbing demographic trends, the future can yet be bright.

While welcoming the decreased focus on national population targets at Cairo, the orthodox side expressed concern that the new focus at Cairo masks a more subtle coercion, namely a new effort to export a secular, materialistic culture to traditional societies. In a letter to heads of state in March 1994, the Pope argued that the Cairo conference was seeking to impose "a lifestyle typical of certain fringes within developed societies ... which are materially rich and secularized" (quoted in Woodward 1994, p. 25). A Muslim author put it even more strongly: "The draft's authors wish to establish a universal dictatorship in which the tastes of what is still a small minority, mostly in wealthy countries, are dictated to the whole of mankind on such crucial issues as sex, love, procreation, marriage and family" (Taheri 1994a).

The orthodox do not share the alarm over population growth. The underdeveloped countries have in the past sounded the concern that population control is an imposition from the Western countries, motivated by racism (eugenics) or by a strategy to protect Western economic dominance and standards of living. This concern was raised again at Cairo, especially by the orthodox; it can be heard, for instance, in the statement of Archbishop Renato Martino quoted above. The massively disproportional use of resources by the West, first linked to questions of overpopulation by ecologists beginning in the late 1960s, was also again voiced at Cairo (Pope John Paul II 1994; views expressed in Crossette 1994, p. 16), though not just by the orthodox (Greene 1994; Kirschten 1994, p. 1019). For the orthodox, however, the moral issue is one of a world made in the image of the West and bent by the West to serve its material interests. This is the vision of the future that they feared Cairo sought to advance and institutionalize.

The Tactics of Conflict

For both sides at Cairo, then, much was at stake. This importance is not just visible in the substance of position statements but in the various tactics used to portray opponents. Many of the quotes already used suggest the effort by both progressives and orthodox to characterize each other's views as unworthy of careful consideration. Briefly, this effort came in four main forms.

1.   Painting enemies with a brush of fanaticism. On the progressive side, for example, the fact that some Muslim groups and governments supported the Vatican on certain issues was loudly ridiculed as undermining the Vatican's moral legitimacy. An oft-repeated but untrue rumor even had it that the Vatican had sent special envoys to the governments of Libya and Iraq. The fact that some Catholics do not follow their leadership on matters of contraception and abortion, and that some Muslim women dissent from Islamic approaches to gender roles were cited as evidence that the orthodox leadership is extremist (e.g., Cohen 1994). The Vatican was also repeatedly accused of trying to force its moral views on others. On the orthodox side, as we have seen, the Cairo conference was criticized as the effort of a "rich and secularized" elite to establish an "international dictatorship" and impose its culture and interests on everyone else.

2.   Treating the moral debate as a distraction from more important issues. This was a progressive charge against the orthodox. Spending so much time wrangling over a few moral issues was seen to distract from the more important work of addressing the real problem, population stabilization. Referring to the debate over abortion, for example, the Egyptian minister of culture said: "It is very unfortunate that all these honest and distinguished people working to save humanity have been distracted by this issue" (quoted in Rensberger and Lancaster 1994).

3.   Viewing the other side as having a hidden agenda. As already discussed, the orthodox saw the Draft Programme as laced with code words disguising morally objectionable positions. But the progressives also found hidden agendas in the moral concerns expressed by the orthodox. They consistently asserted, for example, that religious leaders' concerns were actually rooted in a desire to continue to subjugate women. The former Canadian ambassador to the U.N. called orthodox objections "torrents of thinly veiled misogyny" (quoted in Stackhouse 1994, p. A1; cf. Nafis Sadik in Conners 1994).

4.   Treating certain ideas as not open to discussion. In general, this was the response of the progressives to any suggestion that "overpopulation" is a problematical concept. One critic argued: "The

Vatican's tendency to dismiss the notion of any population crisis at all takes it out of the circle of seriousness on this issue" (Rosenfeld 1994a; cf. Rowen 1994). Responding to a statement from the Cairo-based Council on American-Islamic Relations that criticized Western-imposed population programs, another journalist countered with the progressive trump card on global demographic trends: "The numbers ... speak for themselves" (Waldman 1994, p. 10). On the orthodox side, of course, the moral issues seen to be at stake at Cairo are fundamentally non-negotiable.

POWER AND THE "CONSENSUS" ON OVERPOPULATION

In the period just before the Cairo conference there was much talk of an emerging worldwide consensus on the population problem and the best means to address it. "Consensus" described those portions of the Programme that were not explicitly challenged. By a commonly cited estimate, 92 percent of the Draft Programme was uncontested in this way. Long hours of negotiation on the bracketed phrases during the conference closed the gap even further. It was affirmed that abortion should not be seen as a method of family planning. Ambiguous language was employed in other sections to allow for various readings. The family was affirmed as the basic unit of society. Parental consent was inserted to neutralize the concern over the promotion of adolescent promiscuity. Adding a sentence providing that each nation's laws and practices guide application diffused concerns still further. With a few countries appending reservations, at the conference close a final joint document was signed (U.N. 1994b).

Following Bourdieu (1992), we might view the Cairo conference conceptually as a "field of struggles" in which different actors competed to establish a monopoly defined by their views. Each field, or field of power, has specific types of authority effective in it and recognizes certain types of resources or "capital." Demographic expertise, population control experience and resources, international political standing, and/or a development budget are at least among the major types of "capital" relevant to a United Nations population conference such as Cairo. Dominance in the field is the power to speak on behalf of the international community. The progressives brought considerable "capital" to the conference and exercised great authority at it. Comprised of Western elites and educated, minority elites in developing countries, this alliance dominated the U.N. bureaucracy, the drafting process, the conference itself and the NGO Forum. In their view it was their Programme of Action and their "consensus" that needed to be protected at Cairo from the "narrowly nationalistic or sectarian interests" (New York Times Editors 1994) of the orthodox.

The orthodox, on the other hand, possessed primarily moral capital. Although not in possession of the capital required to achieve dominance, religious leaders were able to use their moral authority to partially block the path to legitimation. Efforts to discredit the orthodox by arguing that they could not speak credibly on behalf of the people that progressive policies affect, failed. This credible representation, coupled with appeals to a higher law, gave orthodox moral suasion bite and put them in a position to obstruct consensus by forcing the moral issues to the surface. Despite their sometimes hostile rhetoric, the progressives recognized this power and actively sought to reach a compromise on the draft language in order to gain orthodox support. This effort can also be seen in the way the United States backed off its abortion legalization advocacy in the face of Vatican opposition, and in the way some Islamic governments, including host Egypt, were at pains to emphasize the conflicts between the Draft Programme and Islam.[16]

For their part, the orthodox also compromised. As argued above, more than a few bracketed statements and their implications were at issue. Different views of human rights and different visions of the future lie behind the specific language debates. These might be described as levels of overt and covert conflict (Lukes 1974). The bracketed issues are an instance of overt conflict. In this case, observable differences were contested within the framework of the conference itself. On the covert level are those grievances publicly expressed but given no entry into the conference proceedings. Traditional Islamic views on gender roles and Catholic opposition to "artificial" means of birth regulation are instances of such concerns.[17] At Cairo, the orthodox walked the fine line that always characterizes the modern Western engagement of religion and politics, a line between too much involvement in the political process—jeopardizing status and legitimacy—and too much detachment—status becomes irrelevant to worldly matters. At Cairo, the orthodox shelved their covert grievances and simply concentrated on using their alliance to contest the bracketed language and gain wording changes. Unwilling to authorize such compromise, four Islamic countries—Saudi Arabia, Lebanon, Sudan, and Iraq—boycotted the conference, as did the female prime ministers of two others—Turkey and Bangladesh. Additionally, several predominantly Catholic or Muslim nations were reported to have downgraded their delegations (Stackhouse 1994, p. A5).

Overall, the orthodox effort to gain limited compromise was quite successful.[18] Referring to the Vatican, a progressive Dutch delegate who led various negotiation sessions, said at the end of the conference: "They are very good. They got all the concessions they could get" (quoted in Lancaster and Rensberger 1994, p. A12). The orthodox claimed some victory in this achievement. The International Right to Life Federation, for instance, described the conference as "clearly a defeat for the Clinton Administration" (Mullen 1994, p. 10), and thus, progressive forces.

In the end at Cairo, however, as the progressive Dutch delegate pointed out: "The gist of the text is still pretty much what it was" (quoted in Lancaster and Rensberger 1994, p. A12). The "largest calculated act of social engineering in history" received its mandate.

CONCLUSION

The alliances that were in conflict at Cairo cut across larger, more historic civilizational distinctions. Convergent moral communities from North and South, East and West joined forces to address basic moral questions and what will become of more traditional ways of life. While the political significance of this development should not be overemphasized—particularly in the orthodox case where the alliance has little if any institutional expression—neither should it be overlooked. If the fault lines between civilizations are of importance to understanding the next phase of conflict in the world, as Huntington argues, then cultural alignments that cross these divides cannot be ignored. Surely they may meliorate conflict on some issues, yet, as demonstrated at Cairo, they open up new fissures on others.

But was Cairo a one-time, if spectacular, moral conflict or the harbinger of more such cross-cultural engagements in the future? Surely, with respect to the question of population control, the conflict that took shape around the Cairo conference did not end when the gavel finally brought the proceedings to a close. Rather it entered a new phase. Cultural change, in part pursued by population and women's movement NGOs, is at the heart of the Cairo approach. Implementing this change, or better, continuing to implement it, will meet with local resistance, international consensus or not. The issues are simply too fundamental to go away. It seems safe to say that at least when various international windows on change taking place at the local level, such as U.N. conferences, briefly open up, the broader conflict will also be revisited.

More generally, Cairo may be seen as an instance of the larger process of globalization and the export of Western culture to non-Western peoples. This process has been under way for a long time and it affects elites and non-elites differently. They have different "ways of life" at stake. This was obvious at Cairo where the basic division followed these lines. In recent years, a host of new movements on behalf of non-elites, quite often under religious leadership, have arisen or been revitalized to resist cultural change. In many countries, the secular legitimation of the nation-state is under new forms of assault (Juergensmeyer 1993) and ethnic consciousness dramatically on the rise. As paradoxical as it seems, in the face of formidable progressivist agenda-setting and the perceived erosion of cultural practices and values, non-elites may increasingly seek to form cross-cultural alliances, as at Cairo, to protect their differences.[19] Cultural distinctions are both real and important. As globalization proceeds, moral conflict rooted in ways of life that cross-cut historic cultural cleavages may find new expression on the global level.

NOTES

1. Population control is here distinguished from "family planning," which has been the focus of various groups since at least the nineteenth century. While population control is usually pursued through family planning groups, the idea of family planning itself is simply concerned with techniques of birth control and spacing in light of individual family needs.

2. For instance, one of the founders of the Population Council, trustee from 1952 to 1968 and president from 1957 to 1959, was eugenics leader Frederick Osborn. Osborn was secretary of the American Eugenics Society from 1928 to 1972 (Shapiro 1985, pp. 45-47).

3. Even some governments—for example, Iran—that otherwise take public positions in opposition to Western population control efforts are now actively engaged in promoting domestic population control (Taheri 1994b).

4. Indicative of the widespread acceptance of population stabilization efforts, the chairman of the "higher committee" of the Cairo conference when asked if the developed countries were pressuring the underdeveloped on the matter of population control, responded: "On the contrary, the developed countries are pressuring developed states to get contributions to population and family programs" (News Agencies 1994b).

5. The Cairo Programme of Action encourages this development: "Governments should use television soap operas and other traditional media to encourage discussion of sensitive topics ..." (U.N. 1994a, para. 11.23).

6. Various incentives and disincentives are used. For example, in Pakistan, poor women are paid to undergo sterilizations (Crossette 1994, p. 16). In Zimbabwe, parents get tax deductions only for the first four children (Drogin 1994, p. 8). Some countries use very coercive measures to control population growth. India, for instance, has used sterilization quotas and China has a legal limit on family size.

7. Governmental-level policy setting is still stressed. There is additionally, however, a new and heavy emphasis on the role of non-governmental organizations (NGOs). Dr. Sadik, secretary-general of the conference, noted the changed focus in a CNN special: "One of the biggest changes in the approach, is how to involve people, communities, NGOs much more in the designing and the implementation of policy, and I would say that the chapter on partnership with NGOs, with a small 'n,' is one of the strongest chapters ever to come out [in a] U.N. document" (CNN 1994).

8. A note on method. This paper focuses on the public debate over Cairo carried on in the English language press. The coverage of the Cairo conference was assessed from the following sample of press sources: (Canada): *Globe and Mail*; (China): *China Daily*; (Egypt): *Egyptian News*; (England): *Manchester Guardian Weekly, The Tablet, The Times*; (Hong Kong): *Asian Wall Street Journal, South China Morning Post*; (India): *Hindustan Times, The Telegraph*; (Ireland): *Irish Times*; (Israel): *Jerusalem Post* [International Edition]; (Japan): *Japan Times*; (Kenya): *Daily Nation*; (Kuwait): *Arab Times*; (Saudi Arabia): *Arab News*; (Singapore): *The Straits Times*; (South Africa): *Johannesburg Star*; (Tunisia): *Tunisia News*; (Turkey): *Newspot*; (United States): *Cable News Network, Christian Science Monitor, Los Angeles News, National Catholic Register, National Journal, National Public Radio, Newsweek, New York Times, Washington Post*; (Vatican): *L'Osservatore Romano* [English Weekly Edition]. These sources represent (1) a sample of prominent U.S. news sources that gave substantial coverage to the Cairo meeting; and (2) all foreign English-language newspapers available to the author.

The most serious weakness of using English language media is the underrepresentation of "orthodox" (see below) voices from the developed countries. As one expert on religious nationalism told the author, most opposition to the conference in these countries was expressed in non-English sources (Mark Juergensmeyer, personal communication). Consequently, the views of the orthodox are overrepresented here by the leadership of the Catholic Church.

9.   Perhaps the strongest statement in this regard was made by Liaquat Baloch, leader of the Pakistani Islamic group Jamaat-i-Islami: "This [Cairo conference] is an American plot against Islamic teachings. It not only wants a military domination but also an intellectual and cultural hegemony over the Muslim nation" (AFP 1994).

10.   This was not just a conflict between governments over governmental policy. Non-governmental organizations of many varieties played a very large role in the preparatory meetings and at Cairo. The three preliminary meetings, for example, were directed by officials of the International Planned Parenthood Federation (Woodward 1994), and the chairman of the committee where the main negotiations took place was Fred Sai, the president of IPPF (Miller 1994, p. 1153). In addition to private family planning groups, more than 200 women's advocacy organizations were involved in the writing of the Draft Programme (Rensberger 1994).

11.   A consistent theme running through opposition coming from developing countries was the grievance that their conference delegates were not representative of popular sentiment (e.g., in the Philippines, see Dikkenberg 1994).

12.   One reporter covering the conference estimated that 10 governmental delegations and "two dozen non-governmental, conservative Catholic, and anti-abortion groups" supported at least some Vatican positions at Cairo (Moffett 1994, p. 4). At the conclusion of the conference about 20 Latin American and Arab countries expressed reservations to the conference program. These official reservations generally raised concerns consistent with orthodox concerns, i.e., about abortion, the family, sex outside marriage and family reunification (U.N. 1994b). Some African nations also supported orthodox positions (Koopman 1995).

13.   An Egyptian Islamic group even threatened violence against all foreigners "taking part in the licentiousness conference" (Georgy 1994).

14.   The IPPF, for instance, had more than 70 representatives as staff or volunteers on the delegations of some 60 countries (Miller 1994, p. 1153). Of course, a great number of countries, delegations were not heard from in the public debate. While many delegations insisted in their opening statements at the conference that they opposed abortion as a method of family planning, their orientation toward many of the other conflicted issues was not publicly voiced in the English language press here reviewed, and they did not enter reservations at the close of the conference.

15.   As noted above, the conference document is not consistent on this new emphasis.

16.   In her widely publicized opening speech to the conference, the Prime Minister of Pakistan, Benazir Bhutto, who was attending the conference over serious objections from some Pakistani Muslim groups (AFP 1994), argued: "Regrettably, this conference's document contains serious flaws striking at the heart of a great many cultural values in the North and in the South and in the church and in the mosque." The final Programme of Action, she said, must not seek to "impose adultery, abortion, sex education, and other such matters" on all countries (quoted in News Agencies 1994a).

17.   The Catholic Church never raised the issue of contraception in the negotiations at Cairo (Lancaster and Rensberger 1994, p. A12).

18.   The effort to gain recognition of a "right" to family reunification, however, was defeated. The final text encourages countries to "promote" family reunification (U.N. 1994b, para. 10.12).

19.   An editorial in a Teheran newspaper a few weeks before the Cairo conference
was suggestive: "Collaboration between religious governments in support of
outlawing abortion is a fine beginning for the conception of collaboration in other
fields" (NCR Editors 1994).

REFERENCES

Agence France Presse (AFP). 1994. "Activists Urge Bhutto to Eschew Cairo
    Conference." *Arab News* (September 3):8.
Associated Press (AP). 1994. "Fighting Population With Women's Rights." *Los
    Angeles Times* (September 4):A29.
Bourdieu, P., and L. Wacquant. 1992. *An Invitation to Reflexive Sociology.*
    Chicago: University of Chicago Press.
Branigin, W. 1994. "Indonesia, Philippines Differ Sharply in Population Dynamics."
    Washington Post (September 5):A20.
Cable News Network (CNN). 1994. CNN Specials: "Beyond the Numbers, Part 2:
    Specific Issues Addressed." *Cable News Network* (July 3).
Catholics Speak Out. 1994. "An Open Letter to Pope John Paul II on the Question
    of Contraception (paid political advertisement). *New York Times* (September
    6):A11.
Chalker, L. "Good Work at Cairo." *The Tablet* (October 1):1218.
Cohen, R. 1994. "Another Urban VIII?" *Washington Post* (September 9):A21.
College of Cardinals. 1994. "Cairo Population Conference." *L'Osservatore Romano*
    (June 22):7.
Conners, L. 1994. "Interview: Nafis Sadik." *Los Angeles Times* (September 4):M3.
Crossette, B. 1994. "U.N. is Facing Angry Debate on Population." *New York Times*
    (September 4):(1)1,16.
Davis, K. 1967. "Population Policy: Will Current Programs Succeed?" *Science*
    157:730-739.
Dikkenberg, J. 1994. "Backing for Vatican at Huge Rally." *South China Morning
    Post* (August 20-21).
Drogin, B. 1994. "Zimbabwe: Family Planning Is African Success Story." *Los
    Angeles Times* (September 5):A1,8,9.
Drozdiak, W. 1994. "Vatican Faces Leadership Test at Population Forum."
    Washington Post (September 5):A1,18,19.
Eberstadt, N. 1994. "Population Policy: Ideology as Science." *First Things*
    (January):30-38.
Elliott, M., and C. Dickey. 1994. "Body Politics." *Newsweek* (September 12):22-26.
European Catholic Bishops. 1994. "Final Declaration of the European Episcopal
    Commissions for the Family." *L'Osservatore Romano* (July 27):2.
Georgy, M. 1994. "Egypt's Islamic Group Warns U.N. Conference." *New York
    Times* (August 28):(1)6.
Goodstein, L. 1994. "The Culture War Goes Global." *Washington Post*
    (September 4):C2.

Greene, W. 1994. "Overconspicuous Overconsumption." *New York Times* (August 28):(4)15.

Hunter, J. 1991. *Culture Wars.* New York: Basic Books.

Huntington, S. 1993. "The Clash of Civilizations." *Foreign Affairs* (Summer):22-49.

International Institute for Culture (IIC). 1994. "An Open Letter to President Clinton: Population Enrichment vs. Population Control" (paid political advertisement). *New York Times* (August 15):A16.

International Women's Health Coalition (IWHC). 1994. "The World After Cairo" (paid political advertisement). *New York Times* (September 6):A19.

Juergensmeyer, M. 1993. *The New Cold War?: Religious Nationalism Confronts the Secular State.* Berkeley: University of California Press.

Katz, M., and M. Stern. 1980. "History and the Limits of Population Policy." *Politics and Society* 10:225-245.

Kirschten, D. 1994. "Women's Day." *National Journal* (April 30):1016-1019.

Koopman, J. 1995. "Dialogue: Interview with Archbishop Renato Martino." *National Catholic Register* (February 5):1,8.

Lancaster, J., and B. Rensberger. 1994. "Cairo Delegates Come to Terms." *Washington Post* (September 13):A12,14.

Lukes, S. 1974. *Power: A Radical View.* London: Macmillan.

Mahbubani, K. 1992. "The West and the Rest." *The National Interest* (Summer):3-13.

Miller, A. 1994. "Silver Linings at Cairo." *The Tablet* (September 17):1152-1154.

Moffett, G. 1994. "UN Population Conference Meets Religious Resistance." *Christian Science Monitor* (September 6):1,4.

Mullen, P. 1994. "Behind U.N. Deal Differences Still Remain." *National Catholic Register* (October 9):1,10.

Murphy, K. 1994. "Empowering Women is Focus of Conference." *Los Angeles Times* (September 4):A29.

National Catholic Register (NCR) Editors. 1994. "Cairo's Odd Couple." *National Catholic Register* (September 4):4.

National Public Radio (NPR). 1994. Morning Edition: "Vatican Criticizes U.N. Approach to Population." *National Public Radio* (August 31).

Navarro-Valls, J. 1994. "The Courage to Speak Bluntly." *Wall Street Journal* (September 1).

New York Times Editors. 1994. "The Cairo Conference." *New York Times* (August 28):(4)14.

News Agencies. 1994a. "Leaders Seek Compromise." *Arab News* (September 6):1.

————. 1994b. "Egypt, Pakistan Press for Changes in U.N. Draft." *Arab News* (September 7):1.

Novak, R. 1994. "The Vatican Flap." *Washington Post* (September 5):A21.

Pope John Paul II. 1994. "Message to UN Population Fund Director" (March 18, 1994). *L'Osservatore Romano* (March 23):1-2.

Rensberger, B. 1994. "Cairo Conference Ends with Broad Consensus for Plan to Curb Growth." *Washington Post* (September 14):A13.

Rensberger, B., and J. Lancaster. 1994. "Vatican's Abortion Stance Riles Many at Forum." *Washington Post* (September 8).

Reuters News Service (RNS). 1994. "Mahran: Most Egyptians Support ICPD." *Egyptian Gazette* (August 23):8.

Rosenfeld, S. 1994a. "Let the Pope Be Catholic." *Washington Post* (September 9):A21.

_____. 1994b. "Cairo Mandate." *Washington Post* (September 16):A20.

Rowen, H. 1994. "Vatican Obfuscation." *Washington Post* (September 8):A19.

Saba, M. 1994. "The 'Clash of Civilizations' Revisited." *Arab News* (September 1):10.

Sadik, N. 1991. "Introduction." *United Nations Population Fund 1991 Report*. New York: UNFPA.

Shapiro, T. 1985. *Population Control Politics*. Philadelphia: Temple University Press.

Stackhouse, J. 1994. "Birth Control Divides UN Talks." *Globe and Mail* (September 5): A1,A5.

Stanford, P. 1994. "John Paul Takes a Last Stand." *Manchester Guardian Weekly* (September 4):7.

Steinfels, P. 1994. "Beliefs: A Language Barrier at the World's Population Conference Involved Much More Than Words." *New York Times* (September 24).

Taheri, A. 1994a. "From Malthus to Alternative Life-Styles." *Arab News* (September 5):10.

_____. 1994b. "Population Meet Defines Attitudes." *Arab News* (September 10):10.

United Nations (U.N.). 1974. *Report of the United Nations Population Conference*. U.N. Sales No. E.75.XIII.3.

_____. 1994a. (*Draft*) *Programme of Action of the International Conference on Population and Development*. U.N. Doc. A/CONF.171/ L.1.

_____. 1994b. *Report of the International Conference on Population and Development*. U.N. Doc. A/CONF.171/13.

U.N. Secretary General. 1994. *Explanations Concerning Population and Development Strategies and Programmes*. U.N. Doc. A/CONF.171/4.

U.S. Bishops. 1994. "Statement Regarding the Cairo Conference on Population and Development." *L'Osservatore Romano* (June 29):2.

Waldman, P. 1994. "Population Summit to Open Amid Religious Uproar." *Asian Wall Street Journal* (September 5):1,10.

Woodward, K. "Hot Under the Roman Collar." *Newsweek* (September 12):24-25.

World Conference on Religion and Peace (WCRP). 1994. *Religion, Population and Development: Multi-Religious Contributions*. New York: World Conference on Religion and Peace.

TRUTH, NOT TRUCE:
"COMMON GROUND" ON ABORTION,
A MOVEMENT WITHIN BOTH MOVEMENTS

James R. Kelly

Although occluded by the escalation of violence, much has changed in
the abortion controversy. The alliance between moral conservatives
opposing abortion and the fiscal conservatives supporting a human life
amendment is close to an end. *Roe v. Wade* is now a permanent part
of American law and some pro-choice supporters have showed some
concern about abortion being used as a means of controlling welfare
populations and costs. In this context, the "common ground movement"
begun in the late 1980s warrants empirical study. This study identifies the
seminal meaning of common ground, describes the groups identified with
"common ground," analyzes the reasons for their eclipse, and appraises
their long-term significance for the American abortion controversy.

"Common ground" seems to be the last term one would expect to find in any sociological account of the abortion controversy. In both (1991, p. 49; 1994, pp. vii, 4) of his widely reviewed examinations of the "culture wars," James Davison Hunter refers to the pro-choice and pro-life movements as fierce warring armies; both are a kind of Weberian "ideal" type representing the nonnegotiable, no-surrender conflicts which are rooted in the "incommensurable and unreconcilable" disagreements about moral authority. According to Hunter, these disagreements threaten the civil discourse necessary for democracy.[1] Making Hunter's thesis all the more prescient, the news about abortion remains not only contentious but deadly. On July 29, 1994 an abortion opponent, Paul J. Hill, murdered Dr. John Bayard Britton outside an abortion clinic in Pensacola, Florida. Just 17 months earlier Michael Griffin killed Dr. David Gunn outside another Pensacola abortion clinic. The government's reaction to this violence seemed designed not so much to increase the civil discourse Hunter recommends but to reinforce the appropriateness of his military analogy.

Although they still haven't had their desired effect, the strong measures passed by the Congress and upheld by the Supreme Court in the period between these murders were designed specifically to make abortion protests a costly form of behavior. First, the Supreme Court ruled that RICO ("Racketeer Influenced And Corrupt Organizations Act") could be applied to abortion protesters. Then, in "Madsen v. Women's Health Center," the Court found no violation of first amendment speech rights in a Florida injunction prohibiting abortion opponents from entering within 36 feet of abortion clinic entrances or initiating a discussion within 300 feet of the entrance. On May 26, 1994, President Clinton signed into law the "Freedom of Access to Clinic Entrances Bill" under which offenders face federal fines of up to $100,000 and a year in prison for a first conviction. While these measures may or may not lead to better police management of protests and counter-protests at local abortion clinic sites, they are not likely, in themselves, to lead to any satisfactory discussions about legal abortion. Whatever else these measures signify, they do not by themselves encourage any gain for the rational discourse or the substantive democracy hoped for by Hunter (1994, p. 35) and others.

News during the summer of 1994 about anti-abortion violence, then, seemed to be a dramatic reminder that in the United States the intractable issue of abortion was irredeemably outside civil discourse. For many reasons, however, this would be a mistaken and misleading judgment. Besides the murders, much else had happened in the abortion controversy in the realms of both law and politics, though these changes scarcely affected the public discourse of the competing pro-choice and pro-life movements. Still, while the particular arguments for and against abortion haven't changed much since the mid 1960s, it would be a mistake to view them as static. Arguments for and against abortion can be arranged to suggest different emphases and different tactics. In changing political and legal circumstances, opponents of abortion must continually rethink the implications of being "pro-life" while abortion supporters must rethink the meaning of being "pro-choice." With one exception, both sides' abortion discourse has lagged behind the politics of the abortion debate.

This one exception is the term "common ground," which emerged not from scholars' detached reflections but, surprisingly, from ranks of grassroots abortion opponents who were animated by their uncompromising allegiance to a conflicting set of pro-life and pro-choice principles. As it first emerged in grassroots negotiations, the term "common ground" represents both cooperation and nonnegotiable principles. This odd juxtaposition makes "common ground" a morally significant term in a "post-modern" era characterized by a loss of confidence in truth claims, an escalation of identity politics, and, subsequently, a recourse to violence (Hunter 1994, Chapter 1; Jelen 1994, pp. 185-193).

In the following paper, I will (1) sketch the emergence of the term "common ground" in the abortion debate, (2) explore the reasons why it caught and then lost the media's interest, (3) appraise the sociological conditions for its continuation in the abortion discourse, and (4) evaluate its significance for the abortion conflict and other conflicts involving limited but fruitful cooperation among principled adversaries whose opposing loyalties to morally non negotiable positions paradoxically lead these adversaries to cooperation. (5) I'll conclude with examples of pro-life/ pro-choice cooperation on the local and regional levels that fit the "common ground" model but do not explicitly use the term "common ground." Last, I will argue that a "strong and non-trivial" use of the expression "common ground" can crystallize and thus extend these examples of cooperation among moral adversaries in such a way that the integrity of the actors on both sides is deepened. As is the case when studying war in the literal sense, it is essential that any discussion of culture war include an appreciation of the moral complexities involved. For example, the pursuit of "common ground" challenges adversaries to realize their conflicting convictions in real world situations of enormous complexity.

THE DISCOVERY OF COMMON GROUND IN THE ABORTION DEBATE

The first national media account of which I am aware that explicitly employed the term "common ground" in a story about abortion was Tamar Lewin's February 17, 1992 front-page *New York Times article* entitled "In Bitter Abortion Debate, Opponents Learn to Reach for Common Ground." In this piece, Lewin described the "breakthrough" common ground event which formally began in St. Louis on July 12, 1990 with Andrew Puzder, a "pro-life" lawyer; Lorretta Wagner, a past president of Missouri Citizens for Life; B.J. Isaacson Jones, Director of St. Louis Reproductive Health Services; and Jean Cavender, also of Reproductive Health Services.

This breakthrough common ground event had its inception when Andrew Puzder, a St. Louis lawyer, applied the term "common ground" to the abortion controversy. Puzder is the one who conceived of and then co-authored an article proposing the Missouri statute which the Supreme Court would eventually uphold in its July 3, 1989 *Webster v. Reproductive Health Services* case. The Court's 5-4 decision upholding the abortion regulations passed by the Missouri legislature (viability tests on fetuses judged to be at least 20 weeks old and permission for public hospitals to perform abortions only in cases where the mother's life was endangered) signaled that the Court would now permit other states to pass abortion regulations that limited, but did not remove, the right to abortion declared in Roe. While abortion opponents hailed Webster as an important step towards reversing Roe and abortion supporters denounced it as an unambiguous defeat, Puzder had a more complicated reaction. Soon after (December 26, 1989) Puzder published in the "Commentary" section of the *St. Louis Dispatch* editorial pages an essay entitled "Common Ground on Abortion."

Puzder recalled (May 24, 1994 interview) that after the Webster decision a *St. Louis Dispatch* reporter, Martha Shirk, asked him whether there was anything positive about the decision. Puzder responded:

> I said, it might advance the mutual goals of all sides. She said, 'There aren't any.' I thought, there's so much animosity, so much energy wasted. Were there ways to expend some of that energy on the women who are pregnant and don't know what to do?

In his *St. Louis Dispatch* article, Puzder wrote that both sides might "redirect to other social problems the enormous energy we expend on this single problem," and that both sides might try to "escape the strictures of a simple win-lose attitude." He called attention to the fact that Missouri had both high rates of female poverty and high abortion rates and that, in fidelity to their principles, both pro-life and pro-choice groups ought to acknowledge and do something about the high rates of female poverty and abortion. To describe this cooperation he used the term "common ground," a phrase, he said, that "just popped into my head." He wrote:

> According to a report by the Children's Budget Coalition dated February, 1989, 20 percent of Missouri's children currently live in poverty (a shockingly high percentage). Yet an astounding 55 percent of Missouri's children living in single female-headed households live in poverty.... Surely these numbers alone suggest the existence of some common ground between the pro-life and pro-choice factions. We who support the right to life over the right to privacy call ourselves 'pro-life.' As the interests we seek to protect begin before and not at birth, these interests surely do not end, but continue, well after birth.... While neither side is going to make concessions on the basic underlying issue (life vs. privacy), it is difficult to see how either side would hurt its position by jointly seeking legislative aid for impoverished women and their children (born and unborn).... While the common ground may be slim, it exists. If we can put aside for a moment our simple win-lose attitudes and approach this issue sensibly and calmly, perhaps we can jointly accomplish some good for those we all seek to protect.[2]

Puzder's December 1989 *St. Louis Dispatch* "common ground" appeal quickly led to the first grassroots Common Ground project when his essay was read by B. J. Isaacson-Jones, the director of the abortion clinic that had been the plaintiff in the Webster decision. It helped that B. J. Isaacson-Jones and Puzder had grown up in the same neighborhood and knew each other. After reading his article, Isaacson-Jones called Puzder, and they decided to meet. After a few conversations together, they widened the group to include two activists from each side, all with well-known movement loyalties. The initiators of this first Common Ground group agreed that all participants must remain movement loyalists; the "common ground" sought by principled abortion opponents was not to be confused with the "middle ground" sought by pragmatic politicians. Accordingly, participants agreed that there could be no successful common ground action that required a loss of integrity or even the appearance of moral compromise. For example, an early participant in the Common Ground project was Loretta Wagner, who had organized the first St. Louis mass protest against Roe and had served for more than a decade as the coordinator of St. Louis' participation in the annual January 22 "March on Washington" protesting Roe and who had been arrested a dozen times for civil disobedience outside abortion clinics. She had also founded two shelters for women with problem pregnancies.

During my conversations with her, Wagner always stressed that the term "common ground" did not signify any type of compromise. She noted that the St. Louis Common Ground project involved no long discussions about the reasons for opposing or supporting legal abortion. Nor did the participants seek mutual respect, although they welcomed it when it happened. Likewise, Puzder agreed with Wagner's assessment, telling a *Kansas Star* (June 14, 1992 p. B-5) reporter that "through Common Ground, you can see that good people can be on both sides." The St. Louis Common Ground project did not aim at contestation, compromise, or even conversion. Joint action, not simply dialogue, was the point of Common Ground. Simply put, the originating purpose of St. Louis Common Ground was to find ways to make abortions less needed and less coerced. Wagner listed some of the solutions upon which both sides agreed: "We need to relieve some of the pressures that cause many women to choose abortion and to make possible a kinder society for them and their children. There are many things we can agree on: more quality pre-and post-natal care; more access to treatment of substance abusing mothers and their children; welfare reforms; day-care; affordable housing; adoption; improved recruitment of foster parents; helping women find jobs and educational opportunities. Neither side wants to see poor women economically compelled to have abortions."

Wagner's last sentence is crucial to understanding the concept of common ground and how it demonstrates an aspiration of abortion adversaries to be simultaneously both cooperative and uncompromising. This complex aspiration towards seeking both cooperative closeness with and moral distance from opponents makes it unlikely that Common Ground participants will be single-issue anti-abortion (see Kelly 1994) or pro-abortion activists, but will be instead *pro-*life (supporting real world changes favoring birth) and pro-*choice* (supporting real world changes that lessen indirect coercion to abort). Among opponents of abortion, "common ground" support is most likely to be based on a "consistent ethic of life" because it probes the connections between abortion, capital punishment, militarism and poverty (Bernardin 1988).[3] Among supporters of legal abortion, support for a common ground approach is most likely to come from feminists who object to the use of abortion as a state policy to reduce welfare costs even when this involves direct or indirect coercion (Petchesky 1990; Pitanguy and Petchesky 1993). In terms of the seminal St. Louis approach, common ground occurs when individuals and groups from the consistent ethic wing of the movement join with defenders of legal abortion who acknowledge that women often feel they have no real alternatives to abortion.

During my conversation with her, Wagner acknowledged (interview, March 31, 1993) that, like most of the activists with whom she worked, she initially did not favor a consistent ethic framework for thinking and talking about abortion.

> I was furious at [Joseph Cardinal] Bernardin [after his address at Fordham University]. People like me resent that he would think there was anything more important than abortion. Poverty? At least poor people were alive. The Republicans, our allies, weren't pro-poverty. They had a different way of working on it. We wanted people to support Republicans because they were against abortion. We resented bishops and people like that who made links with other issues. But I'm beginning to get more enlightened. I do think opposing abortion is a whole garment of issues. These things all fit together.

Wagner advanced Puzder's understanding of the term "common ground." She observed that, while avoiding compromise, the pursuit of common ground leads to a deepening of moral integrity on both sides. In St. Louis the challenge to seek common ground led participants to a more consistent commitment to their pro-life or their pro-choice principles as their cooperation moved both sides beyond any single-issue approach to abortion. Referring to Isaacson-Jones' efforts to include adoption as one of the services offered by Reproductive Health Services, Wagner observed that because of the stimulus of Common Ground, "Maybe clinics would live up to their own (pro-choice) expectations."

THE LONG AND DIFFICULT ROAD FROM CONCEPT TO PRACTICE

Practicing the common ground approach to abortion has proved to be both complicated and elusive. The Common Ground movement in St. Louis started simply enough. Just months after they first met, St. Louis Common Ground members testified in support of state legislation promoting improved follow-up care for babies born to drug dependent mothers and for increased financial assistance for single parent households. In the past, similar legislation had been derailed by abortion politics as moral gridlock had deepened the customary political gridlock. This time, however, with Common Ground support, the legislation passed.

Despite this victory, the St. Louis Common Ground project demonstrates that only modest results can be expected from even successful common ground efforts. This should not be surprising. Even when abortion adversaries agree on a course of action (in itself no easy feat), reducing the pressure on women to abort is no simple matter. It is especially hard to finance programs designed to encourage childbearing and support mothers when public confidence in social programs is low and resistance to taxation is high. For example, the Missouri Legislature originally appropriated $1.8 million for the "Crack Baby Bill" endorsed by St. Louis Common Ground, but later cut the funding by two-thirds. Representative Christopher S. Kelly explained to Common Ground that "Missouri's difficult economic situation, unfortunately, made that (original funding) unaffordable."

In light of these pragmatic obstacles, Wagner candidly describes the St. Louis Common Ground achievements as mostly ideational: "The media thinks common ground is a really dramatic new story but I can't say we've done anything dramatic—just getting the idea out. The St. Louis Common Ground group has been working primarily to promote the concept of common ground and to gain the understanding of the public."

The Seminal Definition of Common Ground

For analytical purposes it's worth summarizing the five emergent characteristics of the seminal Common Ground group in St. Louis. Common Ground (1) resulted from a combined pro-life and pro-choice initiative (2) by activists who publicly distinguished common ground from moral compromise and political accommodation. (3) These actors loyally continued their adversarial abortion activities (4) even as they agreed to cooperate on projects and policies aimed at reducing the pressures on women to abort. (5) Common Ground was pursued by locating the overlaps between an evolving pro-life consistent ethic approach and an emergent pro-choice attention to the real-world structures which constrain reproductive freedom. From these five characteristics we can clearly discern the considerable moral difference separating the term "common ground" from such semantic cousins as "middle ground," "common cause," and especially "compromise."

Common ground is not what most politicians look for in the heat of the abortion wars. Unlike politicians, St. Louis Common Ground participants never described the overlap they sought as "middle ground." The moral distinction is important. The use of the term "common ground" means that individuals or groups, known to be opposed on some significant principle, cooperate but with the clearly understood proviso that this cooperation signifies no weakening, much less betrayal, of either side's principle. Common ground is not where principles are buried beneath compromises. On common ground, principles retain their luminosity and opponents their integrity. Even at its moral best, the term "middle ground" hardly suggests integrity. More typically, it suggests the "best possible deal for both sides." Common ground appeals to moral integrity; middle ground to political advantage. For this reason, we cannot expect that common cause by itself makes for common ground. While the terms "compromise" and "middle ground" can with honor appear in the same sentence as "common cause," their appearance with "common ground" might well signal either an outsider's misunderstanding or an insider's moral laxity. The intended point of the term "common ground" is to proclaim loudly that the cooperative acts blur no principle or violate any integrity. I'll use this strong meaning of common ground as it emerged in St. Louis to analyze the kinds of common ground that followed elsewhere and to reflect on its longer-range significance for the abortion debate.

Other Cooperating Grassroots Groups

Soon after the St. Louis Common Ground emerged, two other independent grassroots initiatives involving abortion opponents also began. Although media stories often classified them as "common ground," it's important to note that they did not (and still do not) exhibit all the characteristics found in the St. Louis seminal group. For example, these initiatives often emphasized dialogue rather than principled cooperation and have not attempted similar changes in public policy or practices at abortion clinics. Unlike St. Louis, their origins were not grassroots; neither did they represent a joint initiative from activists on both sides. Likewise, they seemed to tilt as much toward tactical need as toward principle and thus better fit the more familiar framework of "pragmatism" than of an emergent common ground centered on movement loyalty.

Both of these common ground efforts which appeared in post-St. Louis media stories were initiated by proponents of legal abortion— Magi Cage who directed a Wisconsin abortion clinic and Peggy Green, a San Francisco-based pro-choice activist—during the Reagan-Bush era of abortion politics. Cage said her concern was to "improve respect for diversity" and to lessen the legislative gridlock associated with Wisconsin state abortion politics. Her approach was circuitous. She brought together two pro-choice and two pro-life legislators who each in turn contacted two leaders from pro-life and pro-choice groups. A professional facilitator was present at their meetings. The Wisconsin group functioned as a "focus" or screening group for the state legislative leaders considering family policy and school policy legislation. Although this group is included in all the early media accounts of common ground, and Cage remains a member of the steering committee of the "Common Ground Network for Life and Choice" (see below), it is important to note that the group she started did not originally use the term "common ground." Until the media identified them as a "common ground" group, they called themselves the "Wisconsin Dialogue Group." They disbanded in the

Fall of 1992, just thirteen months after their founding. Unlike the seminal St. Louis Common Ground the Wisconsin group never explicitly developed notions of cooperation based on a philosophy of loyalty to pro-life or pro-choice principles.[4]

The second media-identified "common ground" effort, initiated by pro-choice activist Peggy Green in San Francisco, while not officially disbanded, also quickly lost momentum. Its chief success was a three-day retreat held at the end of March, 1992. Dialogue was the main point of the gathering; an advertisement for the retreat emphasized the role of attentive listening in successful dialogue: "Our opponents see our slogans, know our loves, feel our sadness. They haven't heard our stories." Still, in addition to dialogue, it should be noted that the San Francisco Common Ground group located areas for pro-life/pro-choice cooperation. A report from this gathering mentioned "the relationship between teenage pregnancy and low self-esteem, the lack of services for pregnant women, [and] the lack of support for working mothers." It concluded that "in all these areas we can work together."

So far, however, there has been no follow-up to the retreat. And no joint actions. One of the organizers, Rose Evans, the editor of the "consistent ethic," pro-life journal *Harmony*, acknowledged (interview, March 18, 1989) that "not much is happening at the moment in San Francisco." She mentioned the practical difficulties, especially for mothers, of finding time for a three-day retreat and, for most of the women, retreat expenses. Another factor might be the retreat's focus on understanding differences more than the development of cooperative plans for reducing pressures on women to abort. Dialogue about abortion does not by itself warrant the added characterization of "common ground." By itself, dialogue can aim at compromise and middle-ground rather than common ground.

THE PROFESSIONALS DISCOVER AND SHAPE COMMON GROUND

During the period between the inception of the seminal St. Louis Common Ground group and Clinton's Presidential election, the concept of "common ground" attracted the interest of conflict resolution professionals. In September 1992 the Family Institute of

Cambridge (FIC), a Massachusetts family therapy group seeking to adapt its therapeutic techniques of family counseling to issues causing public controversy, initiated its "Public Conversations Project." The following year Search For Common Ground—a group of "social entrepreneurs" organized by John Marks to seek "innovative ways" to "reframe contentious issues and to develop viable policy alternatives"—added "The Common Ground Coalition for Life and Choice" to its roster of projects.[5] Unlike grassroots groups, these professional mediators publicly entered the abortion controversy with tested frames of references and methodologies.

The Family Institute of Cambridge (FIC) saw parallels between the "stuck" conversational processes in dysfunctional families and the "stalemated" polemics of abortion adversaries. FIC formed experimental groups comprised of four activists, two from each side of the abortion debate. FIC "discourse rules" allowed no arguments about abortion, only the sharing of experiences. An informal dinner, where participants met but did not identify their positions on abortion, preceded the structured interaction (viewed from behind one-way mirrors by staff therapists). According to the FIC staff, it was important for abortion opponents to see each other as "people just like themselves." The only questions permitted were ones of clarification. "What do you mean? Why do you feel that way?" No critical responses to each other's reflections were permitted. FIC staff report that these structured dialogues demonstrate that, "When we carefully communicate to our participants our expectations, create an atmosphere of safety and respect, and structure the session to block old patterns of interaction and old 'stories,' then new patterns of interaction emerge, fresh and unique stories are told, new questions are asked, and shared concerns about the costs of polarization surface" (Becker et. al, 1992, p. 8). By the emergent St. Louis criteria, FIC's project should be described as aiming at a form of "dialogue" rather than common ground.

The FIC project director, Laura Chasin (interview, July 30, 1994), acknowledged that the Public Conversations Project had initially hoped to "move beyond our framework to more problem solving action. We stopped." She said their groups—comprised of 72 people—had remained "one-shot groups." A comparison with the seminal St. Louis group is instructive on this point. Unlike St. Louis Common Ground, which was premised on continued abortion activism and publicly eschewed compromise, FIC explicitly screened out movement loyalties and encouraged participants to respond solely as individuals, not as members of any group. FIC's discourse rules de-emphasize any principle of "loyalty to loyalty" based on movement identities. In fact, FIC's methodology was designed to elicit personal feelings towards abortion and to screen out all moral arguments. It seems likely that any external consequences of a FIC-type of mediation would be closer to a "truce" than to the seminal St. Louis Common Ground focus on changing policies and practices. In this regard, it's worth noting that Chasin is less convinced of the fruitfulness of the term "common ground":

> I don't like the term. Most people are still caught up in the polarization. People must hear of it as compromise. All I can imagine is that people will hear 'common ground' as a shade of gray. John Slatter (a Professor of Communications at the University of New Hampshire) suggests 'a different ground.' The ground that emerges is different, common in the sense of a shared search and then a shared position, but it is created. The "different ground' is not necessarily an option identified in the polarized activities of the organizations. The process introduces new elements resulting in new positions. It is common in that it is created. I prefer a term emphasizing the emerging previously undisclosed options. The 'common' in common ground is heard as pertaining to what people have been fighting over. People haven't put energy into dreaming into what might work (interview, March 18, 1994).

Chasin acknowledged that the St. Louis Common Ground group "does not think of it my way. They talk of it as Venn circles, with overlap as option for both. They never talk about abortion."

While still formally associated with the "Common Ground Network for Life and Choice," The Family Institute of Cambridge left the abortion controversy in 1994 and moved on to other projects.[6]

The Common Ground Coalition for Life and Choice

Unlike FIC, the Common Ground Coalition for Life and Choice (CGCFLC)—now called "The Common Ground Network for Life and Choice)—has goals which are explicitly wider than merely fostering a dialogue centered on increasing mutual understanding. Like St. Louis Common Ground, the GCFLC proposes to "reframe" the abortion controversy so that abortion adversaries "can find a basis on which they can collaborate on specific projects." Indeed, CGCFLC envisions an ambitious national network of local groups "working with a common-ground approach to abortion." On March 5-6, 1993, when it called itself "The Common Ground Project," it sponsored a national meeting of the various local "common ground" efforts. Attending were the familiar groups reported by the media (from St. Louis, Wisconsin, San Francisco, Cambridge and a more recent one, described below, Buffalo.) After this meeting, CGCFLC added the emergent St. Louis meaning of common ground to its parent organization's (in my judgment) more "politically" pragmatic definition of common ground.[7]

On January 10, 1994 the CGCFLC announced that it had become the Common Ground Network For Life and Choice, a national network of the already existing common ground groups. This announcement received some media coverage[8] but not nearly as much as St. Louis Common Ground received during the 1992 Presidential campaign. Foundations no longer showed much interest either. At that time Mary Jacksteit, the co-director of Common Ground Network For Life and Choice, said (Interview, March 18, 1994) that her organization was currently "working on funding and running out of money." Our parent organization (Search For Common Ground) is covering us until end of year. We're trying to organize another conference for November but we're not doing real well." By November 1994 they had succeeded in receiving only a single $20,000 grant from the Tortuga Foundation. But by the fall of 1995 additional foundation support was secured. Showing increased confidence, GNFLC has produced a position paper on adoption co-authored by pro-life and pro-choice members and is working toward one on teen-age pregnancy. (GNFLC may yet succeed in giving some institutionalized form to local common ground initiatives and possibilities. But it won't be easy.)

Buffalo Common Ground

Until 1995, The Common Ground Coalition For Life And Choice has been involved in one grassroots effort, in Buffalo, New York,[9] where it was invited by the Buffalo Council of Churches in response to Operation Rescue's April-May, 1992 "Spring of Life Campaign." This campaign fostered a renewed public interest in the community's many disagreements over legal abortion. Since the planned turmoil generated by Operation Rescue's civil disobedience outside abortion clinics, the Buffalo Coalition for Common Ground has sponsored three weekend workshops (involving about 150 people, mostly from churches) and its steering committee (22 individuals who formally represent no abortion social movement organization) has circulated a (9/1/92) Mission Statement. It builds upon the St. Louis Common Ground model but lacks its sharp focus:

> Buffalo Coalition for Common Ground is a voluntary association dedicated to the promotion of cooperative alternative approaches for addressing problems that deeply divide the Greater Buffalo Community. Without requiring persons of different views to abandon their principles or activities, the goal of the Buffalo Coalition for Common Ground is to diminish polarization through: (1) Identifying mutual concerns. (2) Creating models for collaboration, among persons of different views, for finding solutions that benefit the community. (3) Promoting and facilitating, as needed, projects undertaken by the collaborative partnerships that develop.

Though the Buffalo Coalition for Common Ground seems ready to accomplish the third goal mentioned above—collaborative pro-life/pro-choice projects—it hasn't yet succeeded. Its most visible achievement has been a video of a "common ground" conversation between a pro-choice activist, Karalyn Schmidt, and a pro-life activist, Karen Swallow Prior. Schmidt had been a director of the local Planned Parenthood chapter and Prior was a spokeswoman for the local chapter of Operation Rescue. During the video, which appeared in prime time on Buffalo television, they described themselves as former enemies who have become friends despite their continuing differences over abortion (Warner 1994 p. C4).

In January 1994 Common Ground of Buffalo hired a part-time coordinator, Terese Maciocha. In my interview with her, she acknowledged (interview, May 24, 1994) that: "If you interviewed people in Buffalo, in general our name is not known. We have not established a collaborative project." Machiocha's primary responsibility is fund raising. She had no success to report at the time of our interview. So far, no pro-choice or pro-life national organization has expressed any interest in her organization. "Common ground of Buffalo," she explained," is mostly kept alive by a few people—maybe 100—who are attracted to the idea of common ground and believe strongly in it. They are for the most part associated with the churches of Buffalo."

COMMON GROUND AND PUBLIC DISCOURSE

The public hears little about common ground efforts in the abortion controversy.[10] The periodic appearance of the term "common ground" in media reports regarding abortion has many causes; chief among them is the tactical usefulness of its ironically inclusive connotations for political advantage. When political parties find common ground language and tactics useful, the media employs the term; when common ground tactics and language are not tactically important, the coverage stops.

Use of the term "common ground" peaked during the 1992 Presidential election campaign and then fell below the media horizon. As mentioned earlier, its first national appearance was Tamar Lewin's February 17, 1992 front-page *New York Times* article entitled "In Bitter Abortion Debate, Opponents Learn to Reach for Common Ground." The story and the term quickly moved around the country. Major print media transformed the same handful of examples of pro-choice/pro-life discussions (whose participants did not at the time even use the term common ground) into what suddenly seemed a nascent national movement capable of challenging the entrenched and combative establishments in both movements. Stories appeared in *USA Today*, the *Los Angeles Times*, the *Washington Post*, the *Boston Globe*, the *Christian Science Monitor*, *Glamour*, and countless more local media, such as the *St. Louis Post-Dispatch*, the *Kansas Star*, the *San Jose News*, the *Oregonian*, and the *Cleveland Plain-Dealer*. Just as suddenly, however, the stories stopped and common ground went underground.

First, Conceptual Difficulties

There are many reasons for the virtual disappearance of the term "common ground" in abortion reportage. To begin, it has been difficult for both sides to distinguish "common ground" from "middle ground" and other related terms suggesting moral compromise. Incidentally, no leader of any nationally recognized abortion activist group endorsed the term "common ground." National leaders of Planned Parenthood, the National Organization of Women, the National Abortion and Reproductive Rights Action League have all eschewed the term. So have prominent pro-choice authors. Anna Quindlen entitled her June 23, 1993 *New York Times* column about common ground efforts in the abortion controversy "Going Nowhere." In his widely reviewed book about abortion and euthanasia entitled *Life's Dominion* (Knopf, 1993), Ronald Dworkin, distinguished philosopher of constitutional law and frequent commentator on abortion law, dismissed any hope that common ground could be found between the two sides of the (abortion) debate. He wrote that those

> who urge compromise (sic) urge it, understandably, on terms that protect what they themselves believe to be fundamental principles of justice. Those who believe that women have a fundamental right to make their own decisions about abortion, for example, insist that any acceptable solution must respect that principle. But no proposal that does respect it could possibly be accepted by people who believe that abortion is murder, that it violates the most fundamental rights and interest of unborn children" (1993 p. 9).

The leaders of the most prominent pro-life organizations agreed with Dworkin. In her March 9, 1993 news column, National Right to Life Committee President Wanda Frantz advised the activists in NRLC's 3000 chapters to view common ground as a "clever pro-choice" strategy seeking "to gain acceptance of the pro-abortion position as morally equivalent (or morally superior!) to the pro-life position." In his Operation Rescue newsletter Randall Terry likened common ground initiatives to blacks negotiating with the Ku Klux Klan or Jews with the Nazis.

There was good reason for this caution among right-to-life leaders. In the early 1990s, prominent proponents of legal abortion had adopted the term "common ground" in their books and articles. During this period, the term was not used by any prominent right-to-life leader nor did it appear in any of the many dozens of right-to-life newsletters. Those authors endorsing the term claimed that they were sympathetically portraying both sides of the abortion controversy and presented suggestions for achieving a truce. The most prominent of these authors were Harvard law professor Laurence H. Tribe and PBS commentator and essayist Roger Rosenblatt. Both acknowledged that they were pro-choice. In his *Abortion: The Clash of Absolutes* (Norton, 1990), Laurence Tribe employed the term "common ground" while in *Life Itself: Abortion in the American Mind* (Random House, 1992), Rosenblatt adopted the variant "uncommon ground."

Both acknowledged that the obvious humanity of the fetus was a significant dimension of the legal debate about abortion. Both were conciliatory in tone and explicitly recognized that opponents of abortion could not simply be dismissed as religionists or as opponents of gender equality. But despite their irenic titles and expressed intentions, their recommendations for a "truce" actually precluded common ground. For example, Tribe entitled his penultimate chapter "In Search of Compromise." Recall that by St. Louis "common ground" criteria, compromise is an antonym not a synonym for common ground. In this chapter, Tribe mostly criticized "Casey-type" state restrictions such as informed consent provisions and parental notification. Similarly, Rosenblatt denied the basic premise of "common ground" (of the St. Louis Common Ground vintage) with his one-sided conclusion that "it is time for Congress to make a law like *Roe v. Wade* that fully protects abortion rights but legislates the kind of community help like sex education that would diminish the practice."

Another key factor in the disappearance of "common ground" from abortion reportage were the jarring stories of abortion clinic violence, especially the shootings of abortion doctors. Michael Griffin's March 10, 1992 murder of Doctor David Gunn during a protest at a Pensacola Florida abortion clinic and Rachelle Shannon's August 27 attempt to murder Dr. George Tiller outside his Wichita, Kansas abortion clinic killed any enthusiastic hope that a common ground approach could play a part in the abortion debate. Social movement organizations on both sides of the issue immediately occupied themselves with either turning these events to their advantage or deflecting their damage. Abortion proponents successfully campaigned for "The Freedom of Access to Clinic Entrances Bill" and the application of RICO (Racketeer Influenced and Corrupt Organizations Act) to abortion protest. Leaders of the nationally recognized organizations opposing abortion condemned any use of violence but the media showed less interest in that part of the story. The Communications Director of the National Right to Life Committee, the oldest, largest, and most prestigious of the pro-life organizations, complained (NRLNews, March 30, 1993 p. 4) that after the shooting "no national television program quoted a mainstream pro-life spokesperson—not once."

The Loss of any Tactical Advantage in Common Ground

Besides the jarring incongruence of common ground and clinic violence stories, a crucial reason for the rapid eclipse of common ground was the November 1992 defeat of George Bush. During the Presidential race Clinton's more "inclusionary" language counteracted Republican claims to anti-abortion sentiment, thus making common ground type stories national "news." But when Republicans no longer steadfastly promised to seek reversal of Roe and Clinton found no convincing way of representing anti-abortion sentiments, common ground type stories became less relevant to national politics and thus reportage.

In the author's judgment, the November 1992 defeat of George Bush also permanently ended a successful tactical alliance—an alliance dating back to Ronald Reagan's 1978 promise to support the human life amendment—on abortion between the mostly middle and working class abortion opponents and the national Republican leaders. Moreover, after Clinton's victory there remained no credible fear that abortion would again be illegal, and because of this, there was little tactical advantage for supporters of legal abortion to search for common ground with abortion opponents. As he had promised in his campaign, President Clinton appointed to the Supreme Court two strong supporters of abortion rights, Ruth Bader Ginsberg and Stephen G. Breyer. After Bush's defeat by Clinton, the Republican party was no longer the secure ally of right-to-life groups. On December 15, 1992 a group of prominent Republican moderates, calling themselves "the Republican Majority Coalition," announced that in the next Presidential election the Republicans would be "inclusive." The coalition founders included no abortion opponents.

The political uncoupling of fiscal and moral conservatives on at least the abortion issue[11] can be viewed retrospectively as entirely predictable, much like, for example, the initial caution and then enthusiastic support among the Tories for the 1967 British law legalizing abortions. In the modern era of activist societies, positions taken on legal abortion inevitably raise questions about positions taken on social policies affecting family life, women's equality, and health care more generally. Professed concern for fetal life inevitably raises questions about concern for the welfare of mother and children. In turn, these questions themselves raise further concerns about the economics of impeding the abortion of unwanted children, especially the children of single women or poor women. Opposition to abortion reflects a moral conservatism, but this moral traditionalism clashes with a fiscal conservatism. It has often been difficult to reconcile the desire to regulate abortion with a party platform perennially committed to lower taxes.

THE FATE OF COMMON GROUND

The limited results of common ground efforts so far do not encourage high optimism about common ground's importance in the abortion debate. There is little evidence that common ground initiatives will become a public perspective in the abortion conflict alongside the well known "culture wars" approach followed by the more familiar organizations on both sides. Since dialogue is of little interest to the media, "common ground" is not often in the news. The "man-bites-dog" element of the story—abortion adversaries can talk with each other—has already lost its novelty.

We should expect, of course, that the common ground approach will be either resisted or ignored by all the prominent social movement organizations involved in abortion conflicts. Even when they understand that common ground is meant to be distinguished from moral compromise, social movement leaders (especially when they are salaried) must view common ground as *sociological* compromise in that the approach necessarily entails organizational costs such as increased competition for the always scarce resources of volunteers, donations, or—at the very least—public attention. However different they are in philosophy, all social movement organizations are alike in that they always seek to become an "issue monopoly." Each group in the abortion conflict struggles to become *the* public voice for its side. Frances Kissling (interview,), the president of Catholics for a Free Choice, gave an insider's account of this sociological generalization:

> There's not much steam in common ground. Two years ago, when the Republicans were in office, there was much interest. Now the pro-life side is more likely to show interest. It's a question of power and politics. If your side is winning, you don't need common ground. Those on the political outskirts are the ones who need common ground. Common ground is on nobody's agenda these days.

Moral Realism

Of course, for abortion activists on both sides the common ground approach represents something far more fundamental than a sociological compromise. Abortion rights organizations and right-to-life organizations remain embattled over the most serious political and legal threats to their principles. It matters enormously, for example, whether national health reform finally includes or excludes non-therapeutic abortions. It's not a matter of moral indifference that the national government does or does not subsidize abortion. For right-to-life groups, a national health policy defining abortion simply as yet another kind of medical procedure would represent a deep institutionalization and moral routinization of a practice they find morally reprehensible.

It would be sociologically naive to expect that any social movement organization that can plausibly promise its membership at least some incremental victories would endorse, much less promote, a common ground approach. Viewed solely as a tactic, common ground initiatives make the most sense for organizations in decline. Sociologically speaking, only those losing ground are likely to seek common ground. In this context, we can anticipate that in the post Reagan-Bush era legal abortion activists will have even less interest in common ground than right-to-life groups. With the Supreme Court and the Congress, for the most part, safely and, it seems, permanently pro-choice with regard to the essential holding of Roe, we should expect a much reduced interest in common ground by pro-choice organizations or authors. As we have seen, already two of the pro-choice initiators of the "common ground" perspective—Laura Chasin (interview March 18, 1994) of The Family Institute of Cambridge and Frances Kissling (interview, April 6, 1994) of Catholics for a Free Choice—say the term is no longer helpful. In this cultural climate pro-life activists might be more likely to try to preserve the common ground approach in the abortion debate.

For the foreseeable future, the common ground approach will always be tangential to abortion politics. But tangential does not necessarily mean marginal. While the political and legal confrontations about the scope of legal abortion will always appear far more newsworthy than any morally complex and tactically ambiguous common ground approach, the common ground perspective on the abortion conflict has important moral significance. Moral culture remains more important than quotidian politics, just as the moral aspirations of a civilization are more important than its specific governance at a particular time. For the long run, a common ground approach makes the most coherent sense as a concrete application of "the consistent ethic of life." In fact, common ground is an important link in the vastly unfinished effort to probe the linkages between the violence of abortion and the violence of war, of poverty, and of capital punishment. The argument that abortion was an act of violence that would, chain-like, be linked to other forms of violence has too frequently been regarded as right-to-life polemics. When abortion opponents first argued that the logic of abortion would lead to an acceptance of euthanasia, their arguments were quickly dismissed. But two decades after Roe, influential scholars (Dworkin 1993) and district judges (Rothstein 1994, p. 23) agreed that, indeed, the logic of Roe includes the right to a medically assisted suicide.

As pro-choice activists turn their attention to the sociological conditions necessary for substantive reproductive choice, they too should pay more attention to the common ground perspective. The question that fostered the "nascent" (Alberoni 1984, pp. 16ff) Common Ground organization in St. Louis—"How will this actually help St. Louis women choose birth rather than abortion?"—should inspire principled pro-life and pro-choice activists to work together to help women and protect human life. Since public opinion polls demonstrate the moral ambiguity women and men feel about legal abortion, it is likely that, even without the term, "common ground," some individuals might intuitively act in a common ground way. Using this explicit term in public discourse, however, helps us to notice long-term shifts in the abortion controversy which might otherwise be obscured by the more typical abortion polemics.

Perhaps the most significant instance of common ground (without being called common ground) happened in New Jersey when official representatives of the New Jersey chapters of National Organization for Women, the American Civil Liberties Union, New Jersey Citizens for Life, the New Jersey Right to Life Committee, the N.J. State Catholic Conference, the United States Catholic Conference and others, including the Educational and Legal Defense Fund of the National Association for the Protection of Colored People and the Puerto Rican Legal Defense and Educational Funds, joined to protest the New Jersey welfare reform billed entitled "The Family Development Act (FDA)" passed by the state legislature and signed into law by Governor Jim Florio, Democrat, on January 21, 1992. While the bill contained several provisions agreeable to almost all partisans (such as mandated job training, better coordination of state services, and the removal of the "marriage penalty"), pro-life and pro-choice (but not Planned Parenthood or the National Abortion Rights Action League) organizations formed a coalition to protest the bill's then novel "additional child provision (ACP)." Contrary to its title, ACP was intended to make certain that in New Jersey there would be *fewer* additional children born to women below the poverty level. The phrase "the additional child provision" actually meant "no additional provisions." Henceforth, New Jersey would provide no medical assistance or any increase in family benefits to a woman who became pregnant while receiving welfare. For such a woman, her "choice" was between abortion and even deeper family poverty. NOW and ACLU representatives objected that in New Jersey women had to trade their reproductive rights for welfare assistance. Abortion opponents objected that the ACP would cause more abortions. As a result, both pro-life and pro-choice activists found themselves opposed to the bill, working together for its demise.

The Fiscal Deterrents to Common Ground

In terms of the moral significance and the political prospects of "common ground" efforts it is important to know that the New Jersey coalition, comprised of leading organizations on both sides of the abortion controversy, failed. The powerful forces generated by issues of class, race, welfare, poverty and taxes easily conquered common ground. The future of common ground when it is defined solely as "dialogue" will remain forever rosy. The future of common ground when it is defined by the seminal St. Louis group will remain forever precarious. The former requires that we change only ourselves; the latter that we change society. It is likely that in American society, there will be more legal abortion with less choice, especially for poorer women, but also for all women precariously balancing the conflicting demands of work and family. A capitalist economy and its mostly accommodating politics, by tending to subordinate all family-related concerns to issues of economic efficiency and increased economic productivity, systematically subvert both pro-life and pro-choice principles.

In this most murderous of centuries, the term "common ground" can bear witness to the aspiration that conflicting loyalties do not in themselves preclude the promotion of the common good.[12] In this era of ever decreasing resources and ever increasing collective and private violence, we can scarcely do without a term of such realism and integrity. In its strong sense it indicates a surprising and even ironical overlap between otherwise fiercely antagonistic domains. It's a term that appears when ordinary people rise up to accept the moral burdens of democracy and commit themselves to finding non-violent and non-isolating ways of working with those who have competing moral assumptions. The usual words for this interaction—diversity, tolerance, pluralism, inclusion—remain useful but capture none of the deep moral substance of "common ground." All too often "inclusion," "diversity," "tolerance," and "pluralism" suggest that those with strong commitments are expected to privatize them. Common ground requires civility and measured cooperation amidst fierce moral differences, but never the suppression of principle even in the public domain. This strong meaning of the term is worth pursuing in the midst of the abortion controversy, and other cultural controversies as well.

NOTES

1. Hunter entitled Chapter 1 of his *Before The Shooting Begins* (1994) "A Search For Common Ground" and later (pp. 232-234) briefly discussed some of the groups analyzed at greater length here.

2. Puzder continued to explore a common ground approach in other essays. He focused on the importance of upholding without compromise the pro-life principle in ways that explicitly took into account the Supreme Court's likely future rulings and the public's complicated ambiguity about abortion. While "prudence" is the term in classical political morality, the usual contemporary term for these kinds of considerations is a "principled pragmatism." Puzder anticipated that no post-Webster Court would reverse Roe and that any shifting of public opinion would occur mostly between keeping abortion legal but distinct from birth control. In "State Protection of Unborn Children After Webster v. Reproductive Health Services: A Legislative Proposal" appearing in the *Public Law Review* (1992) Puzder explained that the Court should be expected only to permit the states to balance the rights of the mother and the rights of the unborn. "Even among the strict constructionists (Rehnquist and White), there is support for the proposition that women have a liberty interest in abortion that is entitled to due process protection" (1992, p. 318). To regain even some "Webster" permitted limited protection for the unborn through the state legislation, the pro-life movement had to win the moral favor of the public.

"The pro-life movement achieves nothing if it prevails in the court of law only to be defeated in the court of public opinion" (1992, p. 312). Puzder urged that "the pro-life movement must take every opportunity to emphasize that it is not attempting to oppress women, question their motives or deprive them of essential rights, but rather that it is attempting to protect the lives and rights of innocent unborn children" (p. 314).

3. In fact, since the mid-1980s a "consistent ethic group" in upstate New York has called itself "Common Ground." Like other "consistent ethic groups," they oppose the violence *common* to war, abortion, capital punishment, poverty, and euthanasia. They seek common ground between the progressives of anti-war and anti-poverty groups and abortion opponents. Unlike St. Louis, they did not explicitly address principled pro-choice activists. In terms of the St. Louis criteria, we might say they sought "common cause" with other movements and sought to convert some of their membership to a consistent ethic of life perspective.

4. The point that common ground involves reciprocal challenges based on integrity to principle recalls the early American philosopher Josiah Royce's neglected classic of moral wisdom *The Philosophy Of Loyalty* (1908). Royce placed his hope for an enlightened public order not in cosmopolitan rationalities but in the steadfast loyalty of ordinary people to their traditions and the causes they motivated. His principle of self-criticism for individuals and movements is "loyalty to loyalty" through which one lives a tradition or serves a cause in such a way that "in consequence of your life, loyalty amongst men shall prosper." Even the way we engage in the most serious conflict, Royce writes, should not undermine the principle of loyalty. "If your fellow's cause has, in a given case, assailed your own, and if, in the world as it is, conflict is inevitable, you may then have to war with your fellow's cause, in order to be loyal to your own. But even then, you may never assail whatever is sincere and genuine about his spirit of loyalty .... All the loyal are brethren. They are children of one spirit. Loyalty to loyalty involves the active furtherance of this spirit wherever it appears" (p. 158).

5. *Search For Common Ground* listed the following projects in its 1994 financial report: "The Initiative for Peace and Cooperation in the Middle East," "The Initiative for Conflict Management in Russia," the Management of the Ethnic Crisis in former Yugoslavia, and Common Ground Productions, which included in its 10-part "Search for Common Ground" series for Public Television one on abortion with the executive director of the National Abortion Rights Action League (now the National Abortion and Reproductive Rights Action League), Kate Michelman, and the former president of the National Right to Life Committee, Dr. John Willke.

6. Laura Chasin, the director of FIC's Public Conversations Project explained (interview, 3/18/94) that because of the publicity they had received from their abortion mediation they "began to respond to the opportunities that knocked on their door." They had recently facilitated discussions, for example, among Episcopalian women in North Carolina on race/ gender issues; and among a group of environmentalists, paper manufactures and property owners, discussing ways of preventing what happened in the forests of the far west to New England forests; and in preparation for The United Nations' Conference On Population And Development facilitating the leaders of groups who were in disagreement about the role of women in population control.

7.   In the president's preface to the 1992 annual report of *Search For Common Ground*, John Marks gives as the philosophical basis for common ground a somewhat "morally thin" description of what his organization means by "common ground". Unlike the St. Louis common ground, *Search For Common Ground* explicitly employs only the language of enlightened self-interest: "We are convinced that adversarial ways of dealing with conflict are inadequate and that alternatives exist. We promote 'win-win' approaches. The idea is to find solutions that maximize the gain of involved parties. We believe that once adversaries recognize that they share interests, they can often work together and become partners in satisfying mutual needs." Dworkin's objection—it makes as much moral sense to speak of win-win solutions to abortion as it does for issues such as slavery, apartheid or rape (1993, p. 10)—applies to this morally thin definition of common ground.

8.   Joe Frolik, *The Plain Dealer* (Cleveland, Ohio), January 23, 1994; The Associated Press, "Two Sides of Abortion Issue Find a Way to Communicate," *The Register Guard* (Eugene Oregon), Feb. 12, 1994; *New Age Journal*, "Stop Shouting, Start Talking," March/April 1994.

9.   But there are other developments. In November, 1994 a community group invited CGNFLC to Pensacola, Florida. During the same month they planned to facilitate and video a dialogue between two pro-choice and two pro-life activists in Toronto. CGMFLC gets stronger rather than weaker.

10.   Although the term was used before its 1991 discovery in abortion politics, it was not common. After its use in abortion reportage, it quickly appeared in dozens of *New York Times* articles and elsewhere. It was often trivialized, losing the quality of surprising or ironic overlap and, far more weakly, merely suggested *any* discovered agreement among foes or even competitors. The dangers of trivialization were much in evidence. For example, the March 22, 1993 *New York Times* news' summary described "an interest in restaurants" as the ice-breaking "common ground" found by President Clinton and German Chancellor Helmut Kohn at their first state meeting. A temporary library at the University of California, Los Angeles was described as sharing "common ground" with "student life" because it had no formal dress code and thus "revived informality as an architectural ideal" (*New York Times* 1993, H29). The new head of Apple computer was described as breaking the ice at a "painful and awkward" meeting between older and newer Apple computer employees by "finally searching for some common ground, (and) asking about members of the original Macintosh team" (Markoff, *New York Times*, 1993). A story about Andrew Guiliani's disruption of his father's New York City mayoral inauguration speech opined that many parents suddenly discovered "common ground with a new Mayor whose human side has not always been in evidence in previous public incarnations" (Firestone, *New York Times* 1994, B4). A report about a park beside Long Island Hospital in Brooklyn designated to become a parking lot said that "people of all backgrounds (found it) a common ground that they feel comfortable about using" (1993, New York Times: 10, p. 1).

11.   Republican party fiscal conservatives can be expected to continue to attract the votes of working and lower middle class moral traditionalists by continuing to support their "social" issues when they require, like school prayer or the teaching of creationism, no tax increases or federal aid. Soon after the November 9, 1994 mid-term elections, when the Republican party won control of both the House and

the Senate for the first time in forty years, the expeled Republican Speaker of the House, Rep. Newt Gingrich, announced that he would seek a constitutional amendment overthrowing not Roe, as Reagan had promised, but the Supreme Court decisions prohibiting prayer in public schools. On abortion, Gingrich said, "In the short run, I just don't think the votes are there" (Dowd, November 10, 1994, A1).

12. While numerous instances of the trivialization of the term can be found, so too can numerous examples of its stronger, more valuable meaning. In a debate on welfare between those who wished to dismantle it and those who wished to enlarge it, "common ground was found in reforms aimed at helping young mothers to return to school and obtaining child support from absent males" (Goodman, Walter, *New York Times* 1994, C16). Anglican, Roman Catholic, Presbyterian and Methodist church leaders in Northern Ireland used the term to describe their agreement endorsing the end of employment discrimination, "while recognizing and respecting differences in other areas." (Origins, January 27, 1994, p. 572). Walter Wink suggested (*Engaging The Powers*, 1992, p. 224) that pacifists who oppose all wars and followers of just war theory might be able to find "common ground" in the phrase "violence-reduction criteria." Representatives of the Catholic Bishops, the Synagogue Council of America and the National Council of Churches issued a statement entitled "The Common Ground for the Common Good" which outlined the areas where they could and couldn't agree on welfare reform: "The project's agenda includes strategies for confronting poverty, homelessness, hunger, health care and welfare reform; however, two priorities among Catholics, abortion and educational choice, are not included. 'We had to agree to disagree,' said the representative of the National Council of Churches. 'We put aside that which divides us...There are just things we can't touch.'" After representatives of the American Catholic hierarchy met with President Clinton on the issue of health care reform, the president of the National Catholic Conference of Bishops, Baltimore Archbishop William H. Keeler, used the term to describe the bishops' support for universal health care and their opposition to inclusion of abortion as health care. "We offer cooperation and common ground wherever possible and respectful disagreement when it may be necessary" (Zapor, Patricia, *The Tablete* 1993, March 3: 6).

REFERENCES

Alberoni, F. 1984. *Movement and Institution.* Translated by Patricia C. Arden Delmoro. New York: Columbia University Press.

Allen, M. 1994. "Media Falsely Claim Paul Hill Is Pro-Life 'Leader'." *National Right To Life News.* (August 5).

Becker, C., L. Chasin, R. Chasin, M. Herzig and S. Roth 1992. "Fostering Dialogue On Abortion." *Conscience*, Autumn, Vol. X111, No. 3. Autumn: 2-9.

Bernardin, J. 1988. *Consistent Ethic Of Life.* Kansas City, Missouri: Sheed & Ward.

Blanchard, D., and T. Prewitt. 1993. *Religious Violence and Abortion.* Gainesville, Florida: The University of Florida Press.

Chasin, L., R. Chasin, M. Herzig, S., and C. Becker. 1991. "The Citizen Clinician: The Family Therapist in the Public Forum." *Afta Newsletter.* Winter: 36-42.

DeParle, J. 1994. "Clinton Agrees to Welfare Financing." *New York Times*, May 26, A14.

Dowd, M. 1994. "G.O.P.'s Rising Star Pledges To Right Wrongs of the Left." *New York Times*, November 10, A1.

Dworkin, R. 1993. *Life's Dominion: An Argument About Abortion, Euthanasia, And Individual Freedom*. New York: Alfred A. Knopf.

Firestone, D. 1994. "A Get-Tough Mayor? Tell It To Andrew." *New York Times*, January 4, B4.

Goodman, W. 1994. "A Debate On Welfare As The Root Of Much Evil." *New York Times*, March 21, C16.

Griffin, S. 1993. *A Chorus of Stones*. New York: Doubleday Anchor

Hayes, R. 1994. "Finding Common Ground." *New York Times*, April 24, CY 17.

Hunter, J. 1991. *Culture Wars*. New York: Basic Books.

————. 1994. *Before The Shooting Begins: Searching For Democracy In America's Culture War*. New York: The Free Press.

Jelen, T., and M. Chandler (eds.). 1994. *Abortion Politics in the United States and Canada*. Westport, CT: Praeger.

Karkoff, J. 1993. "Marketer's Dream, Engineer's Nightmare." *New York Times*, December 12, Sec. 3: 8.

Kelly, J. 1993 "Pro-Life and Pro-Choice After Reagan-Bush." *America*. January 30: 11-15.

————. 1994. "Seeking a Sociologically Correct Name for Abortion Opponents." Pp. 15-40 in *Abortion Politics In The United States And Canada*, edited by Ted G. Jelen and Marthe A. Chandler. Westport, CT: Praeger.

Kissling, F. 1990. "Ending the Abortion War: A Modest Proposal." *The Christian Century*. February, 21: 180-184.

Lader, L. 1973. *Abortion 11: Making The Revolution*. Boston: Beacon Press.

Lewin, T. 1994. "A Cause Worth Killing For?" *New York Times*, July 30, p. 1.

Lynch, Msgr. R., Rev. J. Campbell, R. Michelman. 1993. "A Call To the Common Ground for the Common Good." *Origins*. Vol. 23, No. 6, June 24, 1993.

National Abortion And Reproductive Rights Action League. 1994. "Promoting Reproductive Choices: A New Approach to Reproductive Health." Washington, D.C.

New York Times. 1993. "UCLA Temporary Powell Library." August 8, H29.

————. 1993. "A Park, A Hospital And A Controversy." August 10, p. 1.

Origins. 1994. "Appeal For Investment and Fair Employment In Northern Ireland." Vol. 23, No. 32, January 27: 572.

Pear, R. 1994. "G.O.P. Proposal Would Overhaul Welfare System. An End To Entitlements." *New York Times*, November 22, A1.

Petchesky, R. 1990. *Abortion And Woman's Choice*. Boston: Northeastern University Press.

Pitanguy, J., and R. Petchesky. 1993. "Women and Population: A Feminist Perspective." *Conscience*, Vol. X1V, No. 3, Autumn: 5-7.

Puzder, A. 1989. "Common Ground On Abortion." *St. Louis Dispatch*. Dec. 26.

————. 1992. "State Protection Of Unborn Children After Webster V. Reproductive Health Services: A Legislative Proposal." St. Louis University: Public Law Review, Vol. X1, No. 2: 299-328.

————. 1992. "How To Win The War." *The Human Life Review*, Vol. XVIII, No. 1: 7-17.

Royce, J. 1971 (1908). *The Philosophy of Loyalty*. New York: Hafner Publishing Company.

Rothstein, B. 1994. May 3, 1994 ruling, U.S. District Court, Seattle, Washington. "Assisted-Suicide Ban Ruled Unconstitutional." *Origins*. 24: (2): May 26.

Rosenblatt, R. 1992. *Life Itself: Abortion In The American Mind*. New York: Random House.

Steinfels, P. 1994. "Beliefs." *New York Times*. August 6, p. 9.

Tribe, L. 1990. *Abortion And The Clash Of Absolutes*. New York: W.W. Norton.

Warner, G. 1994. "Rivals Over Abortion Issue Find Friendship on 'Common Ground." *The Buffalo News*. March 6: C-4

Zapor, P. 1993. "Bishops to Clinton: Let's Work Together." *The Tablet*, March 13: 6

REFLECTIONS ON
THE CULTURE WARS HYPOTHESIS

James Davison Hunter

To understand the character of conflict in society is, in the final analysis, to understand something of the changing nature and constitution of the social order—the deepest ways in which civilizations are ordered and legitimated. The reason, of course, is that social change, more often than not, occurs in and through that conflict. This conundrum of social conflict, then, takes us right to the heart of sociological theory.

The dominant models for making sense of social change in sociology in America and Europe over the past half century have been economic in character and, more particularly, class-based. Within these models, the dominant axis of political tension existed between those who favored the maintenance of the inequities of the class structure and those who favored its abolishment toward the end of a fundamental redistribution of wealth. Granted, the categories of "Left" and "Right" were useful so long as they reflected this axis of tension in advanced industrial nations, but with the breakdown of state socialism in the Soviet Union and the Eastern bloc countries and the exhaustion of the labor movement here at home, the analytical power of those categories to clarify the nature of social and political development has weakened to say the least. This is especially true in the United States.

Yet old habits die hard. For reasons of professional interest or professionally rooted, ideological bias, mainstream sociological theory and empirical research continues to favor economic analyses of the social order (even when they have been transformed into paradigms of "rational choice"). What the establishment cliques of professional sociology are missing right before their eyes is a basic realignment of the social order and with it a "new" axis of tension and conflict that is fundamentally cultural, if not "religious" in nature. It might seem odd, in a society as seemingly secular as the United States in the late twentieth century, to suggest that "religion" is at all relevant to the discussion. But the institutional manifestations of "religion" merely point to the *normative* foundations by which late twentieth-century America is constituted and legitimated and the way in which those normative foundations are contested. As Durkheim, Weber, Marx, and Simmel well understood, "religion" or moral order was anything but irrelevant to the dynamics of conflict and change in the nineteenth century. Broadly conceived, it remains central today as well.

The Culture Wars Hypothesis and its Critics

The central hypothesis about normative conflict in America today, *in nuce,* is that there has been a fundamental realignment within American public culture (and beyond) that cuts across traditional religious divisions. Where normative conflict in the West previously (and for centuries) existed within a civilization defined principally by the moral parameters of biblical revelation and natural reason— between Protestants and Catholics as well as between Christians and Jews—the primary axis of conflict is now taking shape in the wake of the dissolution of that civilization. The new lines of conflict exist between cultural systems: a world view that seeks to maintain the normative ideals and social institutions of that traditional civilization and a world view that seeks its transformation. This did not emerge out of thin air. These tensions were certainly inchoate in the French, Scottish and American Enlightenment, and they became institutionalized within the dominant religious and moral communities in America in the late nineteenth century. What began as fissures within these communities, however, have now evolved into major fault lines within American public culture at large. One of the most interesting consequences of this are historically unprecedented alliances forming across previously antagonistic traditions along the divide created by the Enlightenment: Evangelical Protestants, conservative Catholics, Orthodox Jews and classical Platonists forming alliances with each other against competing alliances of secular modernists, liberal Protestants, progressive Catholics and Reform and secular Jews and vice versa.

At the heart of this realignment are different and, more often than not, competing moral epistemologies that can be framed as different ideal-typical formulations of moral authority. At the broadest level, one is a culturally conservative impulse rooted in a transcendent metaphysic that is more or less universally binding; the other, a culturally progressivist impulse that grounds moral authority in human experience. Where the former articulates unchanging standards (i.e., truth, the good, etc.) that exist outside of the self, the latter tends to reject the possibility of universals or universally accepted foundations, maintaining instead that ideals are always and necessarily contingent. It is the polarity of *this* axis that accounts for so much of the variation of opinion and position on a wide range of popular domestic disputes.

It is clear, then, that the culture war extends far beyond the realm of "high culture"—the "canon" of Western literature, music and art. While surely significant, they are, in the end, only one field of a wider and deeper realm of conflict—one that even reaches into the normative understandings of everyday life. Though manifested primarily in the battles of public policy over this issue or that, the major fields of conflict are the reality defining institutions of American society—the family, education, the arts, the media, law and the state itself. The reason is that this conflict finally concerns the power to define the terms by which public life is ordered and maintained: the nature of human life, liberty, justice, and community. At the heart of the culture war is a conflict to define the meaning of America.

Three broad criticisms have been leveled at the culture wars hypothesis over the past several years.[1] The first, and least convincing, is still rather basic: there is, its protagonists maintain, no culture war in America today. The reasons adduced are several, but the main one is that the warfare metaphor used in the hypothesis exaggerates the true nature of any conflict that exists. If one is interested in the *real* culture wars of our historical period, they contend, one must turn to the conflicts in Bosnia, Northern Ireland, Israel, Lebanon, and parts of Africa. Here one may find "concerted violence over governmental legitimacy and control in the pursuit of noneconomic interests."[2] In America, by contrast, there is nothing even remotely comparable. Indeed, what is so striking about the United States is the level of civic tranquility that exists. What is described as conflict, then, is really nothing more than the back and forth of a healthy pluralism. "What some pundits call cultural warfare," one comparativist put it, "I see as cultural democracy at work."[3]

A second criticism leveled at the culture wars hypothesis acknowledges the reality of conflict in America but contends that the warfare metaphor permits one to ignore the moderating influences that exist in American democracy. The most important factor, these critics assert, is the existence of a broad middle in the population. "The remarkable characteristic of American culture throughout its history," one critic has asserted, "is that the center has held, whether the center be defined as the middle class, political independents, or, as statistics sometimes show, the Methodists." As another put it, if up to 60 percent of the American citizenry take moderate positions on issues, "[c]an one have a proper war when two-thirds of the army are noncombatants?" Consider too, some critics say, that people's positions really aren't as consistent or coherent as the culture wars hypothesis assumes. The truth of the matter is that there is tremendous expanse of ambiguity in the minds of most Americans for which a simplistic "two party system" fails to account. This, it is said, is especially true in American Protestantism where "the center has held" despite the ebb and flow of the ongoing fundamentalist and modernist controversy in the twentieth century. In the final analysis, it is the "pragmatists" of the center rather than the "polemicists" of the extremes who have carried the day. A final consideration on this count is that the hypothesis fails to appreciate the moderating effects of various institutions such as schools, businesses, and the bureaucratic structure of the state itself. Here, too, the checks and balances built into administrative structures and procedures tend to assuage any bias toward ideological excesses in public opinion, law and public policy.

A third criticism acknowledges the serious nature of cultural conflict in America today but asserts that to use the warfare metaphor is to reify or overly concretize the polarizing tendencies that are already quite destructive to American public life. In a certain sense, scholarly discourse that employs this symbolism provides an academic legitimation for disputes that are on their own terms difficult to resolve, making them even more difficult to mediate. In the end, to use the language of martial engagement to describe the conflicts that admittedly threaten public unity today in America is irresponsible.

The stumbling block, it would seem, is the metaphor of warfare as an explanatory tool for coming to grips with the character of conflict in American public life. The reasons why this language troubles them vary, but all agree that the metaphor itself goes too far. Some have even suggested that the term is nothing more than a marketing tool invented to sell copy.

But is it really the problem?

My sense is that it is not; that, at base, the source of most difficulties with the argument are rooted in a decisive methodological failing. In particular, those who level the first two criticisms tend to operate in the old reductionist model that equates culture with the aggregated attitudes of autonomous individuals. In this, they fail to understand the more complex Durkheimian character of culture and cultural conflict through which the culture wars hypothesis has been advanced.[4]

Those, for example, who speak of a "strong center" in American society invariably make this case on the basis of an examination of public attitudes on specific issues. It may be that there is a "center" to American public opinion but if there is, it is statistical in nature and therefore contentless—it has no coherence or teleology as a system of moral public reasoning. As it concerns public discourse, any reasoned and substantive center that may exist is certainly eclipsed by the polarizing rhetoric produced by the gatekeeping institutions of public culture. The evidence makes it clear that the positions of those individuals or institutions of middling persuasion that *do* gain a public hearing are nearly always forced through caricature into the grid of the extremes. In this situation, people who offer a moderately conservative reflection on homosexuality are still "homophobes," those who offer a moderately liberal position on avant garde art are still hostile to Western civilization, those who operate with a legal philosophy rooted in natural law theory are still reactionaries, while those who favor anti-discrimination law for women in the workplace are anti-family, and those, finally, who take principled positions in the middle of any dispute are still and incontrovertably wishy-washy.

And here we come to the nub of the problem: the form by which the dynamics of faith and culture get played out most sharply is not the accumulated subjective attitudes of independent citizens but rather the competing moral visions in public culture that have evolved and crystallized over the past several decades—the institutions and elites that produce them and the structures of rhetoric by which they are framed and articulated. It is through the social organization and articulation of these moral visions within the culture-forming institutions of public discourse that they become a reality *sui generis*—ultimately a reality larger and independent (in the sense of disembodied) from those who give it expression. The intentions behind speech acts, and any qualification or nuance they might offer, become irrelevant. In this Durkheimian sense we, as citizens, become separated from our own speech. It is for this reason that it is often said that public discourse in America is more polarized than are Americans themselves. It is at this level, and only at this level, that the term "culture war"—with the implications of stridency, polarization, and mobilization of resources, and so on— takes on its greatest conceptual force, which helps to make sense of why common ground efforts such as those pursued by activists on both sides of the abortion debate, as documented in James Kelly's chapter in this volume, were ultimately unsuccessful.

The failure to take into account the Durkheimian premise within which the culture wars hypothesis has been put forward also accounts for the problem some critics have had with what appears to be a simple dualism in the argument's portrayal of American culture (and religion). Culture is certainly complicated. It is true, on the one hand, that there are strong impulses—philosophical and sociological—toward moral and political consistency such that people holding strong opinions on one issue will hold comparable opinions on other issues. Yet, on the other hand, it is very clear that the polarizations of public policy cut differently on different issues. One can quickly observe that people can hold liberal views on some matters and conservative views on others. The same thing can be said about organizations. The *New York Times,* for example, may take progressive editorial positions on some issues and moderate and conservative positions on others. The central point is this: however individuals or organizations align themselves on particular issues, they become subservient to, and if unwilling, must struggle against, the dominating and virtually irresistible categories and logic of the opposing visions and rhetoric of the culture war.

Moral philosophers have long recognized the incommensurable nature of competing moral claims and therefore the intractable character of many contemporary moral disputes. But the perplexities that engage moral philosophers do not remain merely ethereal musings of ivory-tower intellectuals. As anyone can readily see, they very often translate into the concrete but conflicted realities of public discourse and the institutions and gatekeepers that shape and sustain it. Needless to say, these conflicts also translate into antagonisms faced by local communities, families and individuals. The culture wars hypothesis provides a paradigm for making sense of how incommensurable moral disputes actually play out in the larger social world.

Is this culture war in contemporary America anything like Bosnia? Of course not. A culture war need not erupt into military conflict for it to be a culture war. Moreover, it is intellectually facile not to see the disturbing parallels of social forms of conflict in different national settings. It is even more facile not to acknowledge the continua upon which conflict exists, as opposed to forcing conflict into either/or categories. As I have argued elsewhere (Hunter 1994), here (in America) as there (in Bosnia, Northern Ireland, and elsewhere), non-negotiable claims about the ordering of public life are in conflict. Here, as there, the claims made (even if thought of as "secular") are "religious" in character if not in substance—they emerge out of our ultimate beliefs and commitments, our most cherished sense of what is right, true and good. Here, as there, the conflicting claims trace quickly back to competing ideals of community and national identity. Finally in both contexts the tensions have deep historical roots that have long festered just beneath the surface of public life.

To be sure, calling these conflicts and the underlying conflict of moral visions underneath them a "culture war" will likely reify the tensions and render them even more difficult to address. What intellectual constructs do not reify the social reality they seek to describe? In this case at least, the metaphor of martial engagement itself originated from the activists engaged in the conflict. It is, after all, the National Organization of Women that has its "war room," and Focus on the Family that has, from the beginning, declared itself to be in a "battle" over America's children, and so on. They regard it and respond to it as a war to the finish. In this case, then, it would be phenomenologically dishonest to employ other terms.

Those who might imagine that this is "normal discourse" may be more than a tad naive—their naiveté born of distance from what they have observed only from afar; a distance or a (blindness) to the consequences to the lives of real communities and real people for whom these conflicts touch. Such distance is, unfortunately, an occupational hazard in the academy.

Local Engagement and National Culture

If the culture wars hypothesis stands, even against some criticism, it does so not as grand theory but as a broad interpretive paradigm for understanding an important layer of contemporary cultural change in America. The most interesting questions relate to the problem of empirical specification, especially between conflict in local settings (or within particular institutions) and national culture. Here the essays in this volume—concerned with education, media and the arts, sexuality and reproduction, and law—make an important contribution.

The study of conflict over curriculum at the University of California–Berkeley shows that a curious *anti*-ideological impulse was central to the opposition to curricular developments relating to multiculturalism at the university. A comfort with any given status quo may itself be enough to mobilize opposition to change. One wonders in this case, however, whether Yamane's survey dug deeply enough into his respondents' moral universe. Superficially, for example, it is well known that competing epistemologies exist in universities along disciplinary lines—mathematics and the sciences rooted in foundationalist metaphysics where the humanities and increasingly the social sciences are rooted in relativistic pragmatism. These, in turn, would have powerful consequences (even if not explicitly understood) for the shaping of intellectual horizons and, therefore, a sense of what is appropriate and inappropriate in the curriculum. The data he presents are, unfortunately, not multivariate enough to really find out.

The study of educational reform in the public schools of Gaston County, North Carolina, by Sargeant and West demonstrates the sense of irreducible incompatibility of world views even in local communities and how intense social and political hostility can become particularly when children are at stake. Here, especially, we see the role of special interest organizations in scripting, funding and ultimately intensifying the conflict beyond the hope of substantive democratic resolution. Surely this was not a case of "normal discourse" to use Michelle Dillon's phrase. It might have been had the national organizations been kept at bay, but we will never know. In war everyone loses something. The real losers in this situation were the children of Gaston County.

In William Hoynes' study of public television we have a very interesting chronicle of the conservative opposition to public television and the latent ideologies and tactical alliances used to weaken its effect. This, along with Eck's study of the funding controversy over the National Endowment for the Arts, shows the mobilization of resentment on the part of conservatives who are certainly marginal to the workings of high culture but not to the power of patronage held by the state. Yet how long can the alliances between economic conservatives and cultural conservatives endure before the latter realize that the subjugation of aesthetics to the market will ultimately undermine the very foundations of all the traditional moral sensibilities they hold sacred?

J. David Woodard's examination of the legal battles over the rights of homosexuals in Colorado and in Cincinnati brings to light the central importance of law as a tool for the legitimation of a moral position. In the contemporary world, the state has become the final arbiter of moral decisions for it is the only institution capable of backing its decisions with force. The very fact that this matter is debated at all is ample evidence of just how much authority has been lost by traditional cosmology in American public culture. That this matter is now problematized at the highest reaches of judicial deliberation shows how institutionally weak and vulnerable traditional moral sensibilities have become.

The internationalization of America's culture war (or, more accurately, the world-historical character of the conflict between orthodox and progressive) is tellingly examined in Davis' study of moral conflict at the Cairo Population Conference in 1994. Davis makes clear that the conflict there was not over abortion alone, as it was reported widely in the press, but over traditional and progressivist world views as they touch on marriage and family life, sexuality, and development. Within these issues, the conflict extended into competing though latent understandings of human rights, human community, and its future. Though the power of religious and cultural conservatives was much talked about in the press, what is so remarkable—globally speaking—is the power of a minority of secularized cultural elites from the West (or Westernized intellectuals) in defining the parameters and course of population debate worldwide, even against the representatives of countries much larger and more traditional than the West.

The authors of these studies are certainly correct in seeing the conflicts continue on into the future, even as the specific issues contested change. The reason is plain: the debates over public policy contain within them deeper debates over the most fundamental matters of human existence: the nature of community, justice, liberty, and of being itself. One of the key lessons these studies teaches is how nationalizing the disputes tends to intensify the conflicts in ways that alter the democratic engagement with them. Just as federalization intensified the dispute over abortion, it has also intensified the disputes over the media and the arts and public education. As the Colorado dispute finds its way to the Supreme Court, it will also, as Woodard himself contends, complicate and enflame the debates over the legal status and social legitimacy of homosexuality.

Yet the power conservatives retain in the on-going conflicts of the culture war is not all that it seems. For all of the triumphalism of conservatives in the 1994 mid-term election and its aftermath, the power they wield is certainly not a reflection of tradition or traditionalism. It is significant, in this regard, that virtually all of these studies show that in making their appeal for their positions, conservatives rarely invoked explicit references to religion or religious faith. The conservative position at Berkeley was not articulated this way, as Yamane points out. Nor was it a point of leverage in the disputes over public television and funding for the arts (where religious leaders themselves central to the mobilization of popular opinion could not convince the media that they were players). The same pattern of downplaying or avoiding explicit religious symbols or language was found in Gaston County, Colorado, and in Cincinnati. Rather, appeals were made on the basis of equity, justice in public funding, parental rights and other pragmatic considerations. James L. Nolan's historical comparative examination of political discourse goes into depth on this point. Following an argument put forward in *Culture Wars,* he goes on to demonstrate with great detail how conservative political rhetoric has come to embrace a form of public rhetoric that ultimately plays to the opposition's natural strengths. Far from being rooted in an appeal to religious transcendence, even conservative political rhetoric is increasingly grounded in an appeal to the subjectivism and emotivism of what he calls the "therapeutic ethos." In all, the moral vision of the cultural conservative is put forward, contested and, in cases, advanced. But it is so increasingly within a moral universe of public discourse whose horizons are defined by the opposition. These advocates are, in fact, "post-modern" conservatives, their moral vision remaining traditional but only in the most post-modern of ways.

Final Reflections

In early August of 1994, I was invited to the White House for a breakfast meeting with President Clinton and Vice-President Gore. In his opening remarks Clinton stated that before his election he had no sense of how intense, mean-spirited, and unrelenting the culture war really was. He had declared in his campaign that the crucial issues dividing the nation were economic in character. He had found out, two years into his administration, that, in fact, hostility to his efforts was primarily cultural in character. What, he asked, could he do? As it turned out, only thirty-six hours earlier I gave a lecture on the culture war to the Sociological Research Association, the American Sociological Association's most eminent (self-appointed) members. There, one prominent sociologist chosen as the respondent declared to the gathering that there was no culture war. As the President spoke, I wondered whether it was only academic sociologists who could not recognize what is obvious to almost everyone and certainly obvious to the President: that America is experiencing deep fragmentation at its core, and in its wake conflict has emerged to redefine the most basic terms by which public life will be ordered, the terms by which a new *unum* (or at least a working consensus for national life) might yet be established.

There was not much to say to Clinton for, in fact, there is no resolution to the culture war in America. The culture war cannot be resolved because it is the natural expression of a massive cultural transformation (to what we don't know but over which individuals, institutions and, least of all, administrations have no control). One cannot resolve it, one can only cope with it. The question individuals, communities and political and cultural gatekeepers alike can address is whether they will seek to deal with it in ways that are at least in keeping with conventions if not the ideals of American democratic life. If James Kelly's analysis of principled common ground movements in the abortion controversy (in St. Louis, San Francisco, Buffalo, Wisconsin, Cambridge and elsewhere) is any indication, it is not likely that Americans will. When Francis Kissling, whom he quotes, says that "common ground is on nobody's agenda," she speaks for more than the opposing advocates on the abortion issue.

Kissling's observation is not only portentous of the likely longevity of the culture war as a whole but of its likely consequences as well. To be sure, cultural conflict in America has the potential to revitalize democratic institutions and ideals. The problem, of course, is that the very normative foundations and baseline civic mechanisms upon which any revitalization might take place are also disputed. The moral and cultural arguments of our time do indeed "go all the way down," as moral philosophers are fond of saying. The question, it would seem, is whether democracy was ever intended to mediate conflicts as rudimentary as these. If it wasn't and if it can't, then sociological theory will have the challenge of clarifying the cultural and historical contingencies upon which substantive democratic political orders are based. Historical sociology will have the challenge of recounting how, in America, it came to an end.

NOTES

1. See, for example, S. Brint, "What If They Gave a War," *Contemporary Sociology,* pp. 438–40, and Randal Balmer, "By Dualism Possessed," *Evangelical Studies Bulletin* 10:1 (Spring 1993): 1–2.

2. This definition of culture wars, employed by Jay Demerath, ("Lions Among Lambs: America's 'Culture Wars' in Cross-Cultural Perspective," Paper delivered at Messiah College, Grantham, PA, June 2, 1995, p. 2) differs substantively from my own, namely, "political and social conflict rooted in different systems of moral understanding, the stakes of which are the domination of one over others." J. D. Hunter, *Culture Wars: The Struggle to Define America* (New York: Basic Books, 1991), p. 42. These

definitional differences would obviously account for the differences in perspective.

3. Again, see N. J. Demerath, "Lions Among Lambs: America's 'Culture Wars' in Cross-Cultural Perspective," Paper delivered at Messiah College, Grantham, PA, June 2, 1995, p. 1.

4. I addressed this misunderstanding in the preface of *Before the Shooting Begins,*

I would like to emphasize straight away (what some reviewers of the earlier book missed) that the culture war of which I spoke cannot be explained in terms of ordinary people's attitudes about public issues. These moral visions are often enough reflected (imperfectly) in the world views of individuals *but by virtue of the way they are institutionalized and articulated in public life, these moral visions acquire something of a life of their own.* It is at this level that the term culture war—with the implications of stridency, polarization, the mobilization of resources, etc.—takes on its greatest conceptual force (pp. vii–viii, emphasis added).

This was just a reiteration of the argument in *Culture Wars:*

It is that the opposing moral visions at the heart of the culture war and the rhetoric that sustains them, acquire something of a life of their own. The culture war is, it is true, rooted in an on-going realignment of American public culture and has become institutionalized chiefly through special purpose organizations, denominations, political parties and even branches of government. The fundamental disagreements that characterized the culture war, we have also seen, have become even further aggravated by virtue of the technology of public discourse, the very means by which disagreements are voiced in public. In the end, however, the opposing moral visions become, as one would say in the tidy though ponderous jargon of social science, a reality *sui generis*, a reality much larger than—indeed, autonomous from—the sum total of individuals and organizations that give expression to the conflict. It is these competing moral visions and the rhetoric that sustains them that become the defining forces of public life. Certainly there is a strong philosophical impulse toward moral and political consistency, such that people on one side of the cultural divide—the overarching "binary opposition"—cuts differently on different issues, showing that an organization can maintain politically liberal positions on most issues while adopting moderate or conservative positions on others—and vice versa. These "exceptions to the rule" are not uncommon in every field of conflict, but that they exist is ultimately irrelevant. However individuals or organizations align themselves on particular issues, they become subservient to, and if unwilling, must struggle against, the dominating and almost irresistible categories and logic of the opposing visions and rhetoric of the culture war (pp. 290–91).

Rather than failing to acknowledge the "moral nuance, complexity and ambiguity" among activists and the general public, as some critics have suggested, in *Before the Shooting Begins,* I actually explain just how moderate the views of activists can be. I also show further how the constraints of institutional location and agenda compel individuals to speak more extremely than they would and do as private citizens (pp. 45–46). Of the hard-core followers of pro-choice and pro-life positions, Carl Bowman and I went out of our way to demonstrate in the analysis of the survey data that very few are purists (pp. 98–106). Far from being "puzzled" by the muddled middle, as Michele Dillon charges in her essay in this volume, I merely point out that the structure of ambivalence among non-activist citizens has never adequately been explained—a task that I, and my colleague, set out to accomplish with considerable attention to subtlety and nuance. Again, the very fact that these more complex and nuanced views do not typically find expression in public debate is itself evidence of the saliency of the culture wars hypothesis. What, then, is put forth here as a challenge to the culture wars argument actually provides empirical support for it.

REFERENCE

Hunter, J. D. 1994. *Before the Shooting Begins.* New York: Free Press.

DATE DUE

12/3/12			